California Madness

A SAPIENT Being's Guide to the State's Recall, Leftist Policies & Progressive Downward Spiral

By

Corey Lee Wilson

California Madness

California Madness

Fratire Publishing books can be purchased in bulk with special discounts for educational purposes, association gifts, sales promotions, and special editions can be created to specifications. All inquiries for such can be made below.

FRATIRE PUBLISHING LLC
4533 Temescal Canyon Rd. # 308
Corona, CA 92883 USA
www.FratirePublishing.com
FratirePublishing@att.net
1+ (951) 638-5502

FratirePublishing
Relevant Books for **SAPIENT** Beings

Fratire Publishing is all about common sense and relevant books for sapient beings. If this sounds like you and you can never have enough common sense, wisdom, and relevancy, then visit us and learn more about the 50 *MADNESS* series of book titles at www.fratirepublishing.com/madnessbooks.

Printed paperback and eBook ePUB by Ingram Spark in La Vergne, Tennessee, USA
Copyright © 2021: First Edition September 2021
ISBN 978-0-9994017-6-7 (Paperback)
ISBN 978-1-953319-52-4 (eBook)
CaliforniaMadness-01-PDF (pdf)
LCCN 2021918497

Special thanks for the cover design by Jenny Barroso, J20Graphics, j20graphics@gmail.com and ebook conversion by Redeemer SoftTech, redeemer.softtech@gmail.com.

California Madness

Contents

Acknowledgements

I owe a debt of gratitude to the following for "heavily" borrowing at times pieces of their and/or outright sections. I do this unashamedly to use the sapient phrase, "if it ain't broke—don't try to fix it." Most of the borrowed works and research cannot be improved upon—so why try? It's better to assemble these meaningful parts, profound messages, and eloquent arguments into a cohesive whole, told with high school and college students in mind, and that's what I've done and where my talent lies.

Below in alphabetical order are the major contributors to *California Madness* that I borrowed verbatim, quoted, and conceptualized much of their content from a little to a lot. Wherever this happened, I did my best to acknowledge my source. If I didn't at times within the 15 chapters, I did so intentionally because doing so would have distracted from their message. Nonetheless, they are more than acknowledged in the References and Index sections of this textbook.

California Policy Center: Is a public policy think tank located in California that specializes in union policy, pension reform, spending reform, and school choice. Their team includes authors, journalists, fellows, thought leaders, and educators along with government, taxpayer, financial, public union, and pension group experts.

CalMatters: Is a nonpartisan, nonprofit journalism venture committed to explaining how California's state Capitol works and why it matters using compelling stories on policies, personalities, and money in Sacramento.

Hanson, Victor Davis: Is a fifth generation Californian and the Martin and Illie Anderson Senior Fellow in Residence in Classics and Military History at the Hoover Institution, Stanford University, a professor of Classics Emeritus at California State University, Fresno, and a nationally syndicated columnist for Tribune Media Services. Hanson is also the Wayne & Marcia Buske Distinguished Fellow in History, Hillsdale College and is the 2003 author of *Mexifornia: A State of Becoming* plus other books and articles about current events.

Hoover Institution: Is a public policy think tank promoting the principles of individual, economic, and political freedom at Stanford University and ranked as the tenth most influential think tank in the world in 2020 by Academic Influence, and the 22nd of the "Top Think Tanks in the United States" by the Global Go To Think Tank Index Report in 2019.

Independent Institute: Is a non-profit research and educational organization that promotes the power of independent thinking to boldly advance peaceful, prosperous, and free societies grounded in a commitment to human worth and dignity. They are home to the California Golden Fleece® Awards and they published in 2015 *California Dreaming: Lessons on How to Resolve America's Public Pension Crisis.*

1

Kotkin, Joel: Is the Presidential Fellow in Urban Futures at Chapman University and founder of the Center for Demographics and Policy there. He is also executive director of the Urban Reform Institute in Houston, Texas, and a regular contributor to *The City Journal, The Hill*, Real Clear Politics, the Daily Beast, and Tablet. He is the author of nine books including the recently released *The Coming of Neo-Feudalism: A Warning to the Global Middle Class* (2020).

Mac Donald, Heather: Is an American conservative political commentator, essayist, attorney, and author. She is a Thomas W. Smith Fellow of the Manhattan Institute and a contributing editor of the institute's *City Journal*. She has written numerous editorials and is the author of several books.

Malanga, Steven: Is the George M. Yeager Fellow at the Manhattan Institute and City Journal's senior editor. He writes about the intersection of urban economies, business communities, and public policy. Malanga is the author of *The New Left: How American Politics Works Today* (2005).

McQuillan, Lawrence J.: Is a Senior Fellow at the Independent Institute, Director of Independent's Center on Entrepreneurial Innovation, and author of the Independent book, *California Dreaming: Lessons on How to Resolve America's Public Pension Crisis* (2015).

Ohanian, Lee: Is a senior fellow at the Hoover Institution and a professor of economics and director of the Ettinger Family Program in Macroeconomic Research at the University of California, Los Angeles (UCLA).

Public Policy Institute of California (PPIC): Is an independent, non-profit research institution, established in 1994 by Bill Hewlett, of Hewlett-Packard, Roger Heyns, and Arjay Miller, with a $70 million endowment from Hewlett.

Ring, Edward: Edward Ring is a contributing editor and senior fellow with the California Policy Center, which he co-founded in 2013 and served as its first president. He is also a senior fellow with the Center for American Greatness, and a regular contributor to the California Globe.

Walters, Dan: Has written more than 9,000 columns about California and its politics and has written about California and its politics for a number of other publications, including *The Wall Street Journal* and the *Christian Science Monitor*. In 1986, he published *The New California: Facing the 21st Century* that became a widely used college textbook about socioeconomic and political trends in the state.

In retrospect, so many of the issues reported by these authors that are covered in *California Madness* are the inspiration for the majority of the 50 MADNESS sapient textbook topics and issues (see Appendix for a link to all 50 textbook titles). So much so—it's extremely important to understand what's happening here in California—can be used as object lessons and what-if scenarios for the rest of the United States.

A SAPIENT Being's Preface

Today's California represents, by far, when compared to the rest of the United States, the worst that "so-called" progressivism has to offer—and if liberal, leftist, and Democratic Party pundits are correct with their declarations that "California is the wave of America's future"—the decline of our republic in most every category on the "sapience scorecard" is well on its way.

The state has earned many times over its various California "crazy" monikers such as the Left Coast, Californification, Mexifornia and a host of others that bring light to the enormous failures of this once golden state whose California dreamin' utopia is now just a blur in the rear view mirror of California's history. Today, it's a neo-feudal dystopia but still has the world's fifth largest economy. How bizarre!

In most every statistic, from homelessness, housing, income disparity, identity politics, illegal immigration, environmental mismanagement, climate activism, public education, free speech suppression, anti-business and middle class, pro crime and homelessness, underfunded pensions, big labor and government, excessive taxation, irrational governance, etc.—California has fallen from grace to disgrace in the 21st century.

So many of California's Democratic supermajority priorities, approved legislation, and socialist policies are beyond "unsapient"—more than just shear "madness"—they're firmly encamped in the "idiocracy" zone with a one-way ticket to a progressivism nightmare. Nevertheless, together, and united, we can stop this Hollywood horror script from becoming a woke reality show if we take decisive action now.

California Madness provides a perfect object lesson for the rest of the United States as to how the California dream was destroyed, when, and by whom and why it's negative influence, if not corrected now, will eventually destroy the American dream as well.

As a once proud native Californian, I cover the major issues facing California using viewpoint diversity, sapient think tanks, renowned authors, and detailed reports—all free of fake news and false narratives.

For some of you this *MADNESS* book will be a revelation, an epiphany, a sapient being moment. For others, it will be a triggering event, denial of truth, and a painful intervention.

Like all *MADNESS* textbooks, *California Madness* offers an opportunity for Californians to learn about what ails the state and be part of the solution to its many problems. In retrospect, too many of the issues covered in *California Madness* are the inspiration for the critical topics and sapient analyses in the majority of the 50 *MADNESS* sapient textbook series (see Appendix for a link to all 50 textbook titles).

Are you interested in learning about the depth and breadth of California's issues, reasons for recall, leftist legislation, over regulation, population madness, illegal immigration, economic degradation, progressivism madness, etc. and how to work together to reform state policies and change its leadership before they destroy this once golden state?

If yes, please read on and if you also believe in the message of this book and willing to fight for it—please considering joining or participating in one of the three SAPIENT Being programs below.

Make Free Speech Again On Campus (MFSAOC) Program

Provide high school and college students the opportunity to start SAPIENT Being campus clubs, chapters, and alliances where independent, liberal, and conservative minded students can meet, discuss, and debate important issues and develop sapience in the process. Learn more about the process of practicing, protecting, and promoting viewpoint diversity, freedom of speech, and intellectual humility as part of the Make Free Speech Again On Campus (MFSAOC) program for on or off site campus groups at https://www.sapientbeing.org/programs.

World Of Writing Warriors (WOWW) Program

Return free speech, open dialogue and civil discourse to high school and college students and journalists without the cancel culture against those with differences in opinion, ideologies, and practices. Encourage open debate, dialogue, and the free expression of alternative and non-orthodox viewpoints with the goal of creating a World Of Writing Warriors (WOWW) program at https://www.sapientbeing.org/programs that upholds journalistic standards throughout all types of campus journalism and media.

Sapient Conservative Textbooks (SCT) Program

Relevant and current events textbooks program to help return conservative values, viewpoint diversity, and sapience to high school and college students and enlighten them on the many blessings to humankind that are the direct result of American exceptionalism, Western European culture, and Judeo-Christian values. The ethos for every textbook in the Sapient Conservative Textbooks (SCT) program is truth without bias and for more information on the 50 titles please visit the program website at https://www.fratirepublishing.com/madnessbooks.

Are You a Sapient Being or Want to Be One?

Sapience, also known as wisdom, is the ability to think and act using knowledge, experience, understanding, common sense and insight. Sapience is associated with attributes such as intelligence, enlightenment, unbiased judgment, compassion, experiential self-knowledge, self-actualization, and virtues such as ethics and benevolence.

Being a sapient being is not about identity politics, it's about doing what is right and borrows many of the essential qualities of Centrism that supports strength, tradition, open mindedness, and policy based on evidence not ideology.

Sapient beings are independent minded thinkers that achieve common sense solutions that appropriately address America's and the world's most pressing issues. They gauge situations based on context and reason, consideration, and probability. They are open minded and exercise conviction and willing to fight for it on the intellectual battlefield. Sapient beings don't blindly and recklessly follow their feelings or emotions.

Their unifying ideology is based on the truth, reason, logic, scientific method, and pragmatism—and not necessarily defined by compromise, moderation, or any particular faith—but is considerate of them.

Most importantly, per a letter written by Princeton professor Robert George in 2017 and endorsed by 28 professors from three Ivy League universities for incoming freshmen, "Think for yourself!"

George's letter continues:

Thinking for yourself means questioning dominant ideas even when others insist on their being treated as unquestionable. It means deciding what one believes not by conforming to fashionable opinions, but by taking the trouble to learn and honestly consider the strongest arguments to be advanced on both or all sides of questions—including arguments for positions that others revile and want to stigmatize and against positions others seek to immunize from critical scrutiny.

The love of truth and the desire to attain it should motivate you to think for yourself. The central point of a college education is to seek truth and to learn the skills and acquire the virtues necessary to be a lifelong truth-seeker. Open-mindedness, critical thinking, and debate are essential to discovering the truth. Moreover, they are our best antidotes to bigotry.

Merriam-Webster's first definition of the word "bigot" is a person "who is obstinately or intolerantly devoted to his or her own opinions and prejudices." The only people who need fear open-minded inquiry and robust debate are the actual bigots, including those on campuses or in the broader society who seek to protect the hegemony of their opinions by claiming that to question those opinions is itself bigotry.

So, don't be tyrannized by public opinion. Don't get trapped in an echo chamber. Whether you in the end reject or embrace a view, make sure you decide where you stand by critically assessing the arguments for the competing positions. Think for yourself. Good luck to you in college!

Now, that might sound easy. But you will find—as you may have discovered already in high school—that thinking for yourself can be a challenge. It always demands self-discipline, and these days can require courage.

In today's climate, it's all-too-easy to allow your views and outlook to be shaped by dominant opinion on your campus or in the broader academic culture. The danger any student—or faculty member—faces today is falling into the vice of conformism, yielding to groupthink, the orthodoxy.

At many colleges and universities what John Stuart Mill called "the tyranny of public opinion" does more than merely discourage students from dissenting from prevailing views on moral, political, and other types of questions. It leads them to suppose that dominant views are so obviously correct that only a bigot or a crank could question them.

Since no one wants to be, or be thought of as, a bigot or a crank, the easy, lazy way to proceed is simply by falling into line with campus orthodoxies. Don't do it!

To be sure, our overly-politicized culture has a hard time viewing any "verbal cacophony" as a sign of strength and vibrancy. And perhaps nowhere is this truer than on many college campuses where political correctness is rampant, groupthink is common, and social media "mobs" arise in a flash to intimidate anyone who openly strays from the prevailing orthodoxy.

At the SAPIENT Being we're not intimidated—and our primary purpose is to seek the truth by enhancing viewpoint diversity, promoting intellectual humility, protecting freedom of speech and expression while developing sapience in the process—no matter what the cost on the intellectual battlefield, campus classroom, and marketplace of ideas. This is our ethos! Is it yours?

Best regards and sapiently yours,

Corey Lee Wilson

Corey Lee Wilson

S.A.P.I.E.N.T. Being

1 – California: Wave of the Future? Wake of the Past? Or Something in Between?

Credit: Bloomberg.com.

The notion of the Golden State as a "nation-state." It's a valid descriptor given that California has a population (nearly 40 million residents) that's larger than all but 35 countries (California would fall between Sudan and Iraq), the fifth largest economy in the world (ahead of India's and behind Germany's), plus remarkable diversity (92 languages other than English are spoken in the Los Angeles public school system).

From the 2020 research brief by Joel Kotkin and Marshall Toplansky *Beyond Feudalism: A Strategy to Restore California's Middle Class at the* Chapman University Center for Demographics & Policy:

California has always been a state where excess flourished, conscious of its trend-setting role as a world-leading innovator in technology, economics, and the arts. For much of the past century, it also helped create a new model for middle and working-class upward mobility while addressing racial, gender and environmental issues well in advance of the rest of the country.

The notion of California's supremacy remains implanted on the minds of the state's economic, academic, media and political establishment. "The future de- pends on us," Governor Gavin Newsom said at his inauguration. "and we will seize this moment." Progressive theorists like Laura Tyson and Lenny Mendonca laud California as the home of "a new progressive era"—an exemplar of social equity. Others see California as deserving of nationhood; it reflects, as a *New York Times* column put it, "...the shared values of our increasingly tolerant and pluralistic society."

However, if California fails to offer young people and newcomers the opportunity to improve their lot, the consequences will be catastrophic—and not only for California. The end of the California Dream would deal a devastating blow to the proposition that such a widely diverse polity can thrive. Indeed, blue America's model faces its most consequential stress test in one of its safest states, where a spectacular run of almost unbroken prosperity could be killed by a miserly approach to opportunity.

California-based *Atlantic* writer Conor Friedersdorf offers a broad and harsh critique of the state in an article entitled "The California Dream is Dying."

Despite the state's many attributes, he writes, "I fear for California's future." The generations that benefited from California's dizzying ascent into global prominence, he says, "should be striving to ensure that future generations can pursue happiness as they did. Instead, they are poised to take the California Dream to their graves by betraying a promise the state has offered from the start.

While California publicly celebrates diversity and inclusion, Friedersdorf continues, "the state's leaders and residents shut the door on economic opportunity," citing a chronic shortage of housing, high poverty, poor educational services, homelessness, and other factors that limit upward mobility

Friedersdorf warns that "blue America's model faces its most consequential stress test in one of its safest states, where a spectacular run of almost unbroken prosperity could be killed by a miserly approach to opportunity."

Thus, while Governor Newsom still sees California as "America's coming attraction," it's jarring that writers who share his ideological orientation are joining those on the right to warn the nation against emulating the state.

How Does a California Family Survive?

This section is from the July 2019 article "How Does a California Family Survive?" by the California Policy Center's Edward Ring:

It's common enough to discuss the high cost-of-living in California. It's become a serious topic, at last. But for Californians who are used to paying ridiculous prices for everything, it may be helpful to present a comparison in the form of an annual family budget. How much does it cost to take care of a family of four in Los Angeles compared to Houston?

The choice of Los Angeles is logical enough. One in four Californians live there. And while Los Angeles County may be more expensive than most of California's inland counties, it is not cheaper than Orange, San Diego, or any of the nine counties of the San Francisco Bay Area. Altogether there are over 25 million Californians living in expensive coastal counties. Two out of three Californians endure the types of prices depicted here.

The choice of Houston is also logical, not simply as a representative of cheaper Texas, but as a proxy for nearly all of the United States, with the only exceptions being those high-tax (usually coastal) metropolitan areas located in states ran by progressive Democrats. In terms of the cost-of-living, Houston is an authentic stand in for most of America.

Reviewing the budget depicted below, the first thing to realize is that most people don't have a household income of $100,000 per year. The median household income in California is $71,805. That means half of those 25 million people who have to live in places like Los Angeles have a household income that is less than $71,805. Let's see how much it costs to a family of four to live in such a place.

As can be seen, while Texas has no state taxes, the Californian gets a bigger federal deduction because of their much bigger home mortgage payments. Very roughly speaking, these factors cancel out. But where there's a big deduction, there's a big payment. The median price of a home in Los Angeles is a larcenous $617,000, whereas the same home in Houston will only set a family back by $189,000. Based on a 4 percent, 30 year fixed mortgage, this translates into a crippling $2,900 monthly payment in Los Angeles, vs a manageable $915 mortgage payment in Houston.

Making house payments that low used to be normal in California. They still are in those parts of this nation, Houston included, where the progressive Democrats haven't yet taken control. Or if the progressive Democrats have taken control—Houston, after all, is now a battleground county—they haven't yet had enough time to ruin everything. Consider the difference: For a household with an income of $100,000 per year, in Los Angeles, the mortgage costs 36 percent of before-tax earnings. In Houston, only 11 percent.

Comparing Costs Between California and Texas

California and Texas do not have significant differences in costs for family health insurance, but everywhere else, California costs more. Even property taxes, where Texas charges a higher rate, are nonetheless a much more significant burden to the average Californian, because the assessed value is so much higher.

Comparing the other necessities exposes additional evidence of just how difficult it is to survive in California. Electricity costs, $.20 per kWh in California vs $.11 in Texas. Natural gas, $13.60 per thousand cubic feet in California vs $8.25 in Texas. Gasoline? $3.75/gallon vs $2.35. Even food is cheaper in Texas than it is in California, the supposed breadbasket of America. The food price index—as compared to the national average—is 100.4 in Los Angeles, 92.9 in Houston.

Altogether, the average family of four in Los Angeles spends nearly $300 per month more on gasoline, utilities, and food than they would in Houston. They spend over $2,000 per month more to keep a roof over their heads. They roughly break even on health insurance and taxes.

Imagine two hard working parents who manage to bring in $100K per year. In Los Angeles, they'll have about $1,000 per month left, after paying for taxes and the bare necessities. They'll need this money to pay for telephone, internet, and cable services, garbage collection and life insurance, buy and replace clothes, furniture, and appliances, make car payments, purchase car insurance, maintain their vehicles and their home, save for college tuition and their own retirements, cover medical co-pays and deductibles, and maybe dine out from time to time and take an occasional vacation. It's not enough.

Let that sink in. A family of four can barely survive in California on a household income of $100,000 per year. One unexpected financial shock, and they are underwater.

In Houston, by contrast, this same family will still have over $3,500 per month left over after paying for taxes and the bare necessities. This is enough money to make additional purchases and payments and still have some left over for savings. A family making $100,000 per year cannot afford to live in Los Angeles, yet they can live reasonably well in Houston—or pretty much anywhere except in California and other deep blue enclaves across the land.

And what about those families that don't make $100,000? What about households earning at the median California income of around $72,000 per year? What about single parent households, with a working mom trying to keep a roof over her family, perhaps renting a home in Los Angeles, where the average rental home costs $2,371 per month vs $1,092 per month in Houston?

What bravery it must require to be a Californian trying to raise a family. Trying to make ends meet. How did it come to this?

California and Its Contradictions

As reported throughout his chapter section from the November 2020 *City Journal* article "California and Its Contradictions: Rumblings of realignment beneath a solid-blue surface" by Joel Kotkin:

Overall, to be sure, California voters reaffirmed one-party rule in 2020, giving Joe Biden a two-to-one victory and maintaining the Democratic veto-proof majority in both legislative houses. The dominant urban centers, San Francisco and Los Angeles, went ever further into left field, approving radical measures such as increasing wealth taxes and using public funds to fight racism.

They also overwhelmingly backed measures to raise commercial property taxes, expand rent control, and reimpose affirmative action, though these efforts failed miserably elsewhere in the state. San Francisco, where Biden won 85 percent of the vote, also voted for a new tax on companies where CEOs make too much compared with employees, and a measure to allow noncitizens to serve on public boards.

The good news for Californians is that the rest of the state is not quite ready for socialist rule by the public unions and their allies. "It's not so much light pouring through the window, as a small crack opening," suggests Joel Fox, editor of the widely read California political website Fox and Hounds Daily. The opportunity for centrists and conservatives lies in what a Marxist might describe as "heightening the contradictions" within the blue alliance.

Consider the battle over Proposition 22, funded by Uber and Lyft, to overturn the state's onerous AB5 law, which sought to force employers to treat contract drivers as full-time employees. This mandate, as the tech firms understood, would destroy their business model and their fortunes. Tech elites, who also worked tirelessly to defeat Donald Trump, spent an estimated $200 million to push the measure against labor opposition, and they seem to have won the day.

The conflict between the tech elites and labor, though, is not restricted to ride-sharing firms. Taxes remain a major battlefield. With the apparent defeat of Proposition 15, legislators seem likely to consider new statewide measures to raise income-tax rates to as high as 16 percent. This cannot be good news to the tech industry; not only its fabulously rich owners but also many of their well-paid top employees would be affected.

The State's Business Regulations Threaten California Companies

The state's business regulations threaten even the most heralded, emblematic California companies. Disney executive chairman Robert Iger has fought with the state's progressives, who generally favor extreme lockdowns, to keep his businesses open, but Disneyland remained closed for 412 days, resulting in 28,000 layoffs, and reopened on April 30, 2021, long after the company's parks in Florida and abroad were already operating. The state's inflexibility led Disney's Bob Iger to resign from Governor Newsom's coronavirus recovery taskforce.

Tesla's Elon Musk has also dissented, having battled with Alameda County officials about the opening of his plant. More importantly, he seems to be shifting his investment focus, and perhaps even his headquarters, from California. He has already announced big expansion plans for both Tesla and Space X in Texas.

The contradictions between tech and entertainment oligarchs and the hard Left are likely to intensify in the years ahead. The state has neglected the basics of business competitiveness, particularly in creating the mid-skilled jobs crucial to a healthy economy. University of California at Irvine's Ken Murphy estimates that, outside the Bay Area, 85 percent of all new jobs have paid below the area median income of $66,000; 40 percent pay under $40,000 a year. Once a beacon of opportunity, the Golden State suffers the nation's highest cost-adjusted poverty rate.

Governor Newsom's high-profile preening about lockdowns has made things worse, particularly for tourism and hospitality. In September 2020, California's unemployment rate stood at 11 percent, well above the national average of 7.9 percent and better than only four other states in the nation. Since the March 2020 lockdown, California, with 12 percent of the nation's population, accounts for 16.4 percent of its unemployment.

Of the 55 largest metropolitan areas in the U.S., some of the worst job losses from February to August 2020 have occurred in the Bay Area and Los Angeles-Long Beach. Things are particularly grim for the L.A. area, with its huge exposure to losses in hospitality and other low-end service fields. Overall, Los Angeles has lost 11 percent of its jobs, Murphy notes, significantly higher than the 8 percent drop nationally.

At the same time, one sees clear signs that tech growth will be limited, as more companies expand outside the state and some, like Palantir, the data-mining software company, relocate, in its case to Denver. Some 40 percent of Bay Area tech workers say that they would like to move to a less expensive region, which suggests locations outside of California. In a recent survey, three-quarters of high-tech venture funders and founders predicted the same for their workforces.

For many Democrats, the loss of jobs demands not a change in state policies that chase away jobs but further expansion of government, including the creation of a basic income for its vast numbers of underemployed and underemployed. This is particularly critical for the Latino working class that—in sharp contrast with Latinos in Texas—has remained attached to Democrats, giving Trump barely half the percentage he won in the Lone Star State. Rather than push for economic growth, young Latinos, such as millennials elected this week to the city council in predominantly Hispanic Santa Ana, follow a progressive script about racial justice, public spending, and rent control.

Given the lack of upward mobility in California, such positions are not surprising. A population with little hope of starting a business, owning a home, or making a decent income naturally looks to government as its provider. Add to this the state's extreme climate policies, which disproportionately affect industries that employ blue-collar workers, and it's a perfect storm for continued progressive agitation.

California Remains Intellectually Dominated by a Leftist Media and Academic Elite Promoting Class Warfare

If California remains intellectually dominated by a leftist media and academic elite promoting class warfare, it will be hard to create a more diverse, less dependent political culture. Instead, we will see the continued flight of middle and working-class families out of state. They leave behind both an expanding underclass—a recent UCLA report found that there were enough homeless students of grade-school age to fill five Dodger Stadiums—and older, wealthier residents who came to California when the going was good.

Some conservatives rightly hail the rejection of the affirmative action referendum and of AB5 as landmark victories that show a potential pushback to the state's relentless progressivism. "Californians are conservatives who think they're Democrats," suggests the right-of-center California Policy Center.

This hopeful sentiment has some basis, but for now, it's not likely that the state will abandon the high-tax and heavy-regulation policies that impoverish its population. For example, radical new proposals for slavery reparations—though California was admitted to the Union as a free state—are likely to emerge soon. Worse yet, California's political reach seems to be expanding, despite its manifest failures, creating its own system of ideological satellites also known as Californification. Arizona, for example, has raised its state income taxes to among the nation's highest, and states like Colorado and Nevada have shifted steadily leftward.

The Battle to Change Policy Direction Regarding Class Warfare Has to be Won in California

Ultimately, the battle to change policy direction—for the West generally, and maybe in the country as a whole—has to be won in California. This can only be accomplished by convincing young people and minorities that their future aspirations make them allies to the shrinking white middle-class population.

Until ethnic minorities, including Asians—the state's most rapidly growing and economically vigorous minority, which widely opposed the affirmative action proposition—absorb the pro-business and pro-growth ethic that built Californian prosperity, the state will at best continue its sideways drift into malaise.

Similarly, the attempt to drive Uber and Lyft out of business seems likely to alienate at least some of tech honchos and their employees. In an era where tech jobs are more mobile, and other regions are making appeals both to younger workers and high-paid executives, the state faces a severe economic reckoning. But given the progressive proclivities of the tech sector, any shift to a pragmatic center might be gradual, at best.

More critical to change may be an incipient rebellion against progressive policies by working-class voters. Some pushback is evident even from the unions and union-friendly politicians, as well as leading civil rights groups, representing working-class districts. Early opposition to Newsom's proclamation banning gas-powered cars has come from the likes of Democrat Jim Cooper, who represents a largely working-class district south of Sacramento. Cooper recently noted that the greens, "from their leaders to their funders, are nearly all white," and their policies tend to seek "environmental justice" in forms that create a "burden to lower-income, working-class Californians" who more often are non-white.

Even some of the Democrat-aligned private-sector labor unions have become more hostile to Newsom's "visionary" actions. The oil and gas industry employs 152,000 people in California, and these workers, two-thirds without college degrees, make $80,500 a year on average—far more than the average for "green" jobs. "Can we immediately start talking about jobs? We can hate on oil, but the truth is our refinery jobs are really good middle-class jobs," tweeted labor heroine Assemblywoman Lorena Gonzalez, author of AB 5. "Jobs can't be an afterthought to any climate change legislation."

These divisions and contradictions suggest the path exists for a true restoration of California as a beacon of entrepreneurship and opportunity. Election Day 2020 brought some promising results, but a state that retains a veto-proof legislature, a lockstep progressive governor preparing for a future trip to the White House, powerful public unions, and a debilitated political opposition still faces a long road back to sanity—and prosperity.

Making America California? Please Don't!

As reported in this section from the January 2021 *City Journal* article "Making America California" by Joel Kotkin:

As the Biden administration settles in and begins to formulate its agenda, progressive pundits, politicians, and activists point to California as a role model for national policy. If the administration listens to them, it would prove a disaster for America's already-beleaguered middle and working classes. And yet, the Biden administration seems determined to run the country on the ruinous model of the Golden State.

Biden suggests an ecstatic account in the *Los Angeles Times*, seeks to "make America California again," and he will have plenty of help. Californians will run Health and Human Services, the Treasury, Homeland Security, and Energy. Former California senator Kamala Harris is vice president, and San Francisco's Nancy Pelosi rules the House of Representatives. Progressives like Laura Tyson and Lenny Mendonca see the shift as embracing "California's distinctive approach to market capitalism." The Golden State, they insist, can "show the way forward" toward a more socially just future.

As a California native over nearly half a century, I wonder if these worthies see the same state I do. California has its wonderful spots, great neighborhoods, beautiful vistas, amazing entrepreneurs, and great amenities, but it makes a poor advertisement for social democracy. It suffers the nation's highest poverty rate and presents the widest gap between middle and upper-middle income earners of any state. Minorities—notably African-Americans and Latinos—do worse in California's metros than elsewhere in the country, according to a recent study that we conducted at the Urban Reform Institute. In Atlanta, African-American median incomes, adjusted for costs, are almost double those in San Francisco and Los Angeles; Latinos earn $20,000 more in midwestern and southern cities than in the enlightened metros along the California coast.

Simply put, California's performance economically, particularly for its middle and working classes, hardly constitutes a model of social justice or green accomplishment. In actual reductions of greenhouse gases, California is not the environmental icon that it pretends to be. If the largely preventable wildfires are included, the state has increased its emissions; the smoldering fires, as one environmental analyst puts it, "dwarf the state's fossil fuel emissions."

In the end, the California model works only for the few—but if enough of these super-wealthy few stay put, then the Golden State might yet pretend that it can survive the effects of its policies. It's doubtful that the rest of the country could enjoy that luxury.

A New Vision for California? Let's Do It!

More from the 2020 research brief by Joel Kotkin and Marshall Toplansky *Beyond Feudalism: A Strategy to Restore California's Middle Class:*

Our state's leaders describe California as a beacon of social justice, particularly for historically disadvantaged minorities. Yet our examination of the state economic and demographic trajectory clearly does not support these contentions. Viewed from the perspective of race or class inequality, California is increasingly not a paragon, but rather a cautionary tale of over-regulation and excessive geographic and corporate concentration; an exemplar not of middle-class opportunity, but of resurgent feudalism.

Our vision of California starts first and foremost with improving the lives of our middle and working-class people, and of preserving the state as a place where people will choose to raise families. The program we propose would address these needs by reforming energy, tax, housing, and business regulations so that a broader array of companies and better paying job opportunities are created not for the few, but for the broad population. What matters ultimately is not intentions, but results. Rather than proclaim progressive values, California government needs to focus on the impact of regulatory and tax policy on the daily lives of middle and working-class people.

Today, our state is socially, fiscally, and economically unsustainable

As more people give up hope that their own lives will improve, particularly in the wake of coronavirus, they look increasingly to government for succor. This is true even among tech employees in Silicon Valley, many of whom have little chance to replicate the opportunities for wealth accumulation enjoyed by prior generations in the Bay Area. As the middle-class has shrunk and politics have shifted to a redistributionism ideology, California has become painfully dependent on its ultra-rich class, which pays upwards of half the state's income taxes.

Ultimately, California's neo-feudal model can only be sustained by massive transfers of funds from the very rich to the country's largest collection of poor people, many of whom are working. Redistributionism could promise relief for some in the short run, but would slow economic opportunity. After all, this is a state that voted heavily for socialist Bernie Sanders at a time that Democrats elsewhere opted for more moderate candidates.

The redistributionist model can also be seen in housing policies such as rent control and limits on the rights of owners to keep homes empty or even allow squatters; these are not measures likely to encourage housing investment, but can appeal to voters who feel beleaguered by high prices and lack of opportunity. Construction of high-density housing by companies like Google and Facebook has been aptly described by *The Guardian* not as progressive, but as "a looming feudal nightmare." It is fantasy to believe there is any potential for Improvement through such initiatives.

Some argue that California has developed a "fiscally responsible" form of capitalism, as evidenced by a series of annual budget surpluses. But it's questionable whether California has the financial wherewithal to sustain expanded subsidies for its large, and increasingly permanent, poor population.

Even Jerry Brown has remarked that the "Johnny one note" tech economy could stumble, reducing the huge returns on capital gains that are so critical to generating state revenues. This could be imminent, given the recent poor performance of tech IPOs and the $100 billion drop in the value of privately held unicorns. The early results from the Covid 19 pandemic demonstrate the state's high level of fiscal indebtedness, with the state going from a $20 billion surplus to an over $50 billion deficit.

The state's dependence on capital gains and income tax make it particularly vulnerable.

These decline could be catastrophic for many California communities . Even before the pandemic, over two-thirds of California cities do not have any funds set aside for retiree healthcare and other expenses. Twelve of the state's fifteen largest cities are in the red, and for many it is only getting worse. The current coronavirus-induced recession illustrates just how tenuous California's financial condition is: both private and public sector revenue has nosedived.

The state overall suffers a trillion dollars in pension debt, notes former Democratic State Senator Joe Nation. US News places California, despite the tech boom, 42nd in fiscal health among the states.

Much of this debt has benefited a select group of retirees that hold public-sector pensions, some 40,000 members of the "$100,000 club" who will be living large off taxpayers, most of whom have far more meager funds, for decades to come.209 Ultimately, these obligations can be met either though vastly higher taxes or through sustained, broad based growth, which, among other things, would lower the demand for subsidies and other transfer payments.

A Strategy to Transform California in One Election

This section is from the June 2019 article "A Strategy to Transform California in One Election" by the California Policy Center's Edward Ring:

As a statewide political force, California's conservative voters are disenfranchised. Almost no politicians holding state office speak for conservatives, few court rulings favor conservatives, and nearly everywhere, conservative values are discredited or ignored by a hostile press. But California's political landscape could be poised for dramatic shifts. Even now, after more than a decade of national economic expansion that has especially favored California's high tech industries, the negative consequences of liberal political dominance are increasingly visible.

Today Californian voters might reject liberal governance if they were offered candidates offering a new political agenda designed to rescue California's schools and lower the cost of living. A successful agenda to transform California doesn't even have to be labeled "conservative." A new political agenda for California can be presented as nonpartisan, targeting not only conservatives, but independents and disaffected liberals. To fill the big tent, all this agenda has to do is offer big ideas that will have transformative impact.

Proponents of a new political agenda for California will arouse fierce opposition from special interests and ideologues ranging from orthodox libertarians to fanatic leftist "identitarians," to the environmentalist lobby and their profiteering corporate partners. But the ferocity of their opposition can be used against them; surely these common sense solutions can't possibly be as bad as they're saying. Every negative ad they run, and every negative commentary spewed by their acolytes and puppets, will harm their cause as much as it helps because it will expose them: what they object to is an agenda for the people, not the special interests or the fanatics.

To counter the opposition, proponents of a new agenda for California must assert, continuously and without apology, principles they know are right:

- Competitive abundance instead of politically contrived scarcity.

- Equality of opportunity instead of equality of outcome.

- Practical environmentalism instead of extremism.

The rhetoric that can derive from these principles should cascade into every set of talking points, campaign flyers, op-eds, and responses to attacks from California's liberal elites. The rhetoric should occupy and hold the moral high ground:

- There is a moral value to providing opportunity by making California affordable.

- There is a moral value to instilling pride by abandoning race and gender preferences.

- There is a moral value to embracing policies of abundance—by turning the private sector loose to increase the supply of housing, energy, water, transportation.

Here then, are twelve specific proposals that might constitute a political agenda to be aggressively promoted as a way to break the liberal power that is breaking California.

A Bipartisan, Transformative Political Agenda for California

This last section is from the June 2019 article "A Bipartisan, Transformative Political Agenda for California" by the California Policy Center's Edward Ring:

In the end, California's promise can only be restored by developing policies that empower, not suppress, the aspirations of the middle-class. "Happy the nation whose people have not forgotten how to rebel," noted British historian R.H. Tawney. It is a lesson that has been replicated throughout history, and now needs to extend to California.

Californians must counteract policies that have converted the state from an exemplar of opportunity and personal growth to a harbinger of a neo-feudalist society, dominated by a handful of wealthy people and a growing mass of serfs without hope of property ownership. Particularly in tough times, Californians can no longer afford those delusions of California's leaders. These continue to exact real costs on the lives and livelihoods of our people, as anyone who travels this huge and diverse state can see. The time to change course is now.

(1) Public Education Reform:

K-12 Tenure, Layoff, Dismissal Policies: California teachers will be required to complete a minimum of five years of classroom teaching prior to being granted tenure. School principals shall have sole authority over what teachers may be subject to layoff, in order to allow merit instead of seniority to govern layoff decisions. The process for dismissing incompetent or ineffective teachers shall be streamlined.

(2) Enable Charter Schools:

The right of nonprofit institutions to open charter public schools shall not be infringed; no limit shall be set on the number of charter schools. Charter school approval shall be binding based on any one of the following agencies granting approval—the local school district board, the local county board of education, or the California Dept. of Education.

(3) Housing Abundance:

Repeal the "Sustainable Communities and Climate Protection Act" of 2008 and make it easy for developers to build homes on the suburban and exurban fringes, instead of just "in-fill" that destroys existing neighborhoods. Cancel the war on the single family dwelling, and allow developers (or in some cases even require them) to build homes with large yards again. Repeal excessive building codes such as mandatory photovoltaic roof panels. Create a regulatory environment that encourages private investment in new housing developments instead of discouraging it.

(4) Helping the Homeless:

California's attorney general will challenge the decision in Jones vs the City of Los Angeles, that ruled that law enforcement and city officials can no longer enforce the ban on sleeping on sidewalks anywhere within the Los Angeles city limits until a sufficient amount of permanent supportive housing could be built. To help all the homeless, and to get them off the streets, argue for ruling that permits cost-effective shelter, hospitalization, and incarceration, as appropriate.

(5) Restore Law and Order:

Repeal Prop 47 which downgraded property crimes and drug offenses, making it impossible to engage in "broken windows" policing. Repeal Prop. 57, which released thousands of criminals back onto California's streets. Repeal AB 953, which needlessly bureaucratized police work and made it harder to make arrests based on objective criteria.

(6) CEQA Reform:

California's Environmental Quality Act of 1970, "CEQA," will be modified as follows: (a) duplicative lawsuits shall be prohibited, (b) all entities that file CEQA lawsuits will be required to fully disclose their identities and their environmental or non-environmental interest, (c) court rules that still enable delaying tactics will be illegal, (d) rulings that stop entire projects on a single issue will be prohibited, (d) the loser in CEQA litigation will be liable for legal fees.

(7) Renewables Pricing Reform:

Under the current flawed system, California's public utilities are required to purchase an ever increasing percentage of their total kilowatt-hours from "renewable" sources. But then these utilities have to purchase backup power from other sources which can only make money as backup power plants, greatly increasing their prices since they can't operate all the time.

Meanwhile providers of renewable energy only have to invest in relatively inexpensive, intermittent power–solar panels and wind farms. This makes renewable energy appear far cheaper than it is in reality. To fix this, California must require renewable electricity suppliers to include in their pricing the costs for them to deliver reliable continuous power 24 hours per day, 365 days per year, and lower its renewable portfolio mandate to 20 percent until renewables are competitive with other forms of energy using this new pricing model.

(8) Nuclear Power Development:

California's government will use all its powers to promote nuclear power. It will recommission the San Onofre nuclear power station and construct additional reactors. It will cancel the planned decommissioning of Diablo Canyon nuclear power station and construct additional reactors.

It will solicit bids for public/private financing of additional nuclear power capacity with a goal of increasing total California based nuclear power output from the current 2.1 gigawatts to at least 10 gigawatts. The state attorney general will aggressively litigate in support of fast tracking approval and construction of these projects.

(9) Water Infrastructure Funding:

California will issue general obligation bonds in the sum of $30 billion to accomplish the following specific projects: (a) $3.0 billion for the Sites Reservoir (supplementing funds already granted) with storage capacity of 2.0 million acre feet (MAF), (b) $3.0 billion for the Temperance Flat Reservoir with storage capacity of 1.0 MAF, (c) $7.5 billion for desalination plants on the California coast with annual capacity of 0.5 MAF, (d) $7.5 billion to retrofit urban water treatment plants statewide to potable standards with annual reuse capacity of 1.0 MAF, (e) $4.0 billion to retrofit existing aqueducts with priority on the Friant/Kern canal, (f) $5.0 billion for seismic retrofits to levees statewide, with a focus on the Delta. The timeline for submittal of proposals and awarding of funds shall not exceed 12 months. The state attorney general will aggressively litigate in support of fast tracking approval and construction of these projects.

(10) Additional Highway Funding:

California will issue general obligation bonds in the sum of 30 billion to upgrade and add lanes to every major freeway in the state. Priority shall be granted to construction of high speed lanes and smart lanes. These funds will supplement funds already awarded for road construction. The timeline for submittal of proposals and awarding of funds shall not exceed 12 months. The state attorney general will aggressively litigate in support of fast tracking approval and construction of these projects.

(11) Pension Benefit Reform:

The California constitution will be amended to eliminate the so-called "California Rule," which allegedly prohibits modification to pension benefit accruals for future work. Pension benefits for state and local employees, for future work, shall revert to rates of accrual that were in effect in 1998.

(12) Pension Funds Infrastructure Investment:

California's state and local government employee pension funds shall be required to invest a minimum of 10 percent of their assets in general obligation bonds. These investments shall be limited to infrastructure bonds issued by the state to fund water or transportation infrastructure within California.

From a practical standpoint, these is the question of who would promote this sort of political agenda. But it doesn't have to be a political party. It can bypass party organizations. For example, it can take the form of twelve state ballot initiatives, funded by a coalition of donors, or, for that matter, just one of California's 124 billionaires.

With that in place, candidates for office, no matter what party they belong to, could endorse these initiatives and pledge to support them legislatively if elected. There are a lot of ways to skin a cat. California's politically active citizens, from the grassroots to the pinnacles of political and economic power, need to recognize the opportunity that beckons.

2 – Total Recall: Governor Newsom's Totalitarianism & Pandemic Sanctions

Credit: www.RecallGavin2020.com.

Starting this chapter is the February 2021 report "The Economic Unraveling of California's Governor" by the Hoover Institution's Lee Ohanian:

Gavin Newsom was riding high last fall, with 64 percent job approval. Fast forward a few months later and Newsom is now scrambling to salvage his first term, with just 48 percent approval, as a grassroots effort to recall his governorship is on track for qualifying for November's state ballot, with nearly 1.5 million signatures.

What happened? Plenty, and Californians may be on the verge of finally holding politicians accountable for their failure to govern. Newsom began his governorship with ambitious plans: Solve California's housing shortage and reduce homelessness, promising the 21st-century equivalent of a Marshall Plan to expand housing supply. Reduce medical costs. Improve schools. The list went on.

But even before the pandemic, neither Newsom nor the state legislature had moved the needle on any of these issues. Without strong and sensible leadership, California's problems deteriorated further. Housing costs rose further as new housing construction barely budged, remaining a whopping 85 percent below Newsom's goal. California's median home price is now $717,000, and the median priced condominium is $520,000.

Medical costs rose further, reflecting a poorly performing state Medicaid system (the medical care used by low-income households) that now enrolls nearly 13 million Californians. If our Medicaid enrollees were a state, it would be the fifth largest in the country. A recent audit of the system showed that many problems remain, including integrity issues, long after being identified in a previous audit.

So what has been accomplished? A new law that forbids many Californians from working as independent contractors. A ban on single-use shampoos, the kind you find in hotels. New rent controls that will reduce rental housing supply, making it even more difficult and costly for young families to find and afford housing. Ironically, it was socialist economist Assar Lindbeck who remarked that rent control is the most effective way to destroy a city, next to wartime bombing.

There have been also plenty of executive orders, including one that prohibits the sale of new gasoline-powered vehicles starting in 2035, in a state that is responsible for less than one percent of global carbon emissions. It seems the governor is long on dreaming far into the future and short on understanding, much less addressing, Californians' priorities

The Premises of California's Dysfunction

This section is from the March 2020 article "The Premises of California's Dysfunction" by the California Policy Center's Edward Ring:

Anyone unfamiliar with what is really going on in California would have listened to Governor Newsom's State of the State address on February 12, 2020, and gotten the impression that things have never been better. Newsom's opening set the tone for the rest of his 4,400 word monologue:

"By every traditional measure, the state of our state is strong. We have a record-breaking surplus. We've added 3 million jobs since the depths of the recession. Wages are rising. We have more scientists, researchers, and engineers, more Nobel laureates, and the finest system of higher education anywhere in the world."

Newsom, to his credit, immediately qualified his sunny opening with a disclaimer that might be the understatement of the century, saying "But along with that prosperity and progress, there are problems that have been deferred for too long and that threaten to put the California dream out of reach for too many. We face hard decisions that are coming due."

Gavin Newsom, the political party he represents, and the ideology they've embraced, cannot possibly solve these "problems that have been deferred for too long." First, because Newsom and his gang created the problems, and second, because the ideology they adhere to is based on premises that are both economically unsustainable and destined to eventually deliver not solutions, but tyranny.

California's Recall Is 'Not' Because 1.7 Million Signatories Are Racists

This chapter section is from the June 2021 report "California's Recall Election Is On—And Not Because 1.7 Million Signatories Are Racists" by the Hoover Institution's Lee Ohanian:

Out of 1.7 million signatures among California voters to recall Governor Gavin Newsom, only 43 were withdrawn during the state's 30-day "change your mind" period. Newsom and the state's Democratic party would have you believe that the recall is racist and is akin to treason. This is of course not about race, nor is it about treason, as California law permits such a recall. But the fact that Newsom and his party have strategically woven such a tale tells you all you need to know about why so many are so concerned about Newsom's performance.

This recall is about inadequate governance, a failure to lead, and the continuation of economic policies that benefit a few elites at the expense of nearly everyone else. It is about how millions of Californians have economically suffered during the COVID-19 pandemic at the hands of dysfunctional government institutions. And its genesis is a familiar one: a one-party state with virtually no accountability that picks its politicians seemingly without an eye toward whether they will be able to govern or not.

Because of extreme and confusing business closures, California's economy has suffered enormously, including having the highest unemployment rate in the country outside of Hawaii and Nevada, both of which depend enormously on the travel industry. From this perspective no state managed the pandemic worse than California. And California's recovery is far behind the rest of the country. The average state has restored about 2/3 of the number of jobs lost during the pandemic. California has only restored ½ of those jobs, and in the meantime, California is shrinking, losing businesses and people to low-tax and low-cost-of-living states.

California has not only lost more jobs during the pandemic and restored fewer jobs as the economy expands, but it has grossly failed with the basic function of helping the state's unemployed.

While over a million legitimate unemployment claims remained unpaid for months, the state's Employment Development Department has paid out $32 billion in fraudulent claims. Yes, that is "billion," with a "b." The problem? Sixty-year-old software that has been patched so often that it no longer is reliable and has become easy to hack, plus a failure by the department to heed warnings about lax security. A rapper has even recorded a song about how he became rich from unemployment fraud.

What should have been a top priority to fix remains problematic, with more fraud likely to come: "We are nowhere near the end of this particular fraud," notes Eva Velasquez, president and CEO of the Identity Theft Resource Center, a nonprofit that helps victims of identity theft.

Failure to Address Priorities Through Incompetence, or by Making Priority Issues Non-Priorities

Once vaccines became available, the most important job for state government was to efficiently distribute vaccines and get people inoculated. But California was among the worst states in vaccination rates due to a lack of coordination between Sacramento and California's counties, sort of a "left hand doesn't know what the right hand is doing" situation. State performance was so bad—only 22 percent of survey respondents viewed the state's vaccine efforts favorably—that it was largely turned over to Blue Shield and Kaiser Permanente. What does it say about state government when it can't manage the most important public health responsibility it has faced in decades

Another priority should be investing in the state's water supply and infrastructure. But despite being home to some of the most innovative businesses in the world that could surely come up with answers (how about more desalination?), California politicians continue to kick the water can down the road, pray for rain, institute water rationing whenever drought hits (roughly every third year), and spend millions on ads touring the benefits of turning your lawn into a cactus garden, taking short showers, and making sure you only run your dishwasher when it is full.

The 2020–21 winter was one of the driest in many parts of California, so dry that Lake Oroville's hydroelectric plant may need to shut down due to low water levels, and so dry, that algae is blooming in some reservoirs at such rates that drinking water is tasting like dirt. (I didn't know that algae tasted like dirt either.) You'd think this would be cause for concern, yes? With corrective steps taken? Well, no. Consumers are instead advised to add some lemon to mask the unpleasant flavor. Apparently, adding lemon to drinking water is about as far as the state will help.

The above examples are about the state's performance during the pandemic. What about Newsom's first 14 months, before the pandemic? Newsom's signature campaign promise when he was elected in 2018 was a "Marshall Plan" for housing, promising to expand construction enormously to address California's ever-deepening housing shortage. How did that turn out? Housing starts in 2019, Newsom's first year in office, were about 80 percent below Newsom's annual goal. And before the pandemic hit, in March 2020, housing starts weren't looking much better in late 2019 and early 2020.

Well—So Much For Accomplishments

Plenty of California politicians have been able to stay in office by convincing their constituents that they have what it takes, even if they haven't moved the needle.

Going for the proverbial political hat trick, Newsom recently advertised that 90,000 acres of California land susceptible to wildfire have been treated with fire breaks and other preventive measures. The problem? Data obtained by National Public Radio and CapRadio show that only 11,000 acres were treated. Just 13 percent of what was advertised. So far, nary a word from the governor's office about this, despite a detailed letter from NPR spelling out the investigation and the data that were obtained.

Even progressive politicians such as San Francisco supervisor Dean Peterson tweeted about Newsom: "This cynical BS is why people hate politicians and maybe part of why our Governor faces recall."

Governing a state as large as California is difficult. But after two and a half years, it has become clear that Newsom is not the person who should be governing the state. Newsom was handpicked by Democratic party kingmaker Willie Brown to head San Francisco's parking commission, then Newsom became San Francisco city supervisor, then mayor, then lieutenant governor, and now he is governor. California has become a political monarchy, and we all know that monarchies rarely serve the little people well. It is time for voters to demand better.

Meet Governor Preen: Gavin Newsom

Credit: Bill Melugin @ Fox News - Governor Gavin Newsom at the Napa dinner party at the French Laundry Restaurant.

This chapter section is from the November 2020 *City Journal* article "Governor Preen" by Joel Kotkin:

California's Gavin Newsom presides with aristocratic hauteur over a state in crisis—but if Hollywood were to cast a governor and future president, and if a straight white male were still politically acceptable, he would look like California's Gavin Newsom. The 53-year-old governor, a former mayor of San Francisco, Newsom handsomely epitomizes the progressive politics of the California elite class that has nurtured and financed his career from the beginning.

Like aristocrats of the past, Newsom seems oblivious to the realities felt by constituents among the lower orders. In the face of massive wildfires, he postures on climate change, conflating fires with an angry mother Earth—as opposed to poor land management—and uses the conflagration to justify a radical policy of switching to all-electric power over the next decade, with the elimination of gas-powered cars by 2035. In the midst of a near economic free-fall, he favors raising taxes and works to tighten pandemic lockdowns; and, with the state losing its ability to train workers, he backs an education system where almost three out of five California high schoolers graduate unprepared for either college or a career.

Listening to Newsom, or following California media, one would have no idea how badly California's economy has performed during the pandemic. In the most recent statistics, California's unemployment rate stood at 11 percent, well above the national average of 7.9 percent, and better than only four other states.

Since the March 2020 lockdown, California, with 12 percent of the nation's population, accounts for 16.4 percent of all unemployment. California also is recovering jobs slower than all but two states, tourism-dependent Hawaii and Nevada. Since the pandemic, the state's largest metro, Los Angeles–Orange County, has suffered the second-largest job losses in the U.S., and two others, the Bay Area and the Inland Empire, rank in the top ten.

This awful performance has had little impact on the state's politically and economically well-positioned ruling class. Newsom may be far from a popular governor, ranking in the lower third among his compatriots, but he enjoys a solidly Democratic legislature and almost lockstep support in the media. Voters are showing signs of getting restless, though, defeating proposals and taxes that he heartily endorsed along with his public-union and tech-industry allies. Typically, he avoided taking a position on Proposition 22, the ban on contract labor detested by the tech firms but deeply supported by the unions

The Favored Candidate of a Coterie of San Francisco's Wealthiest Families

Conservatives like to ascribe the label "leftist" to politicians such as Newsom. In reality, California's governor is no Marxist firebrand but rather a favored candidate of what the *Los Angeles Times* described as "a coterie of San Francisco's wealthiest families," including the Fishers (who founded the Gap clothing chain), the Pritzkers (whose family includes the current Illinois governor), and especially the Getty family, which essentially adopted Newsom, financed his business ventures, and allegedly paid for his first lavish wedding while helping launch his political career. These families overall have prospered in California's highly bifurcated economy, among the least egalitarian in the nation. Its prime beneficiaries cluster along the state's postindustrial, temperate zones.

Newsom rose, as former assembly speaker and San Francisco mayor Willie Brown suggests, as the favored spokesman for San Francisco's local well-to-do. "He came from their world, and that's why they embraced him without hesitancy and over and above everybody else," Brown told the *Los Angeles Times*. "They didn't need to interview him. They knew what he stood for."

Newsom postures as a social-justice advocate and believer in austere green virtues, but the corporate aristocracy has helped him live in luxury, first in his native Marin, and now in Sacramento. Newsom's passion for the good life caused him some embarrassment recently when he was caught violating his own pandemic orders at the ultra-expensive, ultra-chic French Laundry in Napa. This episode exemplifies America's elite nomenklatura—demanding sacrifices of the masses, whether in the form of lockdowns or housing, but less often from themselves. Look at Nancy Pelosi's.

In addition to woke posturing on race and gender issues, climate change stands as the key driver of this kind of politics. In many regions, notably the Midwest, Democrats face a conflict between siding with the environmental lobby or with workers in fossil fuels, large-scale manufacturing, and construction. That tension is less evident in California, where a draconian tax and regulatory environment has reduced construction, particularly in the big coastal metros, and where manufacturing has stagnated, while policymakers have targeted the heavily unionized oil industry for extinction.

Draconian Climate-Change Policies Allow Progressive Elites to Advertise Their Good Intentions

Draconian climate-change policies allow progressive elites to advertise their good intentions without curtailing their economic opportunities. The state's renewable-energy policies enrich his Newsom's tech backers even when their efforts—such as the Google-backed Ivanpah solar farm—fail to deliver affordable, reliable energy, and bring severe impacts on sensitive habitats, notably in the state's deserts. Even the most impressive of the tech masterminds, Elon Musk, can trace a significant part of his fortune—now estimated at over $100 billion, the world's fifth-largest—to generous subsidy policies for solar panels and electric cars.

Policies that raise energy and housing prices, of course, tend to be politically unpopular—so Newsom, like his predecessors, imposes these regulations administratively, or through executive orders, thus freeing the governor to avoid legislative and political tangles and freeing him of any obligation to explain these positions to the public.

Climate issues have also offered Newsom an ideal way to justify failed progressive policies. Newsom and his ally, Vice President Kamala Harris, blamed the wildfires on climate change and all-purpose bogeyman Donald Trump. The media echoed the charges: the *New York Times* suggests that California is "ground zero for climate disasters," while the *Los Angeles Times* claims that California now fights not just fires and droughts but also "climate despair."

In reality, as the usually left-leaning Pro Publica has revealed, the fires were made far worse by green policies including constant lawsuits against local efforts to clean up old growth, particularly dead trees, and stopping even sustainable logging. The state Legislative Analyst's Office also found that overall, the fires were less driven by global warming and more by policies that allowed for the accumulation of fuel, as well as growing development in certain exurban areas—partly motivated by a desire to escape the extremely high housing prices along the coast.

The fires are certainly not great for the environment or for reaching the state's super-ambitious greenhouse gas (GHG) goals: according to the U.S. Geological Survey, the 2018 fires emitted roughly as much GHG as an entire year of electrical generation. California, though a hotbed of climate extremism, reduced its greenhouse gases between 2007 and 2016 at a rate that ranked just 40th per capita among the states. Even if California wiped out all emissions, it would have an almost-infinitesimal impact on global climate—and in fact, a negative one, if industry relocates to China, where much electricity is still powered by coal.

Newsom Preens About California's Enlightened Commitment to Social Justice

His filmmaker wife Jennifer Newsom, scion of a very wealthy Bay Area family, has made a documentary that brands America a "racist country" from its origins, a nation where racial and gender oppression is systematically rife.

Social justice? It's rarely noted how Newsom's policies, particularly in reference to climate change, have only intensified inequality. California already suffers the widest gap between middle and upper-middle-income earners of any state, while driving up housing costs and narrowing opportunities for working-class people in blue-collar industries. Since 2008, California has created five times as many low-wage as high-wage jobs. It has lost 1.6 million above-average-paying jobs in the past decade—more than twice as many as any other state.

The state's ever-more aggressive green policies seem certain to accelerate that trend. Rather than a sign of bold progressive change, the electrification mandate is likely to consolidate further a new model of high-tech feudalism—one that offers opportunity for powerful regulators and renewable-energy firms but imposes a harsher future on most other Californians. Newsom's defenders praise his energy policies, which in 2017 alone increased prices at three times the national rate. These increases have been devastating to poorer Californians, particularly in the state's less temperate interior, where "energy poverty" has grown rapidly.

The Impact has been toughest on blue-collar sectors. Over the past decade, the Golden State has fallen into the bottom half of states in manufacturing-sector employment growth, ranking 44th last year; its industrial new-job creation has been negative. By contrast, competitors such as Nevada, Kentucky, Michigan, and Florida have seen gains. Even without adjusting for costs, notes the *New York Times*, no California metro ranks in the U.S. top ten in terms of well-paying blue-collar jobs, but four—Ventura, Los Angeles, San Jose, and San Diego—place among the bottom ten.

Newsom's Recent Plan to Impose Forced Electrification

Newsom's recent plan to impose forced electrification on those parts of the economy running on fossil fuels and his efforts to cut off other sources of supply, like natural gas and nuclear power, will put enormous strain on a state already suffering power outages and rising prices. The mandate to use electric trucks, which are expensive and inefficient, threatens jobs at California's three major ports—Los Angeles, Long Beach, and Oakland—which support nearly 5 million California jobs, nearly one in four of the state's total. The new electrical truck mandate, shipping companies note, will threaten the competitive advantage of these ports, with many jobs likely to head for Houston and other ports free of such strictures.

The question now is how long Californians will put up with Newsom's posturing. Over time, high energy prices affect not just blue-collar industries but also the rapidly departing tech sector; artificial intelligence and live-streaming providers are among the largest and fastest-growing consumers of electricity. Ultimately, Newsom's political coalition of greens, the wealthy, and public unions could be strained by the state's deepening fiscal crisis. A high unemployment rate and an already-expansive welfare state will demand more money from the state's already-beleaguered middle class. Some business leaders, notably Disney's Robert Iger, have balked at strict lockdowns on theme parks, which have been devastating to Southern California. Even the state's leading green entrepreneur, Elon Musk, has become increasingly critical of the state's lockdown and regulatory policies.

Dissatisfaction from the middle and working class may present an even greater challenge for Newsom. Dissent over green policies in particular has been growing of late, particularly among minorities and advocates for the poor. Newsom's attempt to raise property taxes on businesses amid the recession was defeated handily—mainly by voters outside Los Angeles County and the urban core of the Bay Area—as was his affirmative action push, financed lavishly by his wealthy backers, which also failed at the polls.

Talk of a major new tax increase—up to 16 percent on top earners—is not likely to appeal to aspiring entrepreneurs. On November 3, 2020, California voted decisively for Joe Biden, but middle-class voters, including minorities, showed a surprisingly independent streak. Minority business groups bitterly noted in a letter to Mark Zuckerberg, the biggest backer for the measure raising property taxes: "Unlike Facebook, restaurants, dry cleaners, nail salons and other small businesses can't operate right now, and many may never open again. The last thing they need is a billionaire pushing higher taxes on them under the false flag of social justice."

Newsom Counting on Labor Union Army to Tank the California Recall

From a June 2021 Politico article "Newsom counting on labor union army to tank the California recall Politico California" by Jeremy B. White:

California Gov. Gavin Newsom has the numbers, but his opponents have the enthusiasm—and Newsom is counting on a union-heavy army of allies to make up the difference.

With a recall vote looming, the Democratic governor's political survival could hinge on activating enough of his base to counteract the fervor of conservative foes. A substantial part of that task will fall to unions that have vowed to defend him with a mass mobilization effort, dispatching members to doorsteps across the state.

"People like to make noise. That doesn't translate to votes," said Orange County Labor Federation Executive Director Gloria Alvarado. "The voters are already in support, so all we need to do is make sure we secure those votes and talk to our members to ensure that base. We're not going to take it for granted."

California's recall election will ask voters two questions: whether they want to oust Newsom and who should replace him if the electorate removes him.

Political winds are gusting at Newsom's back as the coronavirus pandemic steadily recedes. The state's rebounding economy and brimming budget allow Newsom to regularly express optimism and, implicitly, confidence in his leadership. His approval numbers have stabilized, and polls show a durable majority opposed to recalling Newsom, thanks in part to California's overwhelmingly Democratic electorate.

But within those numbers lurks a warning sign: While California Republicans trail Democrats by millions of registered voters, polling shows they are more motivated to vote in a recall election powered by pandemic fatigue and conservative antipathy toward Newsom. It's also the kind of off-year election that tends to skew toward loyal Republican voters.

"It's going to happen at a time when voters aren't used to going to the polls and that means they need an extra nudge," said Democratic consultant Rose Kapolczynski, and "on the Democratic side, labor is one of the most powerful ground forces that exists."

Universal Mail Voting Could Provide Newsom With a Significant Boost

The governor signed a bill this year that ensures ballots will land in mailboxes across the state, relieving his allies of the need to physically get most voters to the polls, though the state will still maintain in-person voting sites. A record 22 million Californians are now registered to vote, and the 88 percent of eligible voters who are registered is the highest share in decades.

"This is a different election and one in which labor's voice can be much stronger because the ballots are sitting in people's hands for 30 days," Democratic Assemblymember Lorena Gonzalez said, adding that "with 30 extra days, I like our odds."

Even before unions launched their get-out-the-vote drive, Newsom's team had reactivated a network of 2,000 volunteers who will encourage voters to turn in their ballots with techniques like peer-to-peer texting. But labor boasts an especially formidable and battle-tested political machine. Unions spent some $12 million to elect Newsom in 2018, and they have so far supplied roughly $2 million to Newsom's recall defense, with more certain to come.

That money is only part of the equation. More consequential than television spots could be the type of methodical, door-to-door voter outreach that has long been a mainstay of union political power. A coalition of prominent labor unions vowed this week to dispatch members to thousands of precincts across the state.

But Republicans believe that the energy is on their side. Anne Dunsmore, who runs one of the principal recall committees, hailed the "unparalleled" volunteer base for a recall that drew more than 2 million signatures despite a relatively bare-bones budget and a less professional operation that other statewide efforts.

List of Newsom's Most Serious Transgressions

From the July 2021 article "'Roaring Back' Is Just a Campaign Slogan, Not Reality" by CalMatters' Dan Walters:

Gov. Gavin Newsom repeatedly chants that California is "roaring back" from pandemic, but ignores the state's stubborn socioeconomic problems. Virtually every day, Gov. Gavin

Newsom shows up someplace in California to proclaim, for the umpteenth time, that the state is "roaring back" from the COVID-19 pandemic.

These highly orchestrated events are billed as official state business, but in fact are merely political campaign appearances aimed at persuading voters to support him in the Sept. 14, 2021, recall election, mostly by touting one of the multi-billion-dollar giveaways in his new state budget.

"As the state comes roaring back from the pandemic, we're laser-focused on getting this assistance out the door as quickly as possible and providing supports across the board to help Californians get back on their feet," Newsom said at a stop in Southern California last week to highlight a new program to pay overdue rent.

One could conclude that Newsom, in parceling out cash from an unexpected windfall of revenue, is trying to buy votes with taxpayer money.

There Are Three Troubling Aspects to Newsom's Self-Serving Effort

One is that blatant campaigning under the guise of official business is unsavory. While not uncommon in other states, until now California governors have been fairly meticulous about separating official business from their re-election campaign events.

The second is that in spending so much money so quickly Newsom may be endangering the state's fiscal health. His predecessor, Jerry Brown, who preached frugality and was wary of launching new programs that could mushroom out of control, warned of the danger in a television interview this month.

Brown said the state faces "fiscal stress" in the years ahead as revenues return to more normal levels. "The word is volatility," Brown said. "Money comes and money goes. The federal government is going deeper into debt, they are spending money wildly. The state is now spending money. It is not sustainable."

Brown noted that the state is highly dependent on a relative handful of high-income taxpayers for its revenue, saying, "the growing utter inequality of the economy because the rich people make so damn much money and California happens to tax the rich people disproportionally... we need a more frugal, sustainable, more prudent way of doing business."

Finally, Newsom's "roaring back" mantra sidesteps the state's very real socioeconomic problems which, if anything, have worsened during the pandemic. California still has one of the nation's highest unemployment rates with well over a million jobless workers. We had the nation's highest level of poverty before the pandemic, and it has surely increased.

The major factor in California's high poverty is the state's very high cost of living, particularly for housing, but for other necessities as well, such as gasoline and utilities. Newsom has offered only token and/or short-term responses to those costs, such as rental and utility bill assistance and cash payments to low-income families that probably, as Brown warns, cannot be sustained.

The state's housing shortage continues to put upward pressure on rents and home prices and the $3.5 billion that Newsom's new budget contains for affordable housing would build fewer than 10,000 units in a state that's at least 80,000 units short of meeting its own housing quotas each year

The key to the housing dilemma is making California more attractive for private investment, but Newsom and legislators have ducked the difficult policy choices to encourage such investment, such as reforming the California Environmental Quality Act and rebuffing efforts by construction unions to claim jurisdiction on housing projects.

California will be truly roaring back when unemployment decreases, housing construction increases, the poverty rate declines, and educational achievement rises. Until then, it's just a campaign slogan.

Newsom Paints Rosy—But Flawed, Economic Picture

From the May 2021 article "Newsom Paints Rosy, But Flawed, Economic Picture" by CalMatters' Dan Walters:

California Gov. Gavin Newsom is celebrating the latest employment report, but it's not as bright as he claims. There is a seamless connection between what Gavin Newsom is saying and doing as governor and his campaign to survive a recall, encapsulated in the slogan "California Comeback."

Newsom's much-revised state budget, unveiled in May 2021, is centered on a "$100 Billion California Comeback Plan" that would, he says, put the COVID-19 pandemic and its economic fallout in the rearview mirror. When new employment data were released by the federal Bureau of Labor Statistics, Newsom immediately hailed them as proof that under his leadership, the state is booming again.

"California is continuing to lead the nation's economic recovery, adding 101,800 jobs in April—38% of all the jobs created throughout the entire country," Newsom crowed. "Over the past three months, California has created 390,300 jobs. But we're not letting up; the California Comeback Plan is the biggest economic recovery package in the state's history and will provide historic investments in small businesses and workers to bring California roaring back."

A closer examination of the latest employment numbers, however, indicates that—as politicians are wont to do—Newsom is cherry-picking the most favorable economic indicator while ignoring others that are less positive.

One of the latter is the state's unemployment rate of 8.3% in April, unchanged from the March level despite the supposed surge in new jobs. It's still markedly higher than the national jobless rate of 6.1% and is the nation's second highest behind Hawaii's 8.5%.

California's unemployment rate had been the nation's third highest in March, but New York improved enough to displace California in April 2020. Four states were tied for having the nation's lowest jobless rates of 2.8% in April. Arch-rival Texas was slightly higher than the national rate at 6.7%.

Jobs Growth Data Point Cited by Newsom is Also Questionable

The data point cited by Newsom, that California added 101,800 jobs in April 2021, 38% of the nation's job gains, is also somewhat iffy.

The California Center for Jobs & the Economy, a business-supported research organization, points out that the jobs number is a "seasonally adjusted" estimate, rather than a hard count, noting that the federal agency "so far has revised their adjustment formula three times in an effort to overlay seasonal factors to data that is overwhelmingly driven instead by the pandemic."

"The underlying unadjusted numbers instead show California gaining a stronger 151,500 nonfarm jobs, and the U.S. doing far better with a gain of 1,089,000," the center's analysis continued. "Using the adjusted data, California had 38% of the national jobs gain. Using the more relevant unadjusted, California had 14%. As of the April numbers, California has regained 48% of the nonfarm jobs lost to the state shutdowns. The U.S. in total has regained 63%."

Newsom's Employment Development Department (EDD) simultaneously released its version of the federal jobs report, which demonstrated just how much ground California must regain to return to pre-pandemic levels.

EDD said that just 38,600 more Californians were employed in April than in March while 1.6 million remained unemployed—and that doesn't count those who have dropped out of the state's workforce

The employment situation is especially daunting in Southern California. The Los Angeles region had the highest unemployment rate of any major U.S. metropolitan area in April 2021 at 11.7%, dragging down the state as a whole.

So, it would seem, California is recovering, bit by bit, the more than three million jobs lost when Newsom, under emergency decrees, closed large segments of the state's economy a year ago to battle the pandemic. However, we still have a very long way to go before he can legitimately claim a California Comeback.

The Election Results of the 2021 Gavin Newsom Recall

From Katy Grimes, the Editor of the California Globe:

The amazing 2021 Recall Election of California Gov. Gavin Newsom is over after 22 million of California's registered voters received vote-by-mail ballots and went to the polls and Newsom decisively survived the recall attempt. However, the issues leading to the recall were not debated or defended by the governor and the California media called the recall election minutes after polls closed at 8:00 pm Tuesday, September 14, 2021 with the latest poll results as follows. Results will be certified by October 22, 2021:

- "YES" to recall Governor Newsom: 37.3%.

- "NO" to recall Governor Newsom: 62.7%.

Forty-six candidates, including nine Democrats and 24 Republicans, ran in the election. Approximately 6.7 million voters selected a candidate on the second question. The five candidates to receive the most votes were: radio host Larry Elder (R) with 48%, YouTuber Kevin Paffrath (D) with 9.8%, former San Diego Mayor Kevin Faulconer (R) with 8.3%, doctor Brandon Ross (D) with 5.4%, and 2018 gubernatorial candidate John Cox (R) with 4.2%. Eight other candidates received at least 1% of the vote.

The Newsom campaign never involved defending the governor's record and instead went on the attack once it was evident that recall candidate Larry Elder was the frontrunner. The issues at the forefront of the California Recall Election were and continue to be spiking crime rates, school lockdowns and mask mandates, jobs lost, and businesses closed due to the governor's COVID lockdowns, the water shortage, record wildfires, and jobs lost due to AB 5, highest taxes in the country, a homelessness epidemic, endless regulation on businesses, and median home price of $800,000… among other pressing issues.

Instead, Newsom's team relied on a deep bench of Democrat heavy hitters invited to the state to campaign for him during the last weeks of the recall including: President Joe Biden, Vice President Kamala Harris, House Speaker Nancy Pelosi, Sen. Elizabeth Warren, Sen. Bernie Sanders, Service Employees International Union (SEIU) California, National Union of Healthcare Workers (NUHW), California Labor Federation, California Teachers Association (CTA), and Stacey Abrams.

Some anti-recall ads went so far as to associate front runner Elder "as the black face of white America" or as a Donald Trump protégé—both ridiculous and false attacks—that showed how far California's progressives will go to defend their failing progressive agenda.

That the recall even made it to the ballot is the real mandate according to supporters, as millions of voters made sure to let the governor know they didn't approve of how he has handled the job governing the largest state in the country.

3 – The State's Democratic Party Supermajority & Governing Madness.

Credit: NBC News.

This chapter starts off with the February 2020 article "Fighting the One-Party State at the Local Level in California" by the California Policy Center's Edward Ring:

It isn't a partisan observation to say that California is a one-party state. It's just stating a fact.

The Democratic Party controls all the levers of political power in California. Consider the evidence: GOP registration is down to 23 percent of registered voters. There is a Democratic "mega-majority" (75% or more) in both chambers of the state legislature. The GOP only holds 11 out of 53 congressional seats in California and the Democrats occupy every state office from Governor on down.

The Congressional delegation of the United States has 53 members, with 42 Democrats and 11 Republicans, including both the Republican House Minority Leader Kevin McCarthy and Democratic House Speaker Nancy Pelosi.

The GOP hasn't elected a U.S. Senator to represent California since 1988. Democrats control the city councils and boards of supervisors in almost every city and county. There are roughly 10,000 elected positions in California, from school boards to utility commissions and special districts, and Democrats run candidates and have professional funded campaigns for all of them, all the time.

The reasons that California is a one-party state are also not hard to understand. For this as well, the evidence is overwhelming. Virtually every financial special interest in California supports Democrats. Public sector unions, which are almost exclusively supportive of Democratic candidates and causes, collect, and spend $800 million per year. California's high tech industry, commanding mind-blowing wealth, is solidly Democratic. California's wealthy and influential entertainment industry is solidly Democratic. The media establishment in California is also solidly Democratic, wielding priceless influence over voters. And as if that weren't enough, politically active billionaires spend amazing sums of money in California to support Democrats.

It takes BIG money to control California politics, and the Democrats have it: California's own Tom Steyer spent $45 million on CA ballot measures in 2012 and 2016. Steyer spent $60 million on U.S. congressional races in 2018, including several in California. New Yorker Michael Bloomberg spent an estimated 80 million on 24 battleground congressional races, and won 21 of them–including 3 in California. These and other major donors coordinated efforts with PACs supported by public sector unions to flip seven congressional seats in California in 2018 and increase their majorities in both chambers of the state legislature.

California's One-Party State, the Blue Wave Machine

This next section is from the November 2020 article "California's One-Party State, the Blue Wave Machine" by the California Policy Center's Edward Ring:

In California, it doesn't matter that only 11.5 million votes have been reported, when 21 million voters received mailed ballots. The ruling party has everything working in its favor.

The Republicans had to scrap for every donation, with most GOP donors considering California a lost cause and sending their money out of state. The Democrats, on the other hand, had mega-donors willing to spend any amount, joined by public sector unions that, year after year, collect and spend nearly $1 billion in dues from government workers.

This outrageous financial disparity—all the more decisive because of its perennial, unceasing reliability—pays for a trained field army of public sector union activists who are mustered by the thousands every election season and joined by activists, often paid, from California's powerful network of environmentalist and social justice pressure groups. There is absolutely nothing remotely comparable on the Republican side.

This translates into ballot harvesting on an epic scale, but it also translates into superior messaging. Political consulting and public relations are a lot like professional baseball. The best players get hired, at astronomical rates, by the richest owners. In California, the A-Team works for Democrats, because year after year, the Democrats throw down more money. A lot more money.

List of top California state executive offices:

- Governor - Gavin Newsom (D)

- Lieutenant Governor - Eleni Kounalakis (D)

- Secretary of State - Shirley Weber (D)

- State Treasurer - Fiona Ma (D)

- State Controller - Betty Yee (D)

- State Superintendent of Public Instruction - Tony Thurmond (D)

- Insurance Commissioner - Ricardo Lara (D)

- Attorney General of California - Rob Bonta (D)

Executive officials in California are part of a three-pronged government structure that includes state legislators and state judges.

The California State Legislature is a bicameral body consisting of the lower house, the California State Assembly, with 80 members, and the upper house, the California State Senate, with 40 members.

Both chambers of the California legislature have been controlled by the Democratic Party since 1959 except from 1969 to 1971 when the Republican Party held both chambers and from 1994 to 1996, when Republicans briefly held a majority in the Assembly. Each member represented about 423,396 residents, as of the 2000 Census.

California has a Democratic state government trifecta. A trifecta exists when one political party simultaneously holds the governor's office and majorities in both state legislative chambers.

In California, there are four federal district courts, a state supreme court, a state court of appeals, and trial courts with both general and limited jurisdiction. These courts serve different purposes which are outlined in the sections below.

California uses two different systems for its selection of state court judges. The state's appellate judges are chosen by gubernatorial appointment followed by commission confirmation. Trial judges are elected by popular nonpartisan vote.

Left and Lefter in California

This section comes from the March 2017 *City Journal* article "Left and Lefter in California" by Joel Kotkin:

To its many admirers back east, California has emerged as the role model for a brave new Democratic future. The high-tech, culturally progressive Golden State seems to be an ideal incubator of whatever politics will follow the Trump era.

Yet as California Democrats exult in what they see as a glowing future, they are turning away from the models that once drove their party's (and the state's) success—a commitment to growth, upward mobility, and dispersed property ownership. California's current prosperity is largely due to the legacy of Governor Pat Brown, who, a half-century ago, built arguably the world's best transportation, water, and power systems, and created an incubator for middle-class prosperity.

Ironically, the politician most responsible for undermining this achievement has been Pat's son, Governor Jerry Brown. Long skeptical of his father's growth-oriented, pro-suburban policies, Brown the Younger put strong constraints on growth, especially when these efforts concerned the fight against global warming—a quasi-religious crusade. Battling climate change has awakened Brown's inner authoritarian; he has lauded the "coercive power of the state" and embraced "brainwashing" on climate issues.

Brown's stridency on climate, however, does not extend to all leftist issues. Like Senator Dianne Feinstein, Brown has some appreciation of the importance of infrastructure, such as the need to increase water supplies, and he exercises at least a modicum of caution on fiscal matters like the state's gargantuan pension debt. He is not a strict identitarian, having vetoed an attempt to enact Title IX standards of evidence for campus sexual-assault cases, a measure embraced by the state's vocal feminist leaders.

As Brown prepares to depart, and Feinstein struggles to retain office, a new dominant coalition—led by tech oligarchs, identity politicians, and Greens—is rising to usurp control of the party. This new coalition of the privileged and aggrieved marks a departure both from Pat Brown's social democracy and his son's more elitist but still measured politics.

State senator Kevin de León, the emergent leader of this new configuration and cat's paw of billionaire Tom Steyer, the San Francisco hedge-fund billionaire epitomizes the new approach. Having made much of his fortune in oil sands and coal, Steyer is now the Democratic Party's prime bankroller, and his largesse extends to the drive to impeach President Trump. He has made common cause with hard-Left politicians like Kevin de León, and even embraced unionism—as long as labor follows his extreme position on climate change.

Steyer & Other Oligarchs Are Working to Eliminate the Last Vestiges of the Old Democratic Party

Climate activists have been targeting, with some success, the so-called Mod Squad—centrist Democrat legislators from the state's less-prosperous interior and working-class suburbs. This shrinking group, occasionally financed by energy, homebuilding, and other pillars of the old economy, sometimes holds the balance of power in Sacramento, and has managed to slow some of the most draconian climate measures.

De León's enthusiastic embrace of climate-change dogma may seem odd for a politician whose impoverished district suffers from Los Angeles's continued de-industrialization, hastened by strict environmental regulation and high energy costs. Instead of backing policies that would create more high-wage jobs, de León's priorities are largely redistributive. This jibes with his support among public employees and from the militant California Nurses Association. He endorsed the union-backed single-payer health-care plan, a measure that assembly speaker Anthony Rendon tabled as impossibly expensive (it would more than double the state budget). Immigration is another key de León issue. He is a fervent supporter of illegal immigrants, in a state that houses one in four of the nation's total, bragging about his own relatives' use of false IDs.

The Golden State's progressive tilt would not be possible without demographic change. The state's majority-minority makeup has made the capture of middle-class and moderate voters less important. As middle-class families leave California, the electorate is increasingly dominated by racial minorities—with whites, 70 percent of the population in 1970, now less numerous than Hispanics and destined to be roughly one-third of the population by 2030.

California's demography is more and more dominated by the poor and near-poor (roughly one-third of the population), the young and unattached, and a residual population of older whites, many luxuriating on generous state pensions or inflated property values.

What makes all this work is the growing power of the tech oligarchs and their more glamorous cousins in the Hollywood glitterati. The tech boom of the last decade has obscured the decline of California's basic industries, such as energy and manufacturing. California's above-average job performance since 2010 is almost entirely a combination of high-income employment growth in the Bay Area and the swelling ranks of low-wage service workers who serve them.

The oligarchs, including tech investor Sam Altman, LinkedIn co-founder Reid Hoffman, and philanthropist Laurene Powell Jobs, widow of the late Apple founder, have lined up behind de León. Tech will bankroll the pliable and well-heeled Newsom, who already gets cash from Airbnb, Twitter, and Salesforce.com.

This Marriage of the Poor and New Rich Appears to be the Dominant Theme Emerging in California

The oligarchs, as Greg Ferenstein has reported, don't even pretend to believe in upward mobility for the masses. Instead, they favor policies—such as forced densification—that will house their largely young, childless workers, including the nation's largest population of H1-B visa-holders. Measures such as State Senator Mark Wiener's SB 827 would largely strip cities of their ability to control development anywhere near transit stops.

Civil rights groups, mainstream environmental organizations, neighborhood associations, and cities themselves have come out in opposition, and even Los Angeles mayor Eric Garcetti, a dedicated densifier, fears a backlash in the city's remaining single-family neighborhoods. Yet the oligarchs and their YIMBY ("yes in my backyard") allies, whom they generously fund, have backed the bill.

At its core, the oligarchs' vision for California represents a kind of high-tech feudalism. Tech companies are starting to dominate sectors like electric and autonomous cars, even seeking monopolies in dense urban areas. They support limiting ownership and consumer choice, even as the bulk of automobiles remain gas-powered. In the longer term, the oligarchs have little interest in creating blue-collar jobs and would prefer to replace employment with algorithms. Deprived of work and unable to pay for housing, the working class and an ever-shrinking middle class would be bought off with income-maintenance payments—twenty-first-century alms for the poor.

Tech oligarchs and activist CEOs have committed themselves to extreme environmentalism, identity politics, and open-borders immigration policy. California's bevy of clueless celebrities, now celebrated by *Time* as "suddenly serious" for following the identitarian party line, have also climbed aboard. As anyone knows who has suffered through awards shows or listened to interviews with stars, the entertainment industry—much like tech—has become homogeneous in its views.

The key issues for the glitterati are not income inequality, upward mobility, or the preservation of middle-class neighborhoods but the feverish pastimes of the already rich: gender and racial issues, climate change, guns, and anything that offends the governesses and schoolmarms of intersectionality.

To the ranks of these over-exposed but influential voices, you can also add California's media and most of its intelligentsia, who seem to get their talking points from progressive sources and work assiduously to limit the influence of moderate (much less conservative) views. With Silicon Valley increasingly able to control content and ever more willing to curb debate, the policy agenda of the state's new elite may well become reality—a nightmarish one for millions of ordinary Californians.

California's Socialist Oligarchy: Who They Are and How to Defeat Them

This eye-opening section is from the October 2018 article "California's Socialist Oligarchy, Part One: Making the State Unaffordable" and "Part Two: Who They Are and How to Defeat Them" by the California Policy Center's Edward Ring:

Touted as the "fifth-largest economy on Earth," and recently heralded as delivering the "greatest increase in average income," these statistics obscure an alarming reality. California has become a feudal state, where the benefits of prosperity are unequally distributed, rewarding corrupt plutocrats and punishing ordinary working families.

Joel Kotkin, a fellow in urban studies at Chapman University in Orange, California, characterized California's current political economy as "Oligarchical Socialism." This is a perfect description of a system that destroys the middle class at the same time it protects the ultra-rich.

California's leftist oligarchy benefits financially from precisely the depredations they accuse conservatives of committing. They have enacted policies that are designed to make California unaffordable to all but the wealthiest residents, and hostile to emerging small businesses, at the same time as their preexisting wealth and politically connected corporations reap enhanced returns and profits.

Left-Wing Oligarchs

At the top of California's ideological pyramid are left-wing oligarchs, crony capitalists who want to protect their business interests. Whether it's renewable energy, "connected" appliances, or homes built on those rare parcels of land that are entitled for development, California's left-wing oligarchs benefit from artificial scarcity. But these direct beneficiaries are only a segment of California's left-wing oligarchy.

The indirect financial benefits of artificial scarcity are even greater. As the prices of real estate assets ascend once again into bubble territory, as the earnings per share of public utilities swell on the strength of selling overpriced kilowatts, and as Silicon Valley firms see their stock values ascend into the stratosphere, wealthy individuals, and investment funds, most assuredly including California's public employee pension funds which manage over $800 billion in assets, see their portfolio values soar.

Which brings us to the final subcategory of left-wing oligarchs in California, the high-tech moguls of social media. These left-wing billionaires of Silicon Valley, along with their only slightly less well-heeled entertainment industry counterparts in Los Angeles, are the most influential opinion makers on earth. They shape values and behavior using tools that make the overwhelming mass propaganda breakthroughs achieved by radio in the 1930s appear as primitive as smoke signals by comparison. What is their agenda?

Social Media and Entertainment Complex

The communications kingpins of California have no allegiance to ordinary Californians—or ordinary Americans, for that matter.

To them, ordinary people are Pavlovian proles, expendable parasites that pollute the environment. To the extent these kingpins have compassion, it is to profitably create for the expendable multitudes a benign zoo; smart cities of high rises, contained in areas as geographically minute as possible, so that only wild nature, corporate farms, and private estates of the super-rich exist outside the urban containment boundaries.

In these algorithmically managed metropolises, human values, including their voting behavior, will literally be programmed, using the most sophisticated and individualized techniques of manipulation ever devised. Borgcubes, aesthetically optimized by AI psychometricians, with soothing soft edges of gingerbread. Metaphorically speaking, Matrix-like cocoons. A *Brave New World*, complete with Sexophones and Soma. Get ready. Another innovation from California.

The Environmentalist Lobby

California's socialist oligarchy probably can continue to consolidate their power without any help, but help is abundant. Most importantly, they have the help of the environmentalist movement.

The power behind this movement, apart from the oligarchs who financially benefit from scarcity, are the trial lawyers who populate and control the boards of major environmentalist nonprofits. Leaving sensible, and vital, environmentalist causes far behind, these misanthropic organizations prevent any significant infrastructure investment or private development of land and other resources.

Collecting legal fees and settlements thanks to a sympathetic judiciary, California's environmentalist organizations have amassed immense financial power and political influence. And when all else fails, they now have the boogeyman of "climate change" to stop literally anything, anything that so much as scratches the earth, dead in its tracks.

Public Sector Unions

Enforcing the edicts of California's socialist oligarchy are public sector unions; their full-time paid armies of lobbyists, operatives, political consultants, PR firms, and litigators. Their membership is both cowed and co-opted. California's unionized public servants, while not entirely immune to the higher costs imposed on them by the oligarchy, are nonetheless exempted from its worst effects, because they are the most lavishly compensated public employees in America, if not the entire world.

The average total compensation (pay and benefits) for a full-time city, county, or state worker in California in 2015 was $121,843. In that same year, the average full-time private sector worker in California made $62,475 (with benefits), which is 51 percent of what the public sector worker earned. That's not all. This pampered class of public servants also enjoys, typically, 72 paid days off per year (no, that doesn't include weekends).

How that breaks down is as follows: A veteran employee typically gets 20 vacation days, 12 designated holidays, two floating holidays, 12 "personal days," and if they are on salary and they work eight hours a day for nine weekdays, through the very common "9/80" program, they get every 10th weekday off with pay. When they retire, if they work 30 years (most private sector workers put in 45 years), their average pension is nearly $70,000 per year, not including health benefits.

Public sector unions, which ought to be illegal, are squarely to blame for "negotiating" pay and benefit packages that threaten to force California's cities and counties into bankruptcy despite sky-high taxes. California's public sector unions are the most powerful in America, collecting and spending more than $800 million per year in dues and fees. These unions are, in most cases, avowedly socialistic, and in virtually all cases these unions have a political agenda in lockstep with the California's left-wing oligarchy. As the most powerful permanent political organizations in the state, they are the brokers and enablers of corporate power.

In stunning irony, these unions also play a vital role in convincing ordinary Californians to vote contrary to their own best interests. There are two big reasons for this.

First, these unions proclaim themselves in solidarity with the working class, despite the fact that they represent workers who are much more likely to have financially transcended the challenges facing ordinary private sector workers. They conflate themselves with private sector unions, despite the fact that unlike private sector unions, they elect their own bosses, they are funded through compulsory taxes instead of through profits earned in a competitive market, and they operate the machinery of government allowing them to use that to intimidate their opponents.

Second, and equally insidious, these unions have taken over public education from kindergarten through graduate school, and they have now infected two generations of Californians with their left-wing ideology.

Thoroughly Indoctrinated Voters

While the elites represented in the above categories do represent millions of Californians, it is the influence they have on tens of millions of California's voters that give them their political power. This starts with college educated liberals, often living in homes they've owned for so long that they aren't adversely affected by property taxes (Proposition 13), and often living on the coast where they don't have to spend thousands of dollars per year to heat and cool those homes.

These people live and work in educational, corporate, and media environments that are saturated with left-wing propaganda, and they don't feel the harmful impacts of these policies enough to question them. Many of these liberals work in entertainment or high-tech, where their business model is primarily virtual, which prevents their exposure to the intrusive, stifling laws and regulations that affect businesses in the real world.

The other voting bloc that determines California's political destiny, perhaps more than any other, are ethnic voters, or, to use a ridiculous, pretentious, obligatory phrase that makes normal people cringe every time they say it, "people of color." The POC vote in California overwhelmingly favors Democratic candidates for public office.

According to the Public Policy Institute of California (PPIC), among California's "likely voters," more whites are registered as Republicans (39 percent), than Democrats (38 percent). But among Latinos, registered Democrats (62 percent) far outnumber Republicans (17 percent). Among blacks, the disparity is even greater: 82 percent Democrat versus a paltry 6 percent Republican. Among Asians, where the disparity is less, the Democrats still have a nearly two-to-one advantage, 45 percent to 24 percent. But can the Democratic grip on ethnic voters endure?

An Alternative Future for California

The California Policy Center's Edward Ring continues from his two-article "Part Two: Who They Are and How to Defeat Them":

If you poke at the supposed unbreakable hold by Democrats on ethnic and racial minorities, you find cracks. Many Latino citizens actually favor immigration reform. Many Asian citizens fear affirmative action will rob their children of opportunities. Black voters in recent polls are supporting President Trump in percentages greater than any Republican in recent history. All "POC" are becoming increasingly incensed at the way the teachers unions have destroyed public education.

It wouldn't take much to persuade California's racial and ethnic minority voters that the Golden State's artificial scarcity and high cost-of-living is something completely engineered by Democrats. California's current Republican candidate for governor, John Cox, is doing a good job of educating voters on that subject.

And for that matter, what does "people of color" even mean, as greater and greater intermarriage occurs? Who is to say that a Mexican-American, with Christian European roots and a shared heritage of settling the American West, would not, does not, embrace American pride and American patriotism just as much as any other proud member of the American melting pot? Maybe all that California's kaleidoscopic electorate needs is a coherent and unwavering pro-growth, pro-freedom vision, from a new coalition of patriots.

Something's Got to Give

The biggest mistake that California's socialist oligarchs can make is to assume they are unassailable. Their certainty could become their downfall.

It's true that someday we will need to move beyond fossil fuel. It's true that someday we will live in a world where borders slowly wither away, and we are one global people. It's true that eventually we will let machines do most of our work for us, and we will need to invent economic models that account for this new reality.

It's even true that someday we may genetically engineer ourselves into transhuman beings. But those future days are not these present days, and for California's socialist oligarchy to proclaim they have all the answers to trends this transformative displays stupefying arrogance.

While ordinary Californians are deciding between buying gasoline or paying rent, these elites are inventing new ways to make everything cost more. While immigrants from abroad and indigent Americans from east of the Sierras come to California to collect taxpayer funded benefits, these elites are prohibiting the types of economic and infrastructure development that might create the wealth to sustain them, along with those already here.

While commuters curse their way to work and back in clogged lanes on neglected freeways, these elites were backing the $100 billion bullet train project. While Californians pay more taxes than anyone else in America, California's Democratic candidate for governor reaffirms his commitment to universal, single payer health care for everyone, free healthcare for non-citizen immigrants, free public pre-schools, and free community college education.

Something's going to give. Preventing broader private sector participation in competitive development of housing, energy, water, and transportation guarantees eventual failure of California's existing socialist schemes, much less the new ones they're promising. But so far,

California's elites benefit from and promote these financially unsustainable policies. It cannot stand. Rebellion is brewing. Resistance is not futile. New alignments and alliances are forming. One economic hiccup could be all it takes.

California's extraordinary potential is diminished by this ruling class of socialist oligarchs, and their coercive utopian supporters. They think they have all the answers when in reality they are flirting with economic and cultural disaster. Republicans, or some new movement, need to offer Californians a vision of abundance instead of scarcity, through competitive development of natural resources, market-driven urban and suburban growth, realistic immigration policies, and a proud, assimilative message to its residents to join together as a united and prosperous people. Concurrent with an agenda of growth that is as pragmatic as it is optimistic, California's socialist oligarchs need to be exposed for their hypocrisy, their hubris, their venality.

Be warned, America. The agenda of the oligarchic socialists is not incoherent, nor is it mere fantasy. They've been building it for years in California.

The Seven Deadly Sins of California's Political Establishment

This final section is from the November 2019 article "The Seven Deadly Sins of California's Political Establishment" by the California Policy Center's Edward Ring:

California's politicians are hardly alone in their quest to destroy America's rights, freedoms, prosperity, culture, traditions, and pride. They just happen to be more advanced in their quest. But since what happens in California often ends up happening later in the rest of the country, it's vital to highlight just how bad it's gotten in the "not-so" Golden State.

Just as a theologian might argue there are more than seven deadly sins that are fatal to spiritual progress, there are more than seven policy areas where California's political leadership have fatally undermined the aspirations of ordinary Californians. But in the interests of brevity and clarity, here are what might be the most damning seven deadly sins of California's political establishment.

1-Law and Order

Californians have prided themselves on being trendsetters in human rights, but the pendulum has swung too far. Thanks to Proposition 47, the "Reduced Penalties for Some Crimes Initiative" which voters approved in 2014, it is nearly impossible to arrest and hold anyone for possession of hard drugs, so long as they claim the drugs are for personal use. Prop. 47 also downgraded the punishment for property crimes if the value of the stolen goods are under $950 per offense.

The consequence of these laws are public drug use and rampant theft to support these drug habits. Other ridiculous laws include Assembly Bill 953, the "Racial and Identity Profiling Act" (2015), which requires police to fill out an extensive questionnaire after every encounter with a member of the public, even if it doesn't result in an arrest. The purpose of this is to prevent disproportionate encounters with members of disadvantaged groups, and the consequence of it is fewer stops, fewer arrests, and more crime.

2-Environment

It's hard to know where to begin when it comes to environmentalist extremism that tyrannizes ordinary Californians. At the heart of California's central planning state is AB 32, the "Global Warming Solutions Act" (2006), and follow-on legislation. These laws aim to reduce California's net "greenhouse gas" emissions to zero by 2045.

To accomplish this, it is becoming almost impossible to develop land outside of existing cities, which is driving the price of land and housing to unaffordable levels. Next on the "climate change" agenda is to charge Californians for "vehicle miles traveled," wherein everywhere people go in their cars will be monitored and taxed.

Well before AB 32 came along, though, California had already gone overboard with environmentalism. The California Environmental Quality Act (CEQA), passed by the state legislature in 1971 and turned into the monster it is today via numerous follow on legislation, requires environmental impact reports to accompany any building permit. Since a separate report is required for every permit application, and since major building projects require approval from dozens of agencies, in California the costs to file applications and pay fees often exceeds the actual cost of construction.

Then there's forestry management, taken over by environmentalist zealots who prohibited logging, suppressed controlled burns with byzantine application gauntlets and endless litigation, and turned California's forests into tinderboxes.

3-Energy and Water

Californians pay among the highest prices for gasoline, electricity, and natural gas in the United States, despite the fact that California has abundant reserves of oil and gas.

But instead of approving new refineries, more connecting pipelines, oil, and gas drilling, and clean natural gas power plants, California's policymakers are shutting down conventional energy in favor of "renewables." Even clean, emissions free nuclear power is forbidden, as California's last nuclear power plant, Diablo Canyon, is scheduled to be shut down by 2025.

Not only does this leave Californians without affordable energy, as they're herded to the nearest retailer to purchase "demand response" appliances that don't work very well, but utilities investing in renewables don't have money left over to upgrade their power lines to better manage wildfires.

As for water, instead of storing more storm runoff behind dams and within aquifers, and investing in reuse and desalination, California's turned to rationing. Starting in 2020, Californians will be restricted to 55 gallons of indoor water use per person per day, with that amount being lowered in subsequent years.

4-Transportation

Freeways in California are among the most congested in the nation, but instead of widening roads and building new freeways, California's policymakers have declared war on the car. Never mind that cars are the future of transportation, destined to be entirely clean, autonomous, capable of driving safely at high speeds while their occupants work, sleep, or entertain themselves.

Instead, California's political leadership remains committed to a high-speed train that will never pay for itself, light rail when light rail ridership is in decline, and zoning that will make it impossible for people to park their cars where they live. California's transportation policy is misanthropic and misguided. Meanwhile, ordinary Californians cope with super commutes on neglected roads.

5-Housing

Despite the fact that most young married couples, given a choice, would prefer to raise their children in a single-family home with a yard, California's elite have decided that single-family homes and suburbs are "unsustainable." Never mind that California spans over 160,000 square miles, of which only around 5 percent is urbanized.

Californians instead are expected to construct all new housing via high density "infill," where there is minimal open space, parking is unavailable, and prices are sky high thanks to the artificially created shortage.

Again, the costs to prepare permit applications and pay fees often exceeds the construction costs, notwithstanding the fact that high rise and mid-rise construction always costs far more per square foot than what it costs to construct one or two story wood frame homes.

6-Homeless

In a state where you can't build anything without paying fees that cost more than the construction costs, and where utility bills and other hidden taxes make the cost-of-living the highest in the nation, it should be no surprise that California has a homeless crisis.

Add to that the best weather on earth, and laws that permit public consumption of hard drugs and prevent detention of petty thieves, and you have a recipe for a homeless population explosion. Moreover, court rulings make it impossible to remove homeless encampments unless you can offer them "permanent supportive housing," and rampant (totally legal) public sector and nonprofit corruption have driven the costs for such housing to exceed on average $500,000 per unit.

To top it off, state laws make it, for all practical purposes, impossible to incarcerate the mentally ill. If these laws and court settlements were overturned, overnight, half of California's homeless would find shelter with relatives and friends, and the rest would get cost-effective help. But it's a meal ticket for the corrupt public sector.

7-Education

To save the worst for last, this is perhaps the most unforgivable sin of all in California. Instead of teaching children to read and write, the public schools excel at indoctrination. Instead of being held accountable, incompetent teachers are protected by union labor laws. Disruptive students are kept in classes to fulfill quotas designed to prevent "discrimination."

The University of California, which—under threat of lawsuits—is about to abandon using SAT scores entirely, has already engineered its admissions policies to circumvent state and federal prohibitions on affirmative action. From higher education down through the K-12 public schools, leftist propaganda and identity politics are the goal of California's unionized public education system, instead of teaching children the skills they will need to become more productive graduates.

California's Soft Fascism

This is the future that awaits America. It is a future abetted by a complicit media, an activist entertainment industry, a unionized public bureaucracy and public education system, and nearly every significant corporate and financial player. The political model it embraces is often labeled as socialist, but might more accurately be described as economic fascism—a merging of public and private, a partnership of corporations, oligarchs, and the public sector.

While people typically cringe at use of the term "fascist," the fascism we're seeing in California is not the hardcore fascism of World War II-era Germany, but rather a soft fascism as envisioned by Aldous Huxley in his novel *Brave New World*. California's citizens are being channeled into high-density apartments, forced to use mass transit, and increasingly made dependent on government subsidies, in exchange for the illusory freedoms of legal drugs and anything-goes gender exploration.

This 21st-century fascism being pioneered in California touts itself as "anti-fascist" at every opportunity, but the system nonetheless fits the definition of fascism. It is corporate, collectivist, centralized, and autocratic. With an equally unhealthy and excessive fervor, it exalts the planet instead of the nation, and celebrates "diversity" instead of one culture. It punishes dissent, protects the oligarchy, and deludes the overtaxed, over-regulated, overpaying majority.

4 – California Statistics & State Rankings: Great, Good, Bad, Very Bad, Ugly & Idiotic

The U.S. Cities With The Most Homeless People

CoCs with the largest number of people experiencing homelessness in 2020*

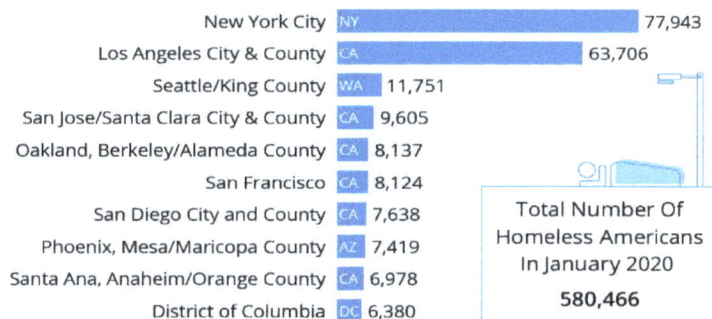

New York City	NY	77,943
Los Angeles City & County	CA	63,706
Seattle/King County	WA	11,751
San Jose/Santa Clara City & County	CA	9,605
Oakland, Berkeley/Alameda County	CA	8,137
San Francisco	CA	8,124
San Diego City and County	CA	7,638
Phoenix, Mesa/Maricopa County	AZ	7,419
Santa Ana, Anaheim/Orange County	CA	6,978
District of Columbia	DC	6,380

Total Number Of Homeless Americans In January 2020
580,466

* CoC - Continuums of Care that are local planning bodies who coordinate homelessness services in certain areas
Source: U.S. Department of Housing and Urban Development

statista

From the 2020 research brief by Joel Kotkin and Marshall Toplansky *Beyond Feudalism: A Strategy to Restore California's Middle Class at the* Chapman University Center for Demographics & Policy:

California's ascent to its rank as the world's fifth (sometimes sixth or seventh) largest economy reflects its status as the hub of the "new" economy. Less often acknowledged, but also painfully true: the Golden State now exemplifies the nation's lurch towards a new form of feudalism in which power and money are increasingly concentrated. Upward mobility is constrained, and sometimes shocking levels of poverty remain widespread.

To be sure, the state has enjoyed faster income and job growth than the rest of the country over the past decade. But over the past few years, even before Covid-19, it has fallen behind other states, such as Texas, Utah, Washington, Nevada, and Arizona. The state is often praised for its elaborate environmental and labor protections, but its record on economic mobility, middle-class disposable income, and even on greenhouse gas reductions, is not encouraging. The gap between middle-class Californians and the more affluent is becoming greater.

Recent trade conflicts, along with the implications of the coronavirus and other potential pandemics, could worsen this reality. In the past decade the hospitality, food service, performing arts and sports/casino sectors have accounted for a quarter of all new jobs, an increase in their share of all employment from 10.6% to 13.4%. Those two million jobs are now gravely threatened. Our position as a hub for trade with Asia and for global tourism is dependent on easy access to Chinese entrepreneurs and other partners world-wide. Damage to those relationships could make us more vulnerable. Our state's population of poor and largely destitute people is also a vulnerability.

Despite these challenges, we are firmly convinced that California has the economic and human resources to withstand these challenges. But this requires developing policies, including educational and regulatory reforms, that foster greater creation of higher wage jobs and address high costs, particularly in housing and in energy.

California's Frightening Rankings

This section is from the January 2020 report "A Perverse Way To 'Solve' California's Housing Crisis: People Are Leaving The Golden State" by the Hoover Institution's Lee Ohanian:

Ironically, California's elected officials claim that they support low earners and historically disadvantaged groups, including African Americans and Latinos. But nothing could be further from the truth. The California of today reflects a very specific failure of governance and policy choices that are enormously biased towards very wealthy political elites who strongly support incumbent politicians and who can easily afford the rising cost of living that comes with their political preferences.

Almost everywhere you look, you will see somebody talking, writing, or complaining about California's housing crisis. Choosing to live in San Francisco, Los Angeles, San Diego, or Silicon Valley will cost you about $1,000,000 if you buy, and about $3,000–$5,000 or more a month if you rent. And that is if you are willing to live in something you would not want to post on Instagram.

California's housing situation has become sufficiently absurd that tech engineers earning six figures are choosing to live in vans.

By now, nearly everyone agrees that the crisis reflects a long-standing supply shortage that is due to extremely high building costs, which in turn are related to poorly designed policies. As 2020 starts, there is virtually no hope that California policymakers will do what it takes to substantially expand supply, as the rate of new home construction here ranks 49th in the country.

For the first time since 2010, when the state's unemployment rate was over 12 percent and exceeded the national average, California is losing population. Over the last year, nearly 200,000 people have left California, primarily for states with much lower housing costs and with better growth opportunities for middle-income earners.

Just how bad are things in California? Here is a partial breakdown:

- Poverty rate: 50th

- Housing affordability: 49th

- Cost of living: 49th

- Inflation-adjusted household income: 27th

- Tax rate for top earners: 50th

- Sales tax rate: 50th

- Business taxes: 49th

- Overall tax burden: 40th

- Business climate: 47th, 48th, 50th

- Infrastructure quality: average grade of D+

- Traffic congestion: 47th

- K–12 learning outcomes: 42nd

- Homelessness rate: 50th

Many families are paying in excess of 50 percent of their household income for rent, which is dangerously high, compared to the industry standard of 30 percent of household income. In Los Angeles, almost 60 percent of renters pay more than the standard 30 percent, and about half of those are paying over 50 percent. These families are a lost paycheck or a car repair payment away from losing their home.

For example, take the state's carbon emission mandates. This includes a new law taking effect this year that requires virtually all new construction to be equipped with solar panels, extremely expensive insulation and energy efficient windows, and extremely efficient appliances that use very little energy.

It has been estimated that these requirements will boost the construction cost of a new home by as much as $40,000. This is a "feel-good" regulation for wealthy households who believe they are making a difference in climate change but is back-breaking for those many households who are paying in excess of 50 percent of their income on rent.

And this expensive regulation is not even a drop in the bucket when it comes to global carbon emissions. California accounts for about one percent of total emissions. It is ludicrous to think that anything California does in this regard will move the global needle.

Wealthy Californians whose cause celebre is climate change would make a much bigger splash in principle by paying China and India to stop using soft coal in their electricity generation rather than forcing meaningless, expensive regulations on the rest of the state.

California Defies Doom With No. 1 U.S. Economy (Great)

This great news article comes from June 2021 Bloomberg News article "California Defies Doom With No. 1 U.S. Economy" by Matthew A. Winkler:

The Golden State has no peers when it comes to expanding GDP, raising household income, investing in innovation and a host of other key metrics to varying degrees amongst its many different economic groupings.

The state's gross domestic product increased 21% during the past five years, dwarfing No. 2 New York (14%) and No. 3 Texas (12%), according to data compiled by Bloomberg. The gains added $530 billion to the Golden State, 30% more than the increase for New York and Texas combined and equivalent to the entire economy of Sweden. Among the five largest economies, California outperforms the U.S., Japan and Germany with a growth rate exceeded only by China.

Enlarging its No. 1 footprint with factory jobs, California GDP from manufacturing gained 13% over the past five years to $316 billion in 2020, an increase unmatched by any of the 10 largest manufacturing states: Texas was No. 2 with 9% growth, followed by Indiana at 8%, according to data compiled by Bloomberg. For all its bluster as being "best for business," Texas can't match California's innovation.

California's New Prosperity is Rooted in Technology and Health-Care Development

California prosperity is rooted in its appeal as a worldwide destination for technology and health-care development. Of the 6,924 corporate locations in the state, 18% are research and development facilities, a ratio that easily beats the U.S. overall (11%), China (15%), U.K. (14%) and Japan (10%). Only Germany, at 19%, has a higher rate, according to data compiled by Bloomberg. The percentage of Texas facilities for R&D is less than half California's at 8.2%.

Corporate California also is the undisputed leader in renewable energy, with 26 companies worth $897 billion, or 36% of the U.S. industry, having reported 10% or more of their revenues derived from clean technology. No state comes close to matching the 21% of electricity derived from solar energy. Shares of these firms appreciated 282% during the past 12 months and 1,003%, 1,140% and 9,330% over two, five and 10 years, respectively, with no comparable rivals anywhere in the world, according to BloombergNEF. The same companies also increased their workforce 35% since 2019, almost tripling the rate for the rest U.S. overall and four times the global rate.

Perennial water shortages and devastating fires drive the perception of dystopia. But California reigns supreme with the GDP-equivalent of $40.2 billion derived from agriculture, forest, and hunting in 2020. That's greater than the output from the next five largest states—Iowa, Washington, Illinois, Texas, and Nebraska—combined, according to data compiled by Bloomberg.

Even with the economic disruptions caused by the pandemic, California cemented its position as the No. 1 state for global trade, with its Los Angeles and Long Beach ports seeing growth that led all U.S. rivals for the first time in nine years in 2020.

The 373 California-based companies in the Russell 2000 Index, which includes small-cap companies across the U.S., appreciated 39% the past two years and 85% since 2016, beating the benchmark's 34% and 67%, respectively. The same California companies reported revenue growth of 56% the past five years, dwarfing the benchmark's 34%, according to data compiled by Bloomberg. More important, California companies invested 16% of their revenues in R&D, or their future, when the rest of the U.S. put aside just 1%.

California Roars Back: Governor Newsom Signs $100 Billion California Comeback Plan (Good)

This July 2021 good news report "California Roars Back: Governor Newsom Signs $100 Billion California Comeback Plan to Accelerate State's Recovery and Tackle Persistent Challenges" comes from the Office of Governor Gavin Newsom:

Governor Gavin Newsom signed SB 129 on July 12, 2021, which is legislation that reflects the majority of the 2021-22 state budget agreement. This transformative budget includes the biggest economic recovery package in California's history–a $100 billion California Comeback Plan.

The California Comeback Plan focuses on providing relief to those that need it most and major investments to address the state's most persistent challenges. The Plan provides immediate cash relief to middle class families and businesses hit hardest by the pandemic, creating the biggest state tax rebate in American history and the largest small business relief package in the nation.

Deploys immediate relief to two-thirds of Californians with Golden State Stimulus payments and provides unprecedented support for small businesses. Major new initiatives and investments to take on persistent challenges including homelessness, disparities in education and opportunity, wildfires, and climate change.

"Harnessing the largest surplus in state history, we're making transformative investments across the board that will help bring all our communities roaring back from the pandemic–and pay dividends for generations to come," said Governor Newsom. "Through this comprehensive plan, the state is taking on the inequities laid bare by the pandemic, expanding our support for Californians facing the greatest hardships, increasing opportunity for every child, confronting homelessness head-on and doubling down on our work to build resilience against the climate change impacts that threaten California's future. I thank Pro Tem Toni Atkins, Speaker Rendon and both houses of the Legislature for their incredible partnership in meeting the unprecedented challenge and opportunity of this moment."

Fueled by a resurgent economy, a surge in state revenues and additional federal recovery funds, the $75.7 billion surplus reflected in the California Comeback Plan stands in stark contrast to the $54.3 billion budget shortfall estimated just over a year ago. The budget is built on a strong fiscal foundation that includes over $25 billion in reserves, pays off educational deferrals and continues to pay down long-term retirement debts. It also appropriately prioritizes one-time spending over ongoing, allocating 85 percent of discretionary funds to one-time spending.

Governor Newsom believes California can't go back to normal, because normal was never good enough. In directly confronting our most stubborn challenges, the California Comeback Plan accelerates the state's recovery by:

- Providing immediate relief to Californians hit hardest by the pandemic.

- Confronting homelessness and the housing affordability crisis.

- Transforming public schools into gateways of opportunity.

- Bolstering wildfire resilience and tackling climate change.

- Building the infrastructure of the next century.

California can now seize this once-in-a-lifetime moment to address long-standing challenges that threaten our state's future and ensure every California family—regardless of their race or zip code—can thrive.

This is a noble strategic plan that only an inconsistent California budget surplus could achieve. In reality, California is subject to economic cycles and budget deficits within its control that make implementing the tactical portion of a grand plan such as Newsom's almost impossible. The rest of *California Madness* starting in Chapter 5 will explain why.

How Los Angeles Descended Into Neo-Feudalism Is a Lesson for Others (Bad)

This May 2021 bad news *Newsweek* article is from "How Los Angeles Descended Into Neo-Feudalism—and How to Fix It" is by Joel Kotkin:

For most of the last century, Los Angeles loomed as the next great American city, a burgeoning paradise riding the shift of world power west. It seemed posed to leave New York and London in the dust, the engines of growth inexorable. There was the city's dominance of the entertainment and aerospace industries, which incited migration from both the rest of the country and abroad, and all this promise was symbolized by a spread of suburban single-family houses that seemed to embody the ideal American dreamscape.

But today, it's clear that the Big Orange was not ready for its closeup. These days, Los Angeles is clearly on the decline, a fact that stems from a persistent lack of leadership, policy stumbles and growing competition from a whole rash of "new L.A.s," from Dallas-Ft. Worth to Nashville, Las Vegas, and Phoenix.

The pandemic provides the most recent snapshot of L.A.'s troubled future. While the COVID-19 pandemic was driving people around the country to less dense places, the leaders of the city that invented the multi-polar urban model remain determined to continue their failing efforts to convert L.A. into a dense, transit-oriented Pacific Rim New York. Little consideration has been given to the fact that Los Angeles had one-third fewer COVID-19 deaths than the New York metropolitan area—in part due to a relative lack of transit riders, warm weather, and the primacy of single-family homes.

L.A. Has Managed to All But Match NYC's Pandemic Paralysis

Rather than seizing on the crisis to promote these elements, L.A. has managed to all but match New York's pandemic paralysis. Last year, it suffered a population outflow among the highest in country, basically matching New York's. It also has suffered the highest unemployment rate of the nation's top ten metro areas, higher even than New York, The Seidman Institute at Arizona State University found.

But the COVID-19 failures are part of a much bigger problem. Persistently weak leadership stands at the root of L.A.'s decline.

For much of the 20th Century, Los Angeles was led by aggressive business leaders. Many were self-made, often somewhat nasty moguls, men like Jack Warner, Walt Disney, Lew Wasserman, Mark Taper, Howard Ahmanson Sr., Donald Douglas, Jerry Buss. They faced derision from eastern elites, but they didn't care; they consistently pushed for all the things that made for L.A.'s ascendency, from roads and bridges to arts institutions and glittering office parks to housing tracts.

Today there are few such figures. Once a beacon for up-and-coming companies, L.A.'s corporate community is diminishing, and the person who had the most potential, Elon Musk, recently announced his departure for Texas. Southern California is home to just 19 Fortune 500 companies today, equal to Denver and Seattle and roughly half the number in the Bay Area, Dallas, and Houston, not to mention New York and Chicago. This year, a long time corporate power, the real estate firm CBRE, decided to move from its downtown L.A. office to Dallas.

And you can see the demise of the city in the fate of Mayor Eric Garcetti, who started the last election season dreaming of becoming President. Garcetti has been reeling from his often-inept handling of the homeless crisis as well as the pandemic, which has been widely linked to the massive bankruptcies of small businesses.

More Troubling is the Decline in L.A.'s Signature Industry: Entertainment.

The increasingly woke nature of Hollywood may satisfy the glitterati's seemingly inexhaustible craving for respectability and acclaim, but the declining audience at the Oscars—down 58 percent from last year's disastrous showing—suggests that Hollywood is losing its place as the dominant cultural capital.

Rather than the middle-class utopia imagined in the last century, L.A. has become sadly more dystopic. It suffers from rising violent crime and a radically left-wing district attorney, George Gascon, who seems determined to lessen enforcement for non-violent crime and has even gone so far as to call for dismantling the county's gang unit (he settled for reducing it in size). LA County, half of which is made up by city residents, home to the top three most unsafe neighborhoods in the country.

The city is likewise beset by rampant inequality, visible in the festering, seemingly unresolvable homeless problem, whose population has risen to over 60,000 souls during the pandemic. The extent of homeless is so severe that some have raised concerns of a comeback of the bubonic plague associated with the Middle Ages; the city ranks second in rat infestation, just edged out by Chicago.

The vast barrios of L.A. also suffer the highest rates of overcrowding, something that proved particularly devastating during the pandemic, where, according to Los Angeles County Department of Public Health data, the fatality rates in south central Los Angeles are ten times or more than what they were in affluent, less crowded Westside neighborhoods.

At root of this neo-feudal reality is an economy that no longer provides much opportunity for most residents. Over the past decade, according to research by Chapman University's Marshall Toplansky, the vast majority of L.A.'s new jobs in the area paid below the median income, many of them under $40,000. In contrast, creation of high wage positions has lagged the national average.

Upward mobility is also stymied by growing "energy poverty" linked to green policies as are the extraordinarily high home prices. L.A., according to a recent American Enterprise Institute study, ranks 48th out of 50 for the worst places for first time homebuyers. So it's not surprising that the region vies with New York for the highest percentage of people in their 20s and early 30s still stuck at home with their parents.

Poverty in California (Very Bad)

This very bad 2021 "Poverty in California" report if from Public Policy Institute of California (PPIC):

This year's California Poverty Measure (CPM) estimates describe poverty in 2019—using the most up-to-date data available—and so do not cover the economic impact of COVID-19 or subsequent policies. Poverty in California declined in 2019, but the effects of COVID-19 are still uncertain.

Unlike the official poverty measure, the CPM, a joint research effort by Public Policy Institute of California (PPIC) and the Stanford Center on Poverty and Inequality, accounts for the cost of living and a range of family needs and resources, including safety net benefits. According to the CPM, 16.4% of Californians (about 6.3 million) lacked enough resources—$35,600 per year for a family of four, on average—to meet basic needs in 2019.

The poverty rate dropped from 17.6% in 2018. In 2020, COVID-19 is likely to have increased poverty due to severely constrained employment opportunity. However, state, and federal responses like the CARES Act in 2020 and the American Rescue Plan Act (ARPA) in 2021 could have mitigated poverty surges by providing economic support.

More than a third of Californians are living in or near poverty and nearly one in six (16.4%) Californians were not in poverty but lived fairly close to the poverty line (up to one and a half times above it). All told, more than a third (34.0%) of state residents were poor or near poor in 2019. The share of Californians in families with less than half the resources needed to meet basic needs (the deep poverty rate) was 4.6%.

Without social safety net programs, more Californians would live in poverty and without the largest social safety net programs, we estimate 6.6% more Californians would have been in poverty in 2019. Most safety net programs are designed to prioritize children, and in 2019 they kept 12.1% of children out of poverty.

The federal Earned Income Tax Credit (EITC) lowered poverty rates most, by 1.6 points overall, and CalFresh lowered the overall poverty rate by 1.3 points. The federal Child Tax Credit (CTC) lowered the rate by 1.1 points; CalWORKs and General Assistance (GA) together lowered the rate by 0.8 points. Among children under age 6, the combined California EITC and Young Child Tax Credit (YCTC) lowered the rate by 0.6 points. These differing effects reflect program scale and scope as well as participation rates among eligible families.

Poverty rates vary widely across California's counties and poverty remains higher among children, seniors, Latinos, and less-educated adults.

Most poor families in California are working in 2019, nearly 80.0% of poor Californians lived in families with at least one working adult, excluding families made up of adults aged 65 and older. For 46.8% of those in poverty, at least one family member reported working full time for the entire year, while 32.4% had a family member who worked part time and/or part of the year.

Public Sector & Teacher Unions: The Other Deep State (Ugly)

This November 2020 ugly news article "Why We Fight Government Unions" comes from the California Policy Center's Edward Ring:

The California Policy Center, established in 2013, exists to expose and undermine the destructive power of government unions. Most Californians still don't understand the threat these unions represent to the integrity of our democracy, the agenda of our politicians, and the solvency of our public institutions.

Government unions, sometimes also referred to as public sector unions, have very little in common with unions that represent employees in the private sector. While there is debate over what sorts of regulations should govern private sector unions, there is general agreement that they have played a vital role in protecting the rights of workers. Government unions are completely different.

Unlike private sector unions, government unions do not have to be reasonable when they negotiate pay, benefits, and work rules. In the private sector, if a union demands too much, the company can become unprofitable and go out of business. But government unions operate in the public sector, where politicians can simply increase taxes and cut services in order to pay whatever the unions demand.

Also unlike private sector unions, government unions do not negotiate with an independent management team. In the public sector, government unions often are the main contributors to political campaigns. Government unions "negotiate" with politicians they helped elect and whom they can easily target and defeat when they run for reelection. In California alone, government unions collect and spend nearly one billion dollars per year in dues, and of that, they use hundreds of millions, per year, to fund political campaigns.

Finally, government unions operate the machinery of government. It's easy to overlook the significance of this obvious fact. But owners of small businesses who must comply with regulations, manage inspections, pay fees, and apply for permits, all to government agencies, cannot afford to be on record as contributing to candidates and causes these government unions oppose.

The negative consequences of government union control over the vast majority of California's local and state elected officials cannot be overstated. Major corporations and wealthy individuals, by and large, have acquiesced to the government union agenda, greatly narrowing the scope of political debate, and limiting the options offered voters.

Fighting Back

In June 2018, in the landmark case of *Janus v. AFSCME*, the U.S. Supreme Court ruled that public sector employees cannot be compelled to pay anything to unions as a condition of employment, not even the so-called agency fees. In the months leading up to this case, public-sector unions made Janus out to be a catastrophe in the making, fueled by "dark money" and poised to destroy the labor movement.

In the months prior to the Janus decision, the mainstream press played up the panic. The *Economist* reported that "Unions are confronted with an existential threat." The *Atlantic* went with "Is This the End of Public-Sector Unions in America?" Even the *Wall Street Journal* was caught up in the drama, publishing a report with the ominous title "Supreme Court to Decide Fate of public-sector unions.

Maybe some union officials actually thought an unfavorable Janus ruling would destroy their organizations, but more likely, they saw it as an opportunity to rally their base and consolidate their power.

The Janus ruling has come and gone, but public-sector unions are as powerful as ever. In ultra-blue states such as California, they still exercise nearly absolute control over the state legislature, along with the city councils and county boards of supervisors in nearly every major city and county. Their control over school boards is also almost absolute.

Deceptive and Misleading Claims–How Government Unions Fool the Public

This September 2015 article "Deceptive and Misleading Claims–How Government Unions Fool the Public" comes from the California Policy Center's Edward Ring:

California's public sector unions collect and spend well over $1.0 billion per year. When you have that much money, you can hire thousands of skilled professionals to wage campaigns, litigate, lobby, negotiate, and communicate. You can hire the best public relations firms money can buy. You can commission research studies that spin facts to support your agenda. You can silence voices of dissent, voices of reason, voices of reform, with an avalanche of misinformation. And it works.

Here is a list of some of the biggest deceptions and misleading claims made by California's government unions that all rate "false" on the (sapience truth meter):

1. Government unions are protecting the middle class.

2. Government unions are a necessary political counterweight to "Wall Street," big business, and billionaires.

3. Government unions represent and protect the American worker and the labor movement.

4. Public employees are underpaid.

5. The average public sector pension is only $25,000 per year (or some similarly low number).

6. California's state/local pension systems are being reformed and will be just fine financially.

7. The teachers unions care about student achievement more than anything else.

8. Billionaires are trying to hijack California's public education system.

9. Proponents of public sector union reform are "anti-government workers."

10. Opponents of government unions are "right wing extremists."

A detailed breakdown of these ten myths promulgated by spokespersons for government unions are covered in *Union Madness* and only begins to chronicle their many deceptions. But each of these myths offer strategic value to these unions–giving them the ability to put reformers on the defensive, change the topic of discussion, redefine the terms of the debate. Each of them has powerful emotional resonance, and each of them–along with many others– is continuously reinforced by a network of professional communicators backed by literally billions in dues revenue.

Compensation reform, pension reform, other fiscal reforms, reforming work rules, education reform—all these urgent reforms must first go through one powerful special interest that stops them in their tracks—government unions. Reformers must confront not only the myths these unions promote, challenging and debunking them, but they must also redefine the role of government unions, if not question their very existence.

Progressivism Madness (Idiotic)

This November 2017 article in regards to the idiocracy of progressivism is "Rhetoric to Challenge California's Statist Elites" and comes from the California Policy Center's Edward Ring:

California's ruling elites have enacted policies that make it impossible for middle class citizens to live here. They have artificially elevated the cost of living, nearly destroyed public education, decimated public services, neglected public infrastructure, and declared war on small business.

To deflect criticism, they've convinced a critical mass of voters that any attempts to roll back these abominable policies are being engineered by racist, sexist plutocrats, and their willing puppets in the Republican party.

Exposing this diabolical, conniving scam won't be easy. The ruling elites are a powerful coalition, comprised of left wing oligarchs including most of Silicon Valley's billionaires, California's public sector unions armed with the billion dollars (or more) they collect every year in forced dues, and the environmentalist lobby and their powerful trial lawyer cohorts.

Defeating California's ruling elite requires a new coalition, comprised of the private sector middle class, enlightened members of the public sector middle class, and members of disadvantaged communities that aspire to the middle class. Attracting members of these communities, especially California's Latinos, Asians, and African Americans, requires convincing them that current policies actually harm their interests.

To do this, there are two moral arguments the elites make that have to be debunked, because they underlie all of the intrusive, statist policies that are destroying California's middle class. The first is the argument that capitalism is inherently evil and must be strictly curbed if not completely replaced by socialism. The second is the argument that unprecedented sacrifices must be made in order to save the planet from an environmental catastrophe.

The Moral High Ground

This fact—that the rhetoric of California's elite does not translate into a better quality of life for the people they govern—is the core moral argument against current policies.

Across virtually every issue, the policies of the elites are failing ordinary Californians. Pouring money into public schools has not helped students. Raising taxes has not improved services. Expanding college curricula that replace academic rigor with what amounts to political indoctrination has not improved employment opportunities for graduates. And creating artificial scarcity in the name of saving the planet has not helped the planet, but it has impoverished millions of California's most economically vulnerable residents.

In claiming the moral high ground, reformers can use the same rhetoric the elites have employed for decades, and by doing so will find the elites have already done much of their work for them. The seditious goal of making California friendlier to small businesses, with more affordable housing, more affordable energy, better jobs, and better schools is furthered by reminding Californians what the elites have done. They have engaged in one of the biggest cons of all time, enriching themselves at the expense of the average worker.

Once the issues of race and environmentalism are exposed as overstated issues, overemphasized in order to manipulate the electorate, then the resentment the elites have inculcated in their constituents can be turned against them.

Pro-growth policies don't have to rely on terminology that has been tainted by the status-quo elites. "Free market," "Libertarian," "Conservative," "Classical liberal," etc. have seductive appeal for many ideologically driven reformers, but they have limited value in California politics. Reformers have to supplement their vocabulary, borrowing more from the left than from the right.

The values and slogans that the ruling class has invested decades in inculcating in the minds of Californians can be used against them, because these elites have engaged in rank hypocrisy. Terms such as "social justice" and "equity" now have tremendous value to reformers, because reform policies will further those goals, whereas the policies implemented by California's elite have condemned ordinary people to poverty.

Examples of using terms popular with the left to advance reformer causes:

- Social justice—charter schools, teacher accountability.

- Civil Rights—the right to a quality education in a school chosen by parents.

- Equity—competitive land development to create affordable housing.

- Micro-aggression—countless taxes, hidden taxes, fees, and regulations.

- Fairness—prices for energy and water competitive with other states.

- Progressive—pension benefits with lower percentage formulas for highly paid public employees.

- Diversity—college curricula that embrace conservative as well as liberal values.

- Anti-Discrimination—merit based, color blind criteria for hiring and college admissions.

A pragmatic, centrist ideology that co-opts the rhetoric of the status-quo elites to attack the ruling class can resist being pigeonholed as left or right, or conservative or socialist. We are pragmatists. We are pro-growth, pro-job Californians and our policies will lead to prosperity, affordable housing, affordable utilities, affordable education, and social justice and equity for all Californians, and not just the elites.

5 – State Polarization, Diversity Politics, San Francisco Madness & Alarming Projections

In the Los Angeles Area, Black and Latinx Californians Have Significantly Less Wealth Than Do Other Groups
Household Median Net Worth by Race and Ethnicity, 2014

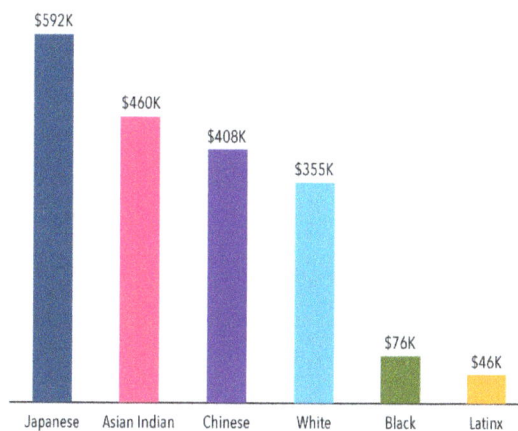

Note: Data are for Los Angeles and Orange counties.
Source: 2014 National Asset Scorecard and Communities of Color survey. See Melany De La Cruz-Viesca et al., *The Color of Wealth in Los Angeles* (Duke University, The New School, the University of California, Los Angeles, and the Insight Center for Community Economic Development: March 2016).

California Budget & Policy Center
Independent Analysis. Shared Prosperity.

Credit: Public Policy Institute of California (PPIC).

This May 2011 article "How Assimilation Works: And how multiculturalism Has Wrecked It In California." comes from Bruce Thornton at the *City Journal*:

California is a concentrated example of the time-honored idea that America is an immigrant nation. From its beginnings as a territory through the twentieth century, California comprised a riotous variety of ethnic groups, nationalities, and religions. The whole world, it seemed, was coming, and contributing to the state's ethnic tapestry: Mexicans, Irish, Australians, South Sea Islanders, Italians, Basques, Portuguese, Chinese, Japanese, Armenians, Volga Germans, Filipinos, Hmong, Laotians, Punjabis, Vietnamese.

And for a long time, immigration worked, because everyone was expected to assimilate, more or less, to the American paradigm. The choice was hard, at times even brutal. Racism, ethnocentrism, and prejudice could make the work of becoming American notoriously difficult. But people understood that to have a nation composed of immigrants, there had to be a unifying common culture in the public sphere. Transmitting that common culture was the job of the schools.

It was at school that the immigrant learned American history and celebrated the culture, leaders, and citizens who had created the world's greatest country, fought in its defense, ended slavery, defeated fascism, turned back communism, and countered racism, and embodied its most cherished values of Judeo-Christian ethics, Western European culture, and American exceptionalism. In short, they learned how to be what his or her parents had freely chosen to become—American.

This process has now been compromised over the past 40 years as the ideology of multiculturalism has colonized schools, government, and popular culture.

Today, immigrants learn to embrace a sense of entitlement and grievance and to demand that schools and government acknowledge and atone for America's sins. School curricula have degenerated into ethnic cheerleading and feel-good symbolism. The effect is to divide, not unify, to pit group against group as each tries to out-victim the other in a zero-sum competition for political clout and slices of the public fiscal pie.

How Multiculturalism Has Wrecked Assimilation In California

For example, most California state university campuses have chapters of a quasi-racist group called MEChA, the "National Chicano Student Movement of Aztlan."

Aztlan is the mythical territory, comprising northern Mexico and the American Southwest, that was allegedly stolen and plundered by Americans. MEChA promotes a politicized Mexican identity called "Chicanismo" that "involves a personal decision to reject assimilation and work towards the preservation of our cultural heritage." As such, MEChA "is committed to ending the cultural tyranny suffered at the hands of institutional and systematic discrimination that holds our Gente [people] captive."

If you need further evidence that this ideology is hostile to American culture and identity, just read a poem published at California State University Fresno in *La Voz de Aztlán*, a state-subsidized campus newspaper that functions as MEChA's house organ: "America the land robbed by the white savage / the land of the biggest genocide / the home of intolerance / the place where dreams come to die / the place of greed and slavery," and so on for another two dozen lines.

The traditional model of immigrant assimilation that helped create California cannot work if our public schools and universities subsidize anti-Americanism. Schools and government must recommit themselves to teaching and reinforcing the common culture and political principles that immigrants once learned to become Americans.

Proposition 16: A New Fight Over Affirmative Action

From the October 2020 article "'Proposition 16: A New Fight Over Affirmative Action" by CalMatters' Dan Walters:

California's failed Proposition 16 is a new skirmish in an old battle over affirmative action. Fundamentally, Proposition 16 is the latest skirmish in a decades-long conflict over the meaning of two words—affirmative action.

If it had passed—the measure would repeal 1996's Proposition 209, which banned discrimination or preferences "on the basis of race, sex, color, ethnicity, or national origin in the operation of public employment, public education, or public contracting."

Proposition 209 advocate Ward Connerly, a black member of the University of California's Board of Regents, said at the time, "Affirmative action was meant to be temporary (but) three decades later, affirmative action is permanent and firmly entrenched as a matter of public policy (and) the battleground for a political and economic war that has racial self-interest as its centerpiece."

Connerly was referring to the 1960s, when President John Kennedy ordered federal government contractors to "take affirmative action to ensure that applicants are employed and that employees are treated during employment without regard to their race, creed, color, or national origin." The term, however, quickly morphed from treatment "without regard" for race, gender or ethnicity into policies granting specific preferences to what were then called "minorities."

Proposition 209 passed in 1996 with support of 54.5% of that year's voters, nearly three-quarters of whom were white and voted for it 63% to 37%.

Interestingly, Why Did Prop 16 Fail?

From the November 2020 article "Why Did Prop 16 Fail?" by Inside Higher Ed author Scott Jaschik we have:

Fast forward 24 years later and the vote was 56.5 percent against Prop 16, almost the same percentage as the yes on Prop 209 vote in 1996. All of which raises the question: Why in a more diverse, politically liberal state did people vote against affirmative action Proposition 16: End ban on affirmative action (in 2020)?

If passed, the initiative would have ended California's ban on affirmative action. It would have allowed schools and public agencies to take race, ethnicity and sex into account when making admission, hiring, or contracting decisions. Supporters of the status quo--or no affirmative action--were quick to say that the vote proves that the current system is working well.

Gail Heriot, a professor of law at the University of San Diego, has been involved in the fight against affirmative action since the campaign for Proposition 209, the measure that banned it in the state in 1996. She was co-chair of the No on Prop 16 Committee.

She noted that the campaign for Prop 16 had far more money than the campaign against it. And that politicians lined up to support it. "I think California voters voted their conscience on the issue," Heriot said. "People think everyone votes according to their race and sex.

Californians reject identity politics."

She added that the University of California system remains a very diverse system. When examining the total number of students it enrolls and graduates, 40 percent are Black and Latinx. She is correct over all, but figures at the University of California campuses at Berkeley and Los Angeles do not support her thesis about the system when all groups are evaluated.

To that point she says, "students were more likely to go to the university campus where they can be competitive and so grad rates have increased."

Yukong Zhao, president of the Asian American Coalition for Education, said, "The resounding rejection of Proposition 16 demonstrates again that we are on the right side of the history."

Fighting for the Asian American vote was a key part of the campaign against Prop 16. While there were prominent Asian American backers of the measure, Zhao noted that many Asian Americans feel that affirmative action in effect legalizes discrimination against them. At Berkeley this year, 42 percent of freshmen are Asian, 21 percent are Latinx, 17 percent are white, and 4 percent are black.

Zhao had a message for politicians in other states.

"Going forward, I'd like to warn liberal politicians in California and nationwide: focus your efforts on devising effective measures to improve K-12 education for Black and Hispanic children, instead of introducing racially divisive and discriminatory laws time and again. You have failed in California in 2014, as well as Washington State and New York City in 2019. Asian Americans will fight fiercely and defeat your racist policies wherever and whenever tried," he said. (The reference to Washington State refers to a push to undo a measure similar to Prop 16 there. The reference to New York City involves a proposal for the high schools that award spots based on standardized test scores).

Interestingly, California's white population is under 40%, white voters make up just 55% of the state's voters in 2020, according to the Public Policy Institute of California (PPIC), and the state's politics have shifted markedly leftward—but the pro "yes" and "no" vote proportions remain almost the same. Proposition 209's critics, alleging that it oppresses women and people of color, sensed time was ripe for change.

The overwhelmingly Democratic Legislature voted to place Proposition 16 on the ballot in legislation carried by a black woman, Assemblywoman Shirley Weber, a San Diego Democrat, now California's Secretary of State. "This is probably an opportune time given people's interest in politics and given the kind of turnout that is anticipated—and given the fact that this is a different generation, that it may be possible for us to begin to work to reverse Prop. 209," Weber said.

Perhaps the timing is not so opportune. Attorney General Xavier Becerra unsapiently gave the measure a very positive official title: "Allows diversity as a factor in public employment, education and contracting decisions."

California's Woke Hypocrisy

This July 2020 *City Journal* article and section "California's Woke Hypocrisy" is from Joel Kotkin:

California's woke leaders offer platitudes and counterproductive policies rather than opportunities and better living standards for the state's minorities.

No state wears its multicultural veneer more ostentatiously than California. The Golden State's leaders believe that they lead a progressive paradise, ushering in what theorists Laura Tyson and Lenny Mendonca call "a new progressive era." Others see California as deserving of nationhood; it reflects, as a *New York Times* columnist put it, "the shared values of our increasingly tolerant and pluralistic society."

In response to the brutal killing of George Floyd in Minneapolis, Los Angeles mayor Eric Garcetti announced plans to defund the police—a move applauded by then Senator Kamala Harris, despite the city's steep rise in homicides. San Francisco mayor London Breed wants to do the same in her increasingly crime-ridden, disordered city. This follows state attorney general Xavier Becerra's numerous immigration-related lawsuits against the Trump administration, even as his state has become a sanctuary for illegal immigrants—complete with driver's licenses for some 1 million and free health care.

Despite these progressive intentions, Hispanics and African-Americans—some 45 percent of California's total population—fare worse in the state than almost anywhere nationwide. Based on cost-of-living estimates from the U.S. Census Bureau, 28 percent of California's African-Americans live in poverty, compared with 22 percent nationally. Fully one-third of Latinos, now the state's largest ethnic group, live in poverty, compared with 21 percent outside the state. "For Latinos," notes longtime political consultant Mike Madrid, "the California Dream is becoming an unattainable fantasy."

Since 1990, Los Angeles's black share of the population has dropped in half. In San Francisco, blacks constitute barely 5 percent of the population, down from 13 percent four decades ago. As a recent University of California at Berkeley poll indicates, 58 percent of African-Americans express interest in leaving the state—more than any ethnic group—while 45 percent of Asians and Latinos are also considering moving out. These residents may appreciate California's celebration of diversity, but they find the state increasingly inhospitable to their needs and those of their families.

More than 30 years ago, the Population Reference Bureau predicted that California was creating a two-tier economy, with a more affluent white and Asian population and a largely poor Latino and African-American class. Rather than find ways to increase opportunity for blue-collar workers, the state imposed strict business regulations that drove an exodus of the industries—notably, manufacturing, and middle-management service jobs—that historically provided gateways to the middle class for minorities.

California is the Worst State in the U.S. When it Comes to Creating Middle-Class Jobs

As a recent Chapman University study reveals, California is the worst state in the U.S. when it comes to creating middle-class jobs; it tops the nation in creating below-average and low-paying jobs.

Following Floyd's death, even environmental groups like the Sierra Club issued bold proclamations against racism, but they still push policies that, in the name of fighting climate change, only lead to higher energy and housing costs, which hurt the aspirational poor. Many businesses, including small firms, must convert from cheap natural gas to expensive, green-generated electricity, a policy adamantly opposed by the state's African-American, Latino, and Asian-Pacific chambers of commerce.

Meantime, California's strict Covid-19 lockdown policies, imposed by a well-compensated (and still-employed) public sector, have imperiled small firms. "There's a sense that there was major discrimination against local small businesses," said Armen Ross, who runs the 200-member Crenshaw Chamber of Commerce in South Los Angeles. "They allowed Target and Costco to stay open while they were closed. Many mom-and-pops may never come back." Many restaurants—roughly 60 percent are minority-owned—may never recover, notes the California Restaurant Association.

In the past, poor Californians, whether from the Deep South, Mexico, or the Dust Bowl, could look to the education system to help them advance. But California now ranks 49th nationally in the performance of poor, largely minority, students. San Francisco, the epicenter of California's woke culture, has the worst scores for black students of any county statewide. Yet educators, particularly in minority districts, often seem more interested in political indoctrination than in improving scholastic results.

Half of California's high school students can barely read, but the educational establishment has implemented ethnic-studies courses designed to promote a progressive, even anti-capitalist, and race-centered agenda. Unless the education system changes, California's black and Hispanic students face an uncertain future. A woke consciousness or deeper ethnic identification won't lead to successful careers. One can't operate a high-tech lathe, manage logistics, or engineer space programs with ideology.

California's failure to improve conditions for Latinos and blacks was evident even before the lockdowns and recent unrest. What the state's minorities need is not less policing, or systematic looting of upscale neighborhoods, or steps to reimpose affirmative action, or kneeling politicians; they require policies that empower working-class citizens of all races to ascend into the middle class.

The state's leaders should prioritize improving middle-class jobs and opportunities, replacing indoctrination with skills acquisition, and encouraging local businesses. Considering the nature of California politics, this can happen only if minority Californians demand something different. That could happen if enough of these residents realize that the state's ruling progressive class is interested in their votes—but apparently not in improving their lives.

California Imposes Diversity Dogma on Corporate Boards

This October 2020 article "California Imposes Diversity Dogma on Corporate Boards" comes from the Independent Institute's Lloyd Billingsley:

On September 30, California governor Gavin Newsom signed Assembly Bill 979, mandating that publicly traded companies place members of "underrepresented communities" on their boards. The bill's author, Pasadena Democrat Chris Holden, claims that "all of California's corporate boards will better reflect the diversity of our state," but in California and across America, people have cause to wonder exactly what Holden is thinking.

For example, one board member could boast proven expertise in economics, another in marketing, manufacturing, and so forth. Or one board member could have proved her worth in New Zealand, another with success in Norway, Ireland, or Italy.

But that is not the kind of diversity the author has in mind. "Underrepresented community" means African-American; Hispanic; Latino; Asian; Pacific Islander; Native American; Native Hawaiian; Alaska Native; and those who self-identify as gay, lesbian, bisexual, or transgender. By contrast, Asians and "whites" are held to be overrepresented in management.

Proportionality dogma dictates that all institutions must reflect the ethnic breakdown of the population. If they do not, the reason must be deliberate discrimination, and the only remedy is government action such as the bill Newsom just signed.

The trouble is proportionality dogma ignores the realities of personal differences, effort, and choice. With those in play, statistical disparities among groups and individuals are the rule, not the exception. For diversity activists, there are "too many" of some groups in college and on corporate boards.

Holden claims that his legislation is "a win-win as ethnically diverse boards have shown to outperform those that lack diversity." A look at California's government could prove instructive.

Ana Matosantos, a Latina from a wealthy family in Puerto Rico, earned degrees in political science and feminist studies. Republican governor Arnold Schwarzenegger established his diversity credentials by naming Matosantos as state director of finance. She brought about little if any improvement, but recurring governor Jerry Brown duly kept her on the job.

In similar style, Newsom named Matosantos as his Cabinet secretary and also made her California's "energy czar." Whatever Matosantos managed to accomplish in that role did not prevent the power blackouts now assailing Californians amid raging wildfires. So in the crucial energy sector, Newsom's "diverse" administration did not exactly set an example of performance.

Assemblyman Holden also claims his new law represents "a big step forward for racial equity."

Californians could believe it's a big step backward.

Californians Exempt From the Consequences of Liberalism

This December 2019 article "Californians Exempt From the Consequences of Liberalism" comes from the California Policy Center's Edward Ring:

When trying to understand why Californians continue to elect liberals, several explanations routinely surface. Chief among them is the theory that conservatives forever alienated California's diverse electorate by championing "discriminatory" policies.

The early example of this was Prop. 187, passed in 1994, which banned providing government services to illegal aliens. Most of Prop. 187 was overturned in court. Claiming it should serve "as a warning to immigrant bashers," the Left is now well into their third decade of using it to bash conservatives in California.

The other, more recent example of a discriminatory policy promoted by California conservatives–and also used ever since to taint them–was Prop. 8, passed in 2008, which banned gay marriage, and which also was overturned a few years later by the U.S. Supreme Court.

Whether you support these social issues or oppose them–and conservatives are by no means monolithic in their positions on either of them, not now, nor at the time–they have come to dominate the political conversation in California. Racism. Sexism. The war on women. Gay bashing. Immigrant bashing. "Transphobia." Conservatives, go away. California is no home for you.

Along with social issues, the California's liberal elites also claim a popular mandate on the issue of "climate change." No public education system in America is more geared towards terrifying the next generation on this topic. When it comes to displays of unanimity, obsession, and panic over climate change, no media region in the world can rival the bloviating hysteria of California's many local news anchors and pundits. California's tech titans and entertainment moguls see profit and power in green technology, and, of course, it's a green gold mine for California's insatiable unionized public sector.

But is it this simple?

Even if California's conservatives are forever tainted as planet destroying racist sexist bigots, aren't the liberals nonetheless failing in California? The highest rates of poverty. The worst roads. The highest taxes. The worst schools. The most homeless. The fewest affordable homes. Water rationing. Mismanaged forests and catastrophic wildfires. The list goes on. California is a tough place to live. And the liberals and the progressives, who have held absolute political power in California for decades, own all of it. What gives?

There's another explanation. A supermajority of Californians are exempt from the consequences of liberalism. These exempt Californians comprise four groups.

- The Technology Elite.

- The Public Sector.

- The Ultra-Low Income and the Undocumented.

- The Prop. 13 Privileged Class.

California May Realign Despite its Exempt Supermajority

The California Policy Center's Edward Ring continues:

This combination–successfully demonizing conservatives while exempting large swaths of the population from the consequences of liberal governance–has worked so far in California. But liberal dominance could come to an end, and it could happen swiftly.

California's low income communities are hit the hardest by the failed public schools, and they are increasingly unwilling to accept the conventional explanations. Why are the worst teachers shuttled into schools in the low income neighborhoods, instead of fired? When are the elected school board representatives going to start telling the truth–that families and hard work and a cultural priority that values educational achievement is the surest guarantee of success, not more BS about discrimination? Low income parents are rising up, demanding charter schools and reform of hiring and management rules imposed by the teachers union. Things are changing.

Similarly, California's low income communities are beginning to hear the message that maybe "climate change" isn't the real reason it's now impossible to build suburbs for all of California's new arrivals; maybe it's greedy landlords and investors who just want to keep home prices high so they can extract higher rents and higher returns. Green activists beware. A backlash could be coming from places where you'll least expect it.

Even many of California's public sector workers are able to see that liberal policies have gone too far. Many of them are still driven by a desire to serve the public, and not just enjoy the lavish benefits, the often lackadaisical workload, and the lucrative pension.

Will California's unionized firefighters really choose to march with the teachers union again, like they did in Los Angeles in January 2019? Don't bet on it. It's becoming increasingly obvious what the teachers union has done to public education in California.

An insurgency is brewing within California's public sector, and significant percentages of them will either demand their union stop exclusively supporting liberal candidates, or–thanks to the Janus decision–they will quit.

Can California's Prop. 13 privileged class see past their exemption to realize how liberals have failed their state? Can the progressive libertarian technology elite? Maybe they will when the liberal mentality of California's state legislature tips fully into a socialist mentality, imperiling their ability to manage their companies and their investments.

But only one of these four groups has to be peeled away to change the political landscape in California. The biggest wild card are low income Californians, who have more reason than ever to make common cause with what's left of California's middle class. That day could arrive sooner than anyone expects.

DO YOU THINK THINGS IN CALIFORNIA ARE GENERALLY GOING IN THE RIGHT DIRECTION OR THE WRONG DIRECTION?

		Right direction	Wrong direction	Don't know
All adults		46%	48%	6%
Likely voters		41	54	5
Party	Democrats	61	34	5
	Republicans	13	85	2
	Independents	39	54	6
Region	Central Valley	39	54	7
	Inland Empire	44	55	1
	Los Angeles	51	46	4
	Orange/San Diego	45	48	8
	San Francisco Bay Area	47	46	7

Credit: Californians & Their Government, PPIC, September 2019

San Francisco Is the Epicenter For Progressivism Madness

This section is from the March 2021 report "Only In San Francisco: $61,000 Tents And $350,000 Public Toilets" by the Hoover Institution's Lee Ohanian:

San Francisco is the unfortunate poster child on steroids for most everything wrong with progressivism madness. The maddening issues below might help to explain why 85 percent of their electorate voted Democrat (i.e., Biden-Harris) in the 2020 election!

In recent years, a contradiction has unfolded in San Francisco. On the one hand, the city continues to practice progressive economic policies. But rather than helping its poor and middle-class—as such policies are advertised as doing—these groups in San Francisco have become more unequal, downwardly mobile, and altogether priced-out. This raises the question of whether the policies themselves are contributing to the problem.

Almost half of San Francisco residents are planning on moving out of the city due to rising crime and a deteriorating quality of life, according to a recent poll. The poll of 500 San Franciscans, commissioned by the San Francisco Chamber of Commerce, showed that just over 40% of residents plan to move out of the city in the next few years.

Additionally, 8 out of 10 people polled said crime has increased in the city, and almost 90% of those polled said they believe that the homeless crisis has gotten worse. Roughly three-quarters of residents in San Francisco said their quality of life has declined over the past year.

According to the San Francisco Chamber of Commerce: "For the second year in a row, 70% of residents feel that the quality of life in San Francisco has declined. Considered in light of the pandemic, these views are somewhat unsurprising. However, what stands out in the polling results is the strikingly high and consistent number of respondents who now view homeless and crime as the leading problems facing the City. Roughly 88% see homelessness as having worsened in recent years, and an overwhelming 80% see addressing this homelessness crisis as a high priority."

San Francisco has the highest per-capita budget of any major city in the country. At $15,650 per person, it is about 40 percent higher than Bill de Blasio's over-the-top New York City budget. You would think San Franciscans would have wonderful city services coming out of their ears. Wrong.

San Francisco represents perhaps the greatest failure of governance in the country, and with this failure comes enormous waste, inefficiency, and dysfunctional politics. Beginning with providing tent living for the homeless, which costs about $61,000 per individual per year. This is not a typo. Not one too many decimal places. Remember, this is San Francisco, which squanders money at a rate that makes your head spin. San Francisco's enormous spending on homelessness has worked about as well as throwing gasoline on a fire.

The city's 2020–21 budget for the Department of Homeless and Supportive Housing is about $852 million. To put that in perspective, Sacramento's city budget is about $650 million, which covers all public services for their population of over 500,000.

Homeless Madness!

This July 2021 news article "40% of San Francisco residents plan to leave due to quality of life: Poll" is by Andrew Mark Miller at the *Washington Examiner*:

The city received more than 42,000 phone calls in 2017 about homeless encampments. Open-air drug markets flourish in plain view, and human excrement, in addition to used needles, line city streets. San Francisco spends about $54 million per year cleaning its streets, and those city workers willing to clean "hot spots," as they are called, can earn as much as $184,000 per year, which gives a whole new meaning to the term "combat pay."

A-San Francisco estimates about 8,000 homeless living in the city. The $852 million budget works out to about $106,500 per homeless individual. Just imagine how much medical treatment and housing could be provided at that level of support. But how the budget is spent would be comedic if the problem weren't so tragic.

During the pandemic, San Francisco distributed 262 tents across six locations. These tents are sheltering just over 300 people. I don't know how much the city paid for these tents, but one can purchase a perfectly fine, very large tent from REI for about $400. The annual budget for these tents is $16.1 million, which comes out to about $61,000 per tent per year. This includes meals, bathroom facilities, and security.

In recent years, a contradiction has unfolded in San Francisco. On the one hand, the city continues to practice progressive economic policies. But rather than helping its poor and middle-class—as such policies are advertised as doing—these groups in San Francisco have become more unequal, downwardly mobile, and altogether priced-out. This raises the question of whether the policies themselves are contributing to the problem.

Criminal Madness!

Police statistics show certain crimes have been increasing in California's fourth-largest city, including a significant surge in car burglaries, which are up as much as 700% in some areas. San Francisco's police chief has pointed the finger at two factors: not enough police on the streets and criminals being let out of jail due to relaxed prosecuting.

"These same people ... are going into the stores and snatching property," San Francisco Police Chief Bill Scott told CNN. "Once we arrest them, we find out they've been arrested over and over again. It's frustrating." In the poll, 76% of San Franciscans said that "it should be a high priority for the city to increase the number of police officers in high-crime neighborhoods."

San Francisco's lax attitude to crime does not start and end with Chesa Boudin, the new 2019 district attorney, refuses to prosecute almost any type of theft less than $950 if no weapon or violence is involved. Never mind that he had never prosecuted a case before; his unabashedly progressive platform—which promised to end cash bail, reduce the size of the city's prison population, "reimagine" criminal justice and stop enforcing so-called "quality-of-life" crimes such as prostitution—garnered international praise.

The problem starts at the state level with the approval of Proposition 47, a 2014 ballot measure that reclassified a range of felonies—including theft of anything worth less than $950 and most drug possession and drug use offences—as "misdemeanors", is also part of the problem; shoplifting is now so rife in the city that Walgreens, a national pharmacy chain, has closed 17 locations in San Francisco. Meanwhile, like other liberal city leaders, San Francisco's mayor London Breed has pulled $120 million from the city's law enforcement budget to reinvest elsewhere.

Justice Madness!

However, not even 18 months into the job, San Francisco's new and overtly progressive district attorney Chesa Boudin has inspired more despair than hope—so much so that he now faces two recall petitions from San Franciscans unhappy with his radical approach to criminal justice. And if he has become a "beacon," it is as a cautionary tale of what happens when voguish ideas of radical reform are put into action.

Boudin, to his credit, has only done what he promised to do. Two days into the job, he fired seven top prosecutors, replacing them with lawyers who had previously worked as public defenders. Within a few months, he had released almost 40% of the city's prison population.

The pandemic further provided Boudin with a public health rationale for his program of decarceration. The consequences speak for themselves: homicides are up, as are burglaries and carjackings. Arson attacks have also increased by almost 50%.

And yet prosecutions are down. Between January 2020, when he took office, and March this year, Boudin has tried just 23 cases. During an equivalent time period, his (already quite liberal) predecessor brought more than ten times as many cases to trial. In 2020, prosecutors in neighboring Alameda County dismissed only 11% of felonies brought to them by the police. In San Francisco, that figure stood at 40%.

It's hardly surprising, then, that San Franciscans have started to turn on Boudin with two recall measures. Of the 131 arrests made for domestic violence felonies in the last three months of 2020, Boudin dismissed 113, prompting anger from campaigners and volunteers at the city's women's shelters. Meanwhile, police in the Tenderloin district, ground zero for the city's homelessness and drug abuse crises, are outspoken in their frustration at Boudin's refusal to prosecute the dealers behind the surge in fentanyl overdose deaths in the city.

Drug Addicts Madness!

This section is from the October 2019 report "Why Drug Addicts Outnumber High School Students In San Francisco" by the Hoover Institution's Lee Ohanian:

San Francisco is one the most productive cities in the world and is the headquarters for several remarkably innovative and creative businesses, including Twitter, Uber, Lyft, and Fitbit, among others. But drug abusers have taken over several of its most densely populated neighborhoods and much of its central business district.

Poorly designed policies are a key reason why San Francisco's drug abuse problem is so much worse than those of other major cities. And new policies aimed at helping drug users may continue this trend.

With an estimated population of nearly 25,000 drug users, there are about 522 drug users per square mile in San Francisco. Drug users outnumber the city's 16,000 high school students by more than 50 percent.

San Francisco's drug abuse problem has become a public health crisis. San Francisco gave out 5.8 million hypodermic needles last year to drug users and collected 3.8 million used needles. Many of the remaining 2 million needles line city streets and pose a risk to those walking on them, particularly children, who are less aware of these issues, as well as the recent interim mayor, who found a hypodermic needle had punctured the sole of his shoe.

Governing Madness!

This November 2014 article "How San Francisco's Progressive Policies Are Hurting the Poor" comes from Scott Beyer at Reason:

With very few exceptions, the political leaders that have been running the "City by the Bay" in the last 40 years have all come out of the same "Democrat machine stable." Many locals refer to it as the Brown-Burton machine, but it is really much more involved and complicated than that, as the likes of Nancy Pelosi, Kamala Harris, and Gavin Newsom are just a few of the beneficiaries of the inbred and self-serving culture that has been at the helm of that city.

"Just opening your business, the amount of red tape puts the Soviet Union to shame... Often times you're hundreds and hundreds of thousands dollars in debt because of delays that were caused by the city and their processes." This is how Ben Bleiman, a small-business owner in San Francisco, described the expense and time involved in opening a small business in San Francisco in 2019.

And small-business nightmares don't end once you have opened your doors. Keeping the business open means paying extraordinary taxes and fees, including a requirement that business owners fund every worker's health insurance at a cost of two dollars an hour, even if workers are covered by the insurance of their parents.

In 2019, San Francisco voters passed Proposition C, the largest tax increase in the city's history. This new tax—about 0.5 percent on gross revenue for businesses with more than $50 million in revenue, or 1.5 percent on payroll expenses for businesses headquartered in San Francisco with greater than $1 billion in revenue—is levied on roughly the largest three percent of the city's businesses. The city estimates that this tax will yield an additional $300 million in revenue in the first year, which would be used to fund additional programs for the homeless. This would roughly double the city's homelessness budget.

This new increase comes on the heels of two other special-purpose taxes in San Francisco, one on gross rental income to pay for childcare services and another on land parcels to increase teacher salaries.

Every sensible government knows the fable about killing the goose that lays the golden eggs. The moral of the story is that one does not set taxes at such a level that they devastate economic activity. San Francisco is doing just that—and one wonders how long it can last.

Let's hope that someday, saner heads will prevail, and San Franciscans will start electing people who are genuinely concerned with the welfare of the people they represent as opposed to politics, and that they have the competence to handle the job.

California Has a Segregation Problem

From the 2020 research brief by Joel Kotkin and Marshall Toplansky *Beyond Feudalism: A Strategy to Restore California's Middle Class* at the Chapman University Center for Demographics & Policy:

A report more than three decades ago from the Population Reference Bureau predicted that the state was creating a two-tier economy, with a more affluent white and Asian population and a largely poor Latino and African American class.

Tragically, none of this was or remains necessary. Perhaps no place on earth has more going for it than the Golden State. Unlike the East Coast and the Midwest, we benefited from a comparatively late industrialization, with an economy based less on auto manufacturing and steel and more on science-based fields like aerospace, software, and semiconductors. The state gained from the best aspects of progressive rule: the nation's elite public university system, the greatest water systems since the Roman Empire, a vast network of highways, ports, and bridges. And, of course, California has incomparable weather.

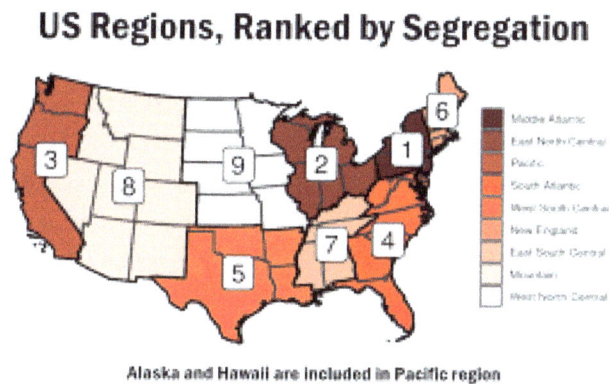

US Regions, Ranked by Segregation

Credit: Othering & Belonging Institute.

The state has drawn ambitious people from the rest of the country and the world. The Californian was, like the American described by eighteenth century French traveler J. Hector St. John de Crèvecœur, a "new man": innovative, independent, less bound by tradition or ancient prejudice. This Californian still exists, but like the state's roads, schools, and universities, is aging, and becoming less mobile and more pessimistic.

Identity Politics vs. Melting Pot Vision

From the November 2020 article "'Identity Politics vs. Melting Pot Vision" by CalMatters' Dan Walters:

Gov. Gavin Newsom was pressed by various identity groups on his appointment to the U.S. Senate seat and this is how the selection process works in an unsapient "identify politics' frame and state of mind. The jousting over Gov. Gavin Newsom's appointment of a U.S. senator to succeed Vice President-elect Kamala Harris became the epitome—or nadir—of identity politics.

It's a mindset in which the personalities, talents, character, and accomplishments of individual human beings are secondary to being defined by their race, ethnicity, gender, age and/or sexual identification—and are expected to automatically reflect the values and mores of their designated categories. Inevitably, then, politics become a competition among identity groups for power and distribution of public goods—a modern version of tribalism that succeeds the earlier vision of America as a melting pot that blends immigrant cultures into a unique society.

Oddly, ordinary Americans increasingly resist such categorization. We intermarry, we happily live in integrated neighborhoods, we have and adopt children of mixed ethnicity, we send our children to integrated schools, and we embrace food and music from disparate cultures. That's especially true in California, the most ethnically and culturally complex of the 50 states.

Then Senator Harris, herself is both a product of the melting pot vision—her mother migrated from India, her father from Jamaica and they met as students at the University of California—and of the politics of identity. Depending on the audience and the moment, she identified herself as Black or Indo-American, but she also married a white man who is Jewish.

Not surprisingly, therefore, Newsom is feeling pressure from identity groups to choose a new senator from within their ranks, each saying Newsom "must" pay homage with an appointment. Willie Brown, the former Assembly speaker and San Francisco mayor who was also Newsom's political mentor, is leading a public drive for a Black woman to succeed Harris, who is also a former Brown protégé.

The odds-on favorite among political handicappers is that Newsom would appoint a Latino, possibly then Secretary of State Alex Padilla, who has a lengthy and close relationship with the governor. And this is exactly what happened.

As the cynics—or realists—see the situation, Newsom has already given a nod to black and LGBTQ groups by naming to a seat on the state Supreme Court. He could placate one of the other groups by naming a successor to Padilla in the secretary of state's office. The same dynamics would apply if he chose another Latino, then Attorney General Xavier Becerra, for the Senate.

While the competition for Newsom's senatorial appointment typifies identity politics, it also demonstrates their unfortunate aspect of ignoring what should be the most important factor. We should have someone in the Senate of good character and demonstrated competence and who approaches the position with an independent mind, as the state's other senator, Dianne Feinstein, has done. But now we don't!

6 – 'Anti' Business, Middle Class & Development—But 'Pro' Green, Crime & Homelessness

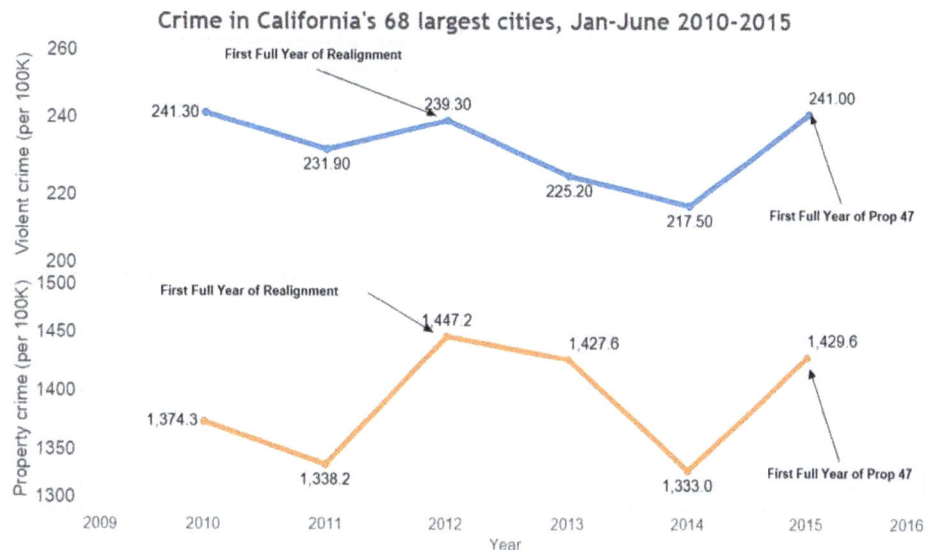

Crime in California's 68 largest cities, Jan-June 2010-2015

Violent crime (per 100K):
- 241.30
- First Full Year of Realignment
- 231.90
- 239.30
- 225.20
- 217.50
- 241.00
- First Full Year of Prop 47

Property crime (per 100K):
- 1,374.3
- First Full Year of Realignment
- 1,338.2
- 1,447.2
- 1,427.6
- 1,333.0
- 1,429.6
- First Full Year of Prop 47

Year: 2009 2010 2011 2012 2013 2014 2015 2016

California violent and property crime rate in California's 68 largest cities in January-June of each year. Violent crime rate includes rapes, which may distort results slightly because of changes in definition

Source: Center on Juvenile and Criminal Justice

Credit: Center on Juvenile and Criminal justice.

California has long been among America's most extensive taxers and regulators of business. But at the same time, the state had assets that seemed to offset its economic disincentives: a famously sunny climate, a world-class public university system that produced a talented local workforce, sturdy infrastructure that often made doing business easier, and a history of innovative companies.

No more. As California has transformed into a relentlessly antibusiness state, those redeeming characteristics haven't been enough to keep firms from leaving. Relocation experts say that the number of companies exiting the state for greener pastures has exploded.

In surveys, executives regularly call California one of the country's most toxic business environments and one of the least likely places to open or expand a new company. Many firms still headquartered in California have forsaken expansion there. Reeling from the burst housing bubble and currently suffering an unemployment rate of 12 percent—nearly 3 points above the national level—California can't afford to remain on this path.

California first began to tarnish its business-friendly reputation in 1974, when Democrat Jerry

Brown became governor. Government's job, in Brown's view, was to restrain growth, not to unleash it. His administration proceeded to scuttle some infrastructure spending, limit development, and expand environmental regulations. In 1977, *Time* declared that "the California of the 60s, a mystical land of abundance and affluence, vanished sometime in the 70s." And by 1978, the Fantus Company, a corporate-relocation firm, was ranking California the fourth-worst state for business.

Brown's two Republican successors determined to restore California's economic luster. George Deukmejian, who served two terms as governor starting in 1983, and Pete Wilson, governor from 1991 through 1998, worked to cut back existing regulations and reject new ones, and they trimmed some taxes and other costs of doing business, including onerous workers'-compensation assessments. Sacramento also created economic "quick-response" teams, whose mission was to persuade companies considering relocation to stay.

California's tax burden, ranked fourth-highest in the nation in 1978 by the Tax Foundation, had dropped to 16th place by 1994. "Companies are once again looking at California as a good place to do business," a Fantus executive declared a few years later.

All that changed for the worse again when Gray Davis, Brown's chief of staff during the late 1970s, became governor in 1999. Elected with heavy support from labor unions and trial lawyers, the Democrat signed 33 bills that the state's chamber of commerce called "job killers."

Rhetoric to Challenge California's Statist Elites

This November 2017 article "Rhetoric to Challenge California's Statist Elites" comes from the California Policy Center's Edward Ring:

California's ruling elites have enacted policies that make it impossible for middle class citizens to live here. They have artificially elevated the cost of living, nearly destroyed public education, decimated public services, neglected public infrastructure, and declared war on small business. To deflect criticism, they've convinced a critical mass of voters that any attempts to roll back these abominable policies are being engineered by racist, sexist plutocrats, and their willing puppets in the Republican party.

Exposing this diabolical, conniving scam won't be easy. The ruling elites are a powerful coalition, comprised of left wing oligarchs including most of Silicon Valley's billionaires, California's public sector unions armed with the billion dollars (or more) they collect every year in forced dues, and the environmentalist lobby and their powerful trial lawyer cohorts.

Defeating California's ruling elite requires a new coalition, comprised of the private sector middle class, enlightened members of the public sector middle class, and members of disadvantaged communities that aspire to the middle class. Attracting members of these communities, especially California's Latinos, Asians, and African Americans, requires convincing them that current policies actually harm their interests.

California to Business: Get Out!

This December 2017 article "California Ranks Second Worst in U.S. on Economic Freedom Index: High Taxes, Overregulation Causing Exodus of Workers and Employers to Other States" comes from the Independent Institute's David J. Theroux:

California's policymakers have enacted policies more harmful to economic freedom and opportunity than those of almost any other state, according to the 2017 Economic Freedom of North America report by the Independent Institute in conjunction with Canada's Fraser Institute.

Not only does California rank 49th out of all 50 U.S. states, but its burdensome combination of high taxes and regulatory overreach is so toxic for economic opportunity that it is causing a major out-migration of both workers and enterprises to other states.

"California's lack of economic freedom helped motivate more than 10,000 businesses to leave the Golden State, reduce operations, or expand elsewhere during the past seven years," said Dr. Lawrence J. McQuillan, Senior Fellow and Director of the Independent Institute's Center on Entrepreneurial Innovation. Census data show that 3.5 million people left California for greener pastures from 2010 to 2015.

While California ranks second worst in economic freedom (only New York was lower), New Hampshire ranked highest for the third year in a row, scoring 8.3 out of 10 in measures of government spending, taxation, and labor market restrictions based on 2015 data, the most recent year available. Rounding out the top five freest states are Florida and Texas (tied for 2nd), South Dakota (4th), and Tennessee (5th).

"The freest economies operate with comparatively less government interference, relying more on personal choice and markets to decide what's produced, how it's produced, and how much is produced," said Fred McMahon, who co-authored the report with economists Dean Stansel of Southern Methodist University and José Torra of the Mexico City–based Caminos de la Liberta.

"The 2017 report shows the public, news media, and policymakers in Sacramento what changes need to be made to make California competitive in the future," said David J. Theroux, Founder and President of the Independent Institute.

This article is from the Autumn 2011 *City Journal* "Cali to Business: Get Out!: Firms Are Fleeing the State's Senseless Regulations and Confiscatory Taxes" by Steven Malanga:

Last year, a medical-technology firm called Numira Biosciences, founded in 2005 in Irvine, California, packed its bags and moved to Salt Lake City. The relocation, CEO Michael Beeuwsaert told the *Orange County Register*, was partly about the Utah destination's pleasant quality of life and talented workforce.

But there was a big "push factor," too: California's steepening taxes and ever-thickening snarl of government regulations. "The tipping point was when someone from the Orange County tax [assessor] wanted to see our facility to tax every piece of equipment I had," Beeuwsaert said. "In Salt Lake City at my first networking event I met the mayor and the president of the Utah Senate, and they asked what they could do to help me. No [elected official] ever asked me that in California."

The Middle Class Squeeze

More from the 2020 research brief by Joel Kotkin and Marshall Toplansky *Beyond Feudalism: A Strategy to Restore California's Middle Class* at the Chapman University Center for Demographics & Policy:

California policies, often steeped in good intentions, have had deeply deleterious consequences, especially on its middle and working-class families. The state's rich have enjoyed an unprecedented bounty. But California also suffers the widest gap between middle and upper-middle income earners of any state.8 California's signatures of upward mobility, homeownership, and the availability of economically sustainable jobs, have fallen well below the national average.

High real estate prices have fostered high rents, and prevented many Californians, notably the young and minorities, from purchasing houses. This is occurring at a time when the vast majority of jobs being produced in the state pay under the median wage, and 40% pay under $40,000 a year. Since 2008 the state has created five times as many low wage jobs as high wage jobs. Yes, the state's employment growth in the past decade has outperformed the rest of the country, but most of the new jobs pay poorly, and now seem to be permanent for many.

California is the single worst state in the nation when it comes to creating jobs that pay above average, while it is at the top of the nation in creating below average and low-paying jobs. High wage jobs have increased marginally in the state during the past decade, but our competitors—Utah, Texas, Arizona, Nevada, and Washington have seen much higher growth. At the same time, middle-skill job growth in California is well below competitive states. California lost 1.6 million above-average-paying jobs in the past decade, more than twice as many as any other state.

Given the sophistication of its economy and its enormous natural advantages, California should lead, not lag, in creating high wage jobs. In this chapter section we identify four critical areas of opportunity: software, international trade, space, and creative industries.

California Feudalism: The Squeeze on the Middle Class

This section is courtesy of the 2018 article "California Feudalism: The Squeeze on the Middle Class" also comes from Chapman University researchers Joel Kotkin and Marshall Toplansky:

Today California's economy is dominated by a handful of Bay Area tech firms that have expanded at one of the most dynamic paces in economic history. Most of these companies are in a relatively constrained geography along the San Francisco Peninsula.

Together, these tech firms—Apple, Netflix, Facebook, Google—along with Microsoft and Amazon, have achieved a combined net worth equal to one-quarter of the NASDAQ and equal to the GDP of France. The S&P 500, the broad index of stocks, has a total market capitalization of approximately $24.2 trillion slightly more than the GDP of the country. They represent 15% of the entire S&P 500 companies' market capitalization.

This has been a heady period for the Bay Area, with San Jose and San Francisco boasting the first and third highest average per capita income in the country. Between 2007 and 2016, according to an analysis of Bureau of Labor Statistics data, the Bay Area created 200,000 jobs that paid better than $70,000 annually. Yet during that same period, high wage jobs dropped in Southern California and statewide; simply put, the Bay Area replaced the high wage jobs lost in the recession while the rest of the state did not.

Part of the problem has been big losses in blue collar jobs, critical to the state's working class. California lost 423,700 manufacturing jobs between 1991 and 2016. Such jobs pay significantly better than the retail and service industry jobs that have characterized the post-recession growth. Minimum or near minimum wage jobs in 2015-6 accounted for almost two thirds of the state's new job growth, notes the state's Business Roundtable. These problems have arisen in "boom times," so we should be particularly concerned about what will happen if, as appears likely, the economy slows.

By late 2017 California's GDP growth rate, once well above the national average, was beginning to fall below it. Growth in high wage sectors like professional and business services is now slower in Silicon Valley and San Francisco than in boomtowns such as Nashville, Dallas-Fort Worth, Austin, Orlando, San Antonio, Salt Lake City, and Charlotte. Most California metros, including Los Angeles, fell in the bottom half of the rankings.

For Latinos, the 'California Dream' Is Becoming Unattainable

Our collective badge of shame is the prevalence of poverty amidst enormous affluence. This correlates with a state that, amidst high living costs, produces a disproportionate number of low wage jobs. Nearly one in five Californians—many working—lives in poverty (using a cost-of-living adjusted poverty rate); the Public Policy Institute of California estimates another fifth live in near-poverty—roughly 15 million people in total.

Most tragic, roughly 17% of California's children live in or near poverty. Poverty rates for California's Latinos and African Americans, most of them working, are well above the national average, and considerably higher than in Texas, our primary competitor, and a state with a similarly diverse population. Over half of all California Latino households, now a plurality in the state, can barely pay their bills, according to a United Way study. "For Latinos," notes long-time political consultant Mike Madrid, "the California Dream is becoming an unattainable fantasy."

The loss of jobs, particularly in hospitality and retail, from the coronavirus could exacerbate this situation further. California's cost adjusted poverty are among the highest in the country, and, even during the recovery, remained higher in 2019 than in 2007.

On the most extreme end, the most obvious expression of pervasive inequality and economic dysfunction lies evident on our streets. Even as homelessness has been reduced in much of the country, it has continued to swell in California. Roughly half the nation's homeless population lives in the Golden State, many concentrated in disease and crime-ridden tent cities in either its largest city, Los Angeles, or San Francisco. This surge, notes the Council of Economic Advisors, is largely attributable to the state's "excessive regulatory barriers."

California's Split Personality

This section is from the Winter 2016 *City Journal* article "California's Split Personality: The Golden State's tech sector is booming, even as its industrial base flees" by Steven Malanga:

Call it a tale of two states. On the one hand, California is briskly creating private-sector jobs, led by a Silicon Valley hiring spree. Sacramento's budget, deeply in the red just a few years ago, is running a surplus, thanks to big income gains by the state's wealthy residents. Meanwhile, however, large areas of the state lag behind. Six of America's ten metro regions with the highest unemployment rates—including blue-collar communities like Merced and Fresno—are in the Golden State.

Nearly two-thirds of Silicon Valley firms said that they were expanding their payrolls in 2015, while just 2 percent were cutting. Their employment gains have fueled increases in other local industries, including construction, retail, and hospitality. The San Francisco Bay Area has accounted for more than half of all job growth in California since 2007, though it accounts for less than one-fifth of the state's population. Robust Silicon Valley earnings have also driven up income among the state's elite and bolstered California's budget.

For other areas of California, especially those with blue-collar jobs, it's a very different picture. Since 2010, the U.S. has added about 800,000 new industrial jobs. But California, for years the leader in manufacturing jobs, has contributed just 30,000 of those new positions, a gain of merely 2.3 percent. The state's mediocre record on creating new industrial jobs may be one reason that its biggest metro region, Los Angeles, has fallen behind.

With nearly 30 percent of the state's population, greater Los Angeles has accounted for just 6 percent of new jobs in California since 2007. Though it has more than half a million industrial jobs, the area has seen no manufacturing growth during the national rebound. Perhaps more ominously, L.A.'s struggles predate the recession of 2008. In the past 20 years, greater Los Angeles has lost 3.1 percent of its jobs, according to a 2014 study by UCLA's Anderson School of Management.

Greater Los Angeles also leads California in business "disinvestments"—that is, firms that close up facilities and move to other states. Government doesn't track relocations by individual companies, but California business-consultant Joseph Vranich—whose Spectrum

Location Solutions provides businesses with site-selection advice—has compiled a list of more than 1,500 firms that have left the state since 2008. Some industry studies approximate that more than five companies relocate for every one that publicly acknowledges doing so, making it possible that some 9,000 businesses have left California since Vranich started tracking the trend.

Though state officials have claimed that there is no exodus, California has consistently ranked as the least business-friendly state in the annual *CEO Magazine* survey of executives nationwide. A 2014 survey by Site Selection magazine, which tracks openings of major new facilities requiring an investment of $1 million or more, estimated that California attracted the third-smallest number of new facilities of any state, when adjusted for population.

Disinvestment may help explain why California's industrial job base is expanding so slowly. The Spectrum Location Solutions study found that industrial firms top the list of companies exiting the state, followed by pharmaceutical and medical-device makers. Firms that operate call centers and data-processing facilities, such as online retailers and providers of cloud services, are also moving out. Their top destination? Texas, followed by Nevada, Arizona, and Colorado.

Extreme Environmentalism vs. Practical Environmentalism

This November 2017 article "Rhetoric to Challenge California's Statist Elites" comes from the California Policy Center's Edward Ring:

Apart from the distraction of race and gender, environmentalism provides the moral argument used as cover for policies that have imposed a punitive cost of living on Californians. It is important to make the distinction between attacks that discredit environmentalism in its entirety, and environmentalist reform that exposes the hidden agendas and inherent futility of California's extremist environmental policies.

Here are examples of two very different ways to apply environmentalist values.

(1) "Stop urban sprawl" vs "California has 163,000 square miles of land and is nearly empty, adding 10 million more people on quarter acre lots (even including new roads and new commercial/industrial centers) would consume less than 2,000 square miles!"

(2) "People need to live in multi-family dwellings" vs "detached single family homes are cheaper per unit to build than multi-family dwellings, and are more popular among buyers."

(3) "There isn't enough water for people to have detached homes and yards" vs "for less than $20 billion, we could build enough desalination capacity to provide water to every home and business in Los Angeles County; farming consumes 80% of all water diversions in California, we are exporting water intensive crops like alfalfa, grown using massively subsidized water, in the Imperial Valley (desert)!"

(4) "The government needs to discourage further development of fossil fuels such as clean natural gas" vs "Californians are paying as much as ten times what energy consumers pay for electricity in low cost states, and that California's CO_2 emissions are a minute fraction of those from other nations such as China and India."

(5) "We have to get people out of their cars and build passenger rail" vs "cars, trucks and buses offer far more convenience and versatility, and are on the verge of becoming 100% clean and sustainable modes of transportation."

(6) "No new mines and quarries should be allowed within California, and existing ones should be phased out" vs "developing in-state natural resources creates in-state jobs and costs less than importing materials from elsewhere in the U.S. and Canada."

When the elites demand "environmental justice" for people of color, ask them (using the San Francisco Bay Area as an example) what any of that has to do with why we can't build homes on the eastern slopes of the Mt. Hamilton Range, or in San Jose's Coyote Valley, or along the Interstate-280 corridor in the Santa Cruz mountains.

Ask them why they're paying 60% of their income for rent or a mortgage, when California has 163,000 square miles of land and is nearly empty. Ask why money that is being spent on high speed rail, using imported materials, isn't instead being used to create high paying jobs in road and infrastructure projects that will actually improve lives. Ask why thousands of people aren't working in high paying jobs in mining and quarrying, so building materials can cost less.

For aggressive reformers, good questions are plentiful. What have California's elites done for working families? Have they gotten you better jobs? Have they nurtured robust and competitive housing markets to lower the price of a home? Have they widened the freeways? Have they enabled competition to drive down the cost-of-living? Have they made your communities safe and prosperous and affordable? Have they done anything other than bribe your so-called leaders with campaign contributions, so they'll do what they're told?

It comes down to this: These purported spokespersons for true environmentalist values have become personally successful by fomenting environmentalist panic, but they do not represent the best interests of ordinary Californians, and they do not articulate a realistic or practical vision of environmentalism.

California's elite has declared war on the working class. They have used race as a distraction, and extreme environmentalism as the phony moral justification for their self-serving policies. They must be exposed!

California's Homeless Crisis and Beyond

This section is from the December 2019 article "The Manger vs The Monster–Housing California's Homeless" and also comes from the California Policy Center's Edward Ring:

Advocates for the homeless frequently invoke biblical passages in order to appeal to the

Christian compassion that still guides the hearts of most Americans, whether they are religious or secular. "No room at the inn," is a phrase the American Left relies upon to justify everything from open borders and immigration amnesty to affordable housing and homeless shelters.

But what sort of inn? An inexpensive manger that is warm, dry, and safe? Or an overbuilt monstrosity? Both options are warm, dry, and safe, but the monster is so grossly expensive that only a few find shelter. California's policies currently favor these overbuilt monstrosities, with the biggest losers the homeless. The average cost for "permanent supportive housing" in California is now easily in excess of a half million per unit as these examples show:

- A recent audit in the City of Los Angeles estimated the average cost at $550,000 per unit.

- According to a program overview released by the Santa Clara County's Office of Supportive Housing, their average cost is in excess of $500,000 per unit.

- In San Francisco, according to a report released by the Bay Area Council Economic Institute, over $700,000 per unit.

- Across the Bay in Alameda County, a 2018 report released by the City of Oakland discloses average costs of over $600,000 per unit.

- On Federal property in Los Angeles County, remodeling an existing building to provide permanent supportive housing is estimated to cost over 900,000 per unit.

- But the champion of all monstrosities is in Venice Beach, California, where developers propose to construct housing for the homeless at a cost of approximately $1.4 million per unit.

It doesn't require a cynic to recognize that something's rotten: The incentive to build monsters instead of mangers is because with these monsters, project developers and financiers have a larger monetary denominator to work with. Much larger. That's more budget to accommodate overhead, fat consultancy contracts, huge payoffs to litigators, hefty payments to the public sector for permits and fees, lucrative deals with subcontractors, and the promise of endless additional work since at this rate, and at this cost, the problem will never get solved. But how is this ever justified morally?

Here's where one of the more insidious manifestations of socialist ideology comes into play. Like all socialist principles, it reeks with compassion but is utterly impractical if not nihilistic in the real world. Building homeless housing and low income housing on some of the most expensive real estate on earth is to fulfill the ideals of "inclusionary zoning." Relying on "scientific studies" that defy common sense, the role of inclusionary zoning is to "encourage the development of affordable housing in low poverty neighborhoods, thereby helping foster greater social and economic mobility and integration."

In practice, this means if you work hard your entire life to live in a neighborhood where your children can go to decent schools and feel safe walking the streets, if you skip vacations and take on a 2nd job to pay off an astronomical mortgage, it does not matter. If you lose the inclusionary zoning lottery, prepare to have an apartment house dumped onto the lot where your neighbor's single family home just got demolished. Then, while investors pad their profits with property tax exemptions for creating "inclusionary" housing, prepare to have this property occupied by tenants who pay little or no rent out of their own earnings–if they work at all–because your taxes will be paying their rent for them. Prepare for them to openly consume drugs and watch your belongings since petty theft and heroin use is now decriminalized in California.

That Is What Happened and It's Coming to Your Neighborhood

There is nothing compassionate about this. In the real world, people congregate in low income neighborhoods because they have low incomes. This is where developers build, at no cost to taxpayers, de facto low income, market housing. This is where charities build and operate shelters because they are affordable. And when people are fortunate enough to be able to afford to move from low income neighborhoods to middle income neighborhoods or beyond, they expect to be rewarded for their efforts, not have to wonder if the Homeless Industrial Complex will destroy their new neighborhood.

The obligations of compassion don't end when the Homeless Industrial Complex is finally forced to build inexpensive mangers instead of overwrought monsters. What if baby Jesus was born in a barn filled with addicts injecting heroin and smoking methamphetamine? What if the three wise men didn't have to bring gifts, because gangs of thieves had set up lucrative criminal enterprises to pay for their drugs, and instead of the hospitality of the innkeeper providing food, King Herod dispensed free government meals?

Compassionate Christians who reelect these corrupt politicians should imagine that scene defining their next Christmas pageant. And while this all sounds horribly cruel during the holiday season of giving, true cruelty is to accept the solutions currently being pursued. They are wasting billions while suffering only increases.

These are the tragic consequences of a perfect storm of flawed legislation and court rulings. In California, the practical effect of Prop. 47, sold to voters in 2014 as criminal justice reform, has been to decriminalize possession of hard drugs and petty theft. At the same time, court rulings such as Jones vs. City of Los Angeles prohibit law enforcement from relocating or detaining anyone camping in a public space unless they can offer them "permanent supportive housing." The final straw is the "housing first" regulations originating at HUD during the Obama administration that require virtually all federal grant money get spent on housing, rather than also on parallel treatment for substance abuse and mental health.

Tolerate vagrancy, drug use and petty crime. Permit an alliance of developers, service nonprofits, and government bureaucrats to hijack and waste every dollar taken from taxpayers to help the homeless, abetted by useful idiots who believe this impossible, toxic intersection of futile, corrupt strategies somehow constitutes "compassion." The result? Billions have been spent, additional billions will be spent, and the population of homeless in California, already numbering over 130,000, will only get bigger and more unmanageable.

This is the fraud presided over by supposedly compassionate politicians such as California governor Gavin Newsom and Los Angeles Mayor Eric Garcetti. Hiding behind supposedly compassionate principles such as "inclusionary zoning" they are spending billions of dollars to construct monstrous housing boondoggles where homeless people will be given "permanent supportive housing" in order to "integrate with the community." At the same time, California's unsheltered homeless, the majority of whom are either mentally ill, substance abusers, criminal predators, or all three, shall be subject to minimal expectations.

Nothing about California's homeless policies today qualifies as genuine compassion because compassion has to be rational. Compassion has to have a winning strategy, not become an endless, losing war. California's housing for the homeless policy is corruption masquerading as compassion.

Progressive extremists believe that simply providing a safe, well-appointed dwelling will cause the pathology afflicting homeless people to subside. They also believe that dispersing homeless people into subsidized dwellings in tranquil neighborhoods everywhere will be "inclusive" and further alleviate their pathology. And there are powerful financial incentives for them to pursue this policy

Pretending the Homeless Crisis is Inextricably Linked to a Shortage of Housing

By pretending the homeless crisis is inextricably linked to a shortage of housing, and because it is considered heresy to expand the urban footprint, draconian new state zoning guidelines are poised to become laws that will override local ordinances. It will become permissible to demolish single family homes in single family neighborhoods and replace them with multi-family dwellings. At the same time it will become mandatory for landlords to accept Section 8 and other subsidized renters.

The U.S. Department of Housing and Urban Development (HUD) operates a housing voucher program under Section VIII of Title 24 of the Code of Federal Regulations. This voucher program is commonly known as Section 8 assistance, and is designed to help low income, elderly, and disabled people afford decent, safe, and sanitary housing. Unfortunately, some tenants commit fraud, which wastes government resources and can create unpleasant situations for landlords and neighbors. Once you have identified Section 8 fraud, it is easy to report it to the authorities.

California's progressive lawmakers are planning to seed California's suburbs with high density dwellings, randomly placed, and fill them with taxpayer subsidized renters. This is where they will relocate the homeless, including substance abusers and mentally ill. The cost of supervising these people when they are disbursed throughout the cities and suburbs will make it scarcely less wasteful than constructing gargantuan palaces at $500,000 (or more) per unit, but progressive ideology and corrupt financial opportunism make this an attractive Plan B for the woke.

Across the suburbs of California in the coming years, expect homes to become worth more to buyers to demolish and replace as a Section 8 fourplexes. And as these suburbs fall prey to increased crime, the state will move in, extending to residential courts and cul de sacs the same pervasive surveillance that already blankets our cities.

There are alternatives to destroying our cities and suburbs in order to feed profits to investors and power to corrupt politicians and bureaucrats. But it will require more than a revolution that merely moves policy from the obviously unworkable Plan A (expensive palaces that "help" only a few) to the insidious yet feasible Plan B (rezone suburbs for subsidized multifamily units).

It will require a realignment that allows conservatives and liberals to join together to demand quick, decisive, cost-effective action. Call in the national guard who can work with law enforcement to round up the homeless, move them into quickly erected tent cities on state-owned land away from residential areas, and use the billions in savings to get them treatment. If the governor declared a state of emergency, it could be done in a matter of weeks.

From an ideological standpoint, that will require a common recognition that the rights of hard working and responsible people have to be given, at the very least, equal priority to the rights of drug addicts and psychotics.

The Sanctuary State for Gangs, Criminals, Drugs & Illegal Aliens

This section is borrowed from *Crime Rate Madness*:

The election of Donald Trump as President in 2016 reignited a key debate about American immigration policy. Do illegal aliens commit crimes at a higher rate than native-born U.S. citizens and lawful immigrants? And, if so, how should that influence any proposed changes to our immigration system?

Advocates of open borders are fond of claiming that illegal aliens commit fewer crimes than native-born U.S. citizens and cite many reports and studies backing this claim. That makes perfect sense, they assert, because illegal aliens do not wish to be brought to the attention of law enforcement and risk deportation from the United States. In reality, however, this is a weak argument, and the studies are questionable.

While the Trump administration has taken unlawful migration seriously, most illegal aliens still have little to fear. The vast majority of recent enforcement efforts have been directed at narrow groups of individuals who fit a specific profile, e.g. gang members, those working without authorization, etc. And, as the protests following President Trump's rescission of the Deferred Action for Childhood Arrivals (DACA) program clearly demonstrate, many illegal aliens feel perfectly comfortable announcing their unlawful status and making demands of the

United States government. Hence, their motto, "Undocumented and unafraid!"

Nevertheless, despite evidence to the contrary, open-borders advocates have persisted in their claims that fear of deportation means illegal aliens are inherently pre-disposed to avoiding criminal behavior. (This argument conveniently ignores the fact that improper entry by an alien is, in and of itself, a federal crime). Are these assertions legitimate?

Hard data indicate that they are not. Research conducted by the Federation for American Immigration Reform (FAIR) strongly suggests all claims that illegal aliens commit crimes at a lower rate than native-born U.S. citizens, or lawfully-present immigrants, are a myth.

In fact, the February 2019 FAIR report by Matt O'Brien, Spencer Raley and Casey Ryan, titled "SCAAP Data Suggest Illegal Aliens Commit Crime at a Much Higher Rate Than Citizens and Lawful Immigrants" finds that in the states examined, illegal aliens are incarcerated up to five and a half times as frequently as citizens and legal immigrants.

California Becomes a Sanctuary State

This *Time* October 2017 article "California Just Became a 'Sanctuary State.' Here's What That Means" is by Katy Steinmetz:

California Gov. Jerry Brown on October 4, 2017, signed a so-called "sanctuary state" bill, officially titled the California Values Act, also Known as SB 54, that will limit cooperation between local officials and federal immigration enforcement. "These are uncertain times for undocumented Californians and their families, and this bill strikes a balance that will protect public safety, while bringing a measure of comfort to those families who are now living in fear every day," Brown said in statement, according to the *Associated Press*.

While other states have passed laws that shore up protections for immigrants, the California bill, formally known as SB54, has been described as the most comprehensive in the country. Measures range from treating schools, courthouses, and hospitals as "safe zones" to restricting the ability of local police to detain people on behalf of federal immigration agents. The law does nothing to curtail the ability of federal agents to come into the state and deport people or carry out raids, but it does make such actions more difficult for agencies with limited resources.

An estimated 10 million immigrants live in California, more than the entire population of states such as Michigan, and about 25% of them are thought to be undocumented. The author of the bill, state Senate Leader Kevin de Leon, has positioned it as a safety measure to ensure undocumented residents are unafraid to report crimes to the police or send their kids to school. De Leon said at a press conference that the new law "will put a large kink in Trump's perverse and inhumane deportation machine," according to the *Associated Press*.

The main criticisms of SB54 have also been about safety, as organizations such as the California State Sheriffs' Association have argued that dangerous criminals might slip through the cracks if local authorities are limited in their ability to interact with federal officials. Before signing the bill, Gov. Brown negotiated changes meant to assuage some of those concerns, such as allowing for cooperation in cases that involve particular crimes.

Regarding California's municipalities, there is nothing unlawful in a city declaring itself a sanctuary city; the declaration is not the problem, the actions which may follow are. Usually, all a sanctuary city is asserting is that their city's resources will not be utilized in helping the federal government enforce federal law, something the Supreme Court has said the federal government cannot force a state or city to do (refusing to cooperate is called "anti-commandeering").

However, it is a federal felony, punishable by five years in prison for each violation, for any person to conceal, harbor, or shield from detection any illegal alien. The word "harbor" is defined as any conduct that tends to substantially facilitate an alien's remaining in the U.S. illegally.

The California Values Act, Also Known as SB 54

California Senate Bill 54 effectively makes California a "sanctuary state" by legalizing and standardizing statewide non-cooperation policies between California law enforcement agencies and federal immigration authorities.

- Prohibits state and local law enforcement from holding illegal aliens on the basis of federal immigration detainers, or transferring them into federal custody, unless they've been convicted in the last 15 years for one of a list of 31 crimes, or are a registered sex offender: if not, they may only be held with a warrant from a federal judge.

- Prohibits state and local law enforcement from asking anyone about their immigration status.

- Prohibits state and local law enforcement from sharing any information with federal immigration authorities that is not available to the general public.

- Prohibits state and local law enforcement from using any of their money or personnel to "investigate, interrogate, detain, detect, or arrest persons for immigration enforcement purposes."

- Prohibits state and local law enforcement from allowing federal immigration authorities to use space in their facilities.

- Limits how and when state and local law enforcement can contract with federal immigration authorities.

- Grants discretion to state and local law enforcement to cooperate even less with federal immigration authorities than the bill authorizes them to, but not more Is near-universally recognized and described by both its supporters and opponents as a sanctuary state bill: protects illegal aliens at the expense of citizens, will increase illegal immigration to California, and sends the message that illegal aliens are welcome everywhere in the state.

The release of these illegal aliens came before passage of The California Values Act, also known as SB 54, which limits law enforcement's ability to cooperate and share immigration information with ICE. It is logical to conclude that refusals of ICE detainer requests and the release of aliens previously convicted of crimes or have pending criminal charges from police custody will only rise now that sanctuary policies are state law in California.

'Sanctuary' California Failed to Honor Over 5,600 ICE Detainers

IRLI investigation shows state released detained aliens with previous convictions or pending criminal charges. Per another disturbing report by Brian Lonergan in February 2019, "'Sanctuary' California Failed to Honor Over 5,600 ICE Detainers" he notes the following:

An investigation by the Immigration Reform Law Institute (IRLI) has revealed that California law enforcement agencies have refused to honor a shocking number of immigration detainer requests for illegal aliens charged with serious felonies, an indictment of the state's deadly and unconstitutional sanctuary laws.

In response to a Freedom of Information Act lawsuit filed by IRLI, U.S. Immigration and Customs Enforcement (ICE) released records regarding law enforcement agencies that failed to honor ICE detainer requests. For a 27 month period ending on December 31, 2017, many California police and sheriff's departments refused to honor over 5,600 immigration holds, of which over 3,400 were classified by ICE as threat level 1 and 2 offenses. These included, but were not limited to, homicide, kidnapping, sexual assault, robbery, aggravated assault, drugs, burglary, and fraud.

IRLI is awaiting additional data from ICE, which would show how many illegal aliens charged with serious felonies were released from jail and later charged with additional crimes.

New Study Concludes Prop 47 Caused California's "Smash-and-Grab" Crime Wave

This June 2018 article "New Study Concludes Prop 47 Caused California's 'Smash-and-Grab' Crime Wave" comes from the Independent Institute's Lawrence J. McQuillan:

Many Californians had high hopes for Proposition 47, a ballot initiative passed in November 2014 with 60 percent voter approval. The measure reduced penalties for some crimes, including certain drug violations, to help relieve overcrowding in state prisons.

While Prop 47 succeeded in meeting those objectives, it also triggered a major unintended consequence: It set in motion a wave of "smash-and-grab" motor-vehicle burglaries and a surge of retail shopliftings. For this reason, Prop 47 has earned the dishonor of receiving Independent Institute's fifth California Golden Fleece® Award, recognition given quarterly to state or local government programs or laws that swindle taxpayers or break the public trust.

The main reason Prop 47 spurred an epidemic of property theft and destruction was its weakening of criminal penalties: By raising the monetary threshold for a felony theft to $950 in property value, up from $500 before the measure passed, Prop 47 lowered thieves' expected cost of criminal activity.

"By reducing penalties associated with car break-ins, shoplifting, and other property crimes—and by making it more difficult to issue felony sentences—Prop 47 de-prioritizes justice for California residents and businesses, who are now increasingly victims of vandals and thieves operating with near impunity," writes Independent Institute Senior Fellow Lawrence J. McQuillan, in his new report, California Property Crime Surge Is Unintended Consequence of Proposition 47.

"Property crimes produce true victims. Californians deserve a legal system that provides true justice," McQuillan's report concludes.

7 – Population Madness, Legal vs. Illegal Immigration & Demographic Challenges

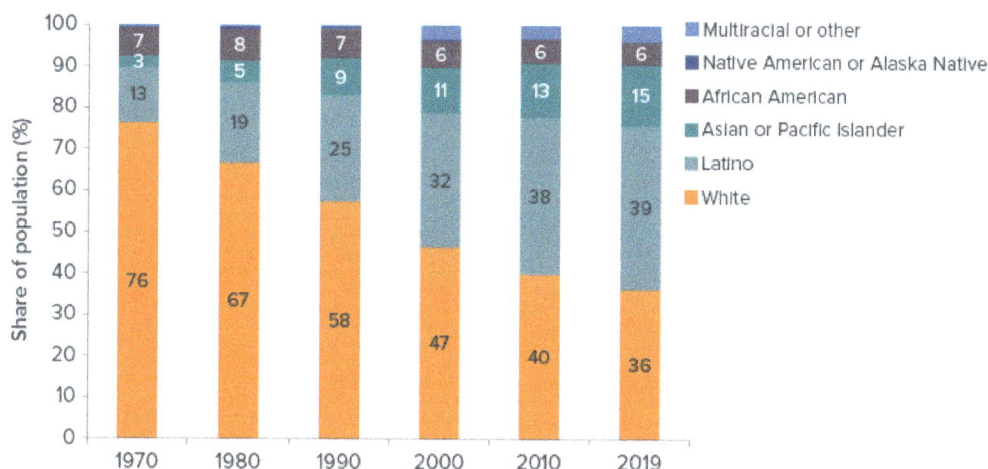

Credit: Public Policy Institute of California (PPIC).

Per the August 2021 "Census 2020: California population grows 6%, becomes more diverse" article by Amanda Ulrich at the *Desert Sun*:

The Golden State's population has expanded by about 2.3 million people over the past decade, with Los Angeles County holding onto its title as the nation's most populous.

With 39,538,223 residents, California remains the state with the most people. And as the state has grown—expanding by 6.1% over the last 10 years, a slower pace than in previous decades—its diversity has increased, too.

New 2020 data released by the U.S. Census Bureau shows that the state's number of white residents dropped by 24% between 2010 and 2020. Meanwhile, Californians who identify as being two or more races grew by a whopping 217.3% to about 5.8 million people.

The Asian population also rose by 25.2% to more than 6 million people, while the Black population decreased slightly, by 2.7%, to about 2.2 million. The number of American Indian residents rose by nearly 74% to more than 630,000 people.

The overall Latino or Hispanic population grew by around 11% to about 15.6 million people, or 39.4% percent of the state's total residents. The Census Bureau counts race, such as black or Asian, apart from ethnicity, which is either Hispanic or Latino, or not. The percentages for each race, such as black or Asian, on *USA Today* network websites reflect both Hispanics and non-Hispanics of that race. In some presentations, the Census Bureau shows only non-Hispanic members of each racial group, then includes one total for Hispanics of all races.

On a diversity index, which measures the probability that two random individuals will be from different race and ethnicity groups, California ranked second, behind Hawaii but ahead of Nevada.

On a county-by-county level, the new 2020 data also showed that Los Angeles County's total population has grown by 2% to 10,014,009 residents. San Diego County ballooned to roughly 3.3 million people, and Orange County to about 3.2 million.

Riverside County, which encompasses the Coachella Valley, saw a jump of more than 10% since 2010, for a current total of about 2.4 million people.

Though California saw a net increase in population over the past ten years, it is losing a seat in the U.S. House of Representatives for the first time, shrinking to a delegation of 52, as other states grow more rapidly.

Redistricting, or the process of drawing boundaries around legislative areas, happens every 10 years based on results from the census. In 2021, it will be up to the California Citizens Redistricting Commission to redraw the state's political boundaries for congressional, state Senate and Assembly and State Board of Equalization districts in time for next year's election cycle.

The U.S. Census, Illegals and Counting Congressional Seats

Per the March 2020 "The U.S. Census, Illegals and Counting Congressional Seats" article in FrontPage Magazine by Bruce Hendry:

The U.S. census is held every 10 years in order to count people, not citizens, and to then allocate congressional seats based on the count.

There are at least 22 million legal non-citizens and 12 million (or perhaps 22 million per 2018 Yale, MIT study review in the next section) illegal immigrants in our country or 10.4% total (or 13.3% total) of our population of 330 million. They are all non-citizens who will be counted in the census for the purpose of reallocating the 435 U.S. House seats. This means that 34 U.S. congressional seats will be attributed to "non-citizens." Minnesota, by comparison, gets just eight congressional seats.

This system of counting helps sanctuary states like California gain more congressional seats than if only citizens were counted because of their large illegal alien populations. No wonder California treats their illegal immigrants with such respect, as those illegals get them additional congressional house seats and all of the power and Federal money that comes along with those seats.

At different times in our past, a question on citizenship has been included on the census, but when the Commerce Department announced plans to ask that question on the 2020 census it brought a storm of left-wing protests and lawsuits from New York State and California to stop that question from being asked.

This is one of the reasons a state like California treats its illegal immigrants with so much respect. There are many sapient beings who think that non-citizens should not be represented in the United States Congress, and states that encourage illegal entry into our country should not be the beneficiary of federal largess for them.

Yale, MIT Study: 22 million, Not 11 million, Undocumented Immigrants in US

Per the September 2018 article "Yale, MIT Study: 22 million, Not 11 million, Undocumented Immigrants in US" in *The Hill* from Rafael Bernal:

The undocumented population in the United States could be twice as large as the most commonly-used estimate, according to a research study published in the scientific journal Plos One.

The paper, led by Mohammad M. Fazel-Zarandi, a researcher at Yale and Massachusetts Institute of Technology, estimates there are 22.1 million undocumented immigrants in the United States.

Fazel-Zarandi's study compared inflows and outflows of immigrants as well as demographic data. According to the report, the number of undocumented immigrants could be as low as 16.5 million, or as high as 29.1 million.

"We combined these data using a demographic model that follows a very simple logic," Edward Kaplan, a co-author of the report, told Yale Insights. "The population today is equal to the initial population plus everyone who came in minus everyone who went out. It's that simple."

Most previous estimates, based on the U.S. Census Bureau's annual American Community Survey (ACS), place the undocumented population at around 11 million people. The ACS is generated annually through interviews with about 3.5 million people.

"You find it's based on one very specific survey and possibly an approach that has some difficulties. So we went in and just took a very different approach," Jonathan Feinstein, another co-author, told Yale Insights.

Still, the new study found similarities in growth patterns of the undocumented population to the ACS reports of the past two decades. Most immigration researchers have reported a plateau in growth of that population since 2007, spurred mainly by the decrease in Mexican illegal immigration to the United States.

The reduction in illegal crossings by Mexican citizens coincided with an increase in illegal immigration from Central America and Asia. But the overall undocumented population has leveled off, and possibly slightly decreased.

The Pew Research Center, which provides regular updates on immigration statistics--based in part on ACS numbers--estimated last year that the undocumented population dropped to 11.3 million from a high of 12.2 million. The Yale study, which goes as far back as 1990, found the same upward and downward trajectory as the ACS studies, with the undocumented population ballooning through the 1990s and plateauing after 2007.

"The trajectory is the same. We see the same patterns happening, but they're just understating the actual number of people who have made it here," said Fazel-Zarandi. The researchers emphasized the new number does not imply a growth in illegal immigration but a longstanding miscount of existing undocumented immigrants.

"We wouldn't want people to walk away from this research thinking that suddenly there's a large influx happening now," said Feinstein. "It's really something that happened in the past and maybe was not properly counted or documented."

California Migration: The Story of 40 Million

This section comes from the June 2020 "California migration: The story of 40 million" report by Judy Lin and Adria Watson at CalMatters:

California, it has been written, is America, "only more so." How much more so? That's a complex question—and an important one. From immigration laws to school spending, some of our biggest decisions depend on an accurate count of this giant state's population—of who we are, of whether we're coming or going and of what we need from each other and our government.

Nationally, California's population numbers determine how many seats we get in Congress. That clout is partly why our stakes are so high for the 2020 census. They also carry cultural and economic weight. One American in eight is a Californian, and as we go, so goes our economy.

These numbers tell stories: As a state we are getting richer, for instance, because the working class is fleeing the high cost of living. They define choices: How we prioritize government services is being impacted by the twin dynamics of a slowing birth rate and an aging population. The latest state report shows California remains shy of 40 million residents due to slowing immigration and more people moving to other states.

And if you're curious about the future, that's in the numbers, too. Wondering what the next generation of Californians will look like? Answer: Like this generation, only more so. We won't just be racially diverse, but racially mixed. And in that picture, there's a hint at America's future, too.

California Is Home to 39,538,223 People Per 2020 Census

State demographers had anticipated we would cross the 40 million threshold sometime in the fall, but it hasn't officially happened. For scale, it would take combining 21 of the smallest states plus the District of Columbia to match the size of California. And if you're worried that Texas, the runner up with nearly 29 million people, is catching up, don't fret: At its current growth rate, it would take Texas until 2047 to match California (assuming California doesn't grow at all).

The state's $2.9 trillion economy is the nation's largest and the world's the fifth-largest, surpassing the United Kingdom. Silicon Valley, Hollywood, sports franchises, and other hallmark California sectors are usually credited for that. But we don't just entertain, we also feed the nation. And people from around the world come to California to seek their fortunes. Los Angeles, San Diego, San Jose, and San Francisco are among the nation's most populous cities.

But living here comes at a high cost. There's a housing crisis and widespread poverty exacerbated by a yawning wealth gap.

Where Do Californians Come From? And Going To?

A century ago, people mostly migrated to California from midwestern states such as Illinois, Missouri, and Ohio. But now, most people are coming in from Mexico, China and Taiwan, Philippines, and other countries: In 2017, there were 11 million foreign-born Californians. That's more than quadruple the migration into the state from all sources, foreign and domestic, in 1920.

Today, 56% of Californians were born in the state. But the proportion of foreign-born residents (28%) is nearly double that of transplants from other states (16%).

Depends on how you look at it. California is losing residents to other states and as the population ages, but those losses are being more than offset by new births and foreign-born immigration. The number of Californians is still increasing, but our once-robust growth rate has slowed.

California added 141,300 residents between July 2018 and July 2019, bringing the state population to an estimated 39.96 million people, according to the California Department of Finance. But while foreign immigration remains high, more Californians are leaving for other states than vice versa, and have been since the 1990s. The 0.35% growth rate was also a record low.

For the better part of three decades, Californians who leave the state have mostly gone to other parts of the country, notably to Texas and neighboring states such as Oregon, Nevada, and Arizona. The dot-com bust, Great Recession and recently soaring housing prices all have helped fuel the exodus. Now more than 7 million people born in California call other states home.

California's College Graduates Mostly Stay In-State

Over the past five years, California has attracted 162,000 more adults with at least a bachelor's degree from other states than it has lost, according to the Public Policy Institute of

California. The Golden State stands alone in this regard.

"This interstate migration pattern—gaining large numbers of college graduates while losing large numbers of less educated adults—doesn't happen anywhere else in the country," the report states.

Departing Californians tend to be younger and poorer—working class families in households whose breadwinners are under 35 years old and making less than $50,000, according to the latest migration data from the Internal Revenue Service.

All states experience shifts in population. California's numbers are large because the state's population in general is large. When departures are put into the context of the overall number of households, California ranks 50th in the nation. And if you look at net migration (people leaving compared to people entering), California ranks squarely in the middle of the pack at 27th. Nothing to boast about, but hardly a mass exodus.

There Are More Than 1 Million Millionaires In California

This is a perennial question and a popular topic for pundits, but so far California is still attracting the rich for its economic opportunities. At face value, there are more than 1 million millionaires in California—more than any other state. San Francisco has the highest density of billionaires of any city in the world.

Now, there are concerns that overtaxing the rich will drive them out of state. So Charles Varner, associate director of the Stanford Center on Poverty and Inequality, took a look at what happened when California voters passed two millionaire income taxes in 2004 and 2012. He found more millionaires in California after the 2004 hike, but a slight tax flight response after the 2012 increase. Specifically, the state lost an estimated 138 millionaires out of 312,000 in that group.

That's a 0.04% increase and the Varner's study concluded the opportunity to make money outweighs higher taxes.

"We often think that the only way for a state to be 'competitive' is to be like Texas—a low-tax, low-infrastructure, low-services state," he and co-authors wrote. "But the reality is that the most competitive places in the U.S., the leading drivers of the economy, and the centers for top talent are New York and California—and they have been for generations, despite higher taxes on top incomes."

Millionaire Migration In California

Perhaps what the study did not capture is all the ways the rich can avoid California income taxes, including by avoiding residency. Generally, a taxpayer who spends more than nine months in a year in California will be presumed to be a resident. If a person stays less than six months—no more than 183 days—and maintains a home outside California without doing much other than visit Disneyland, then they can declare nonresidency.

But let the case of Gilbert Hyatt serve as a cautionary tale. Hyatt was a wealthy inventor who took up residency in Nevada just before cashing in on a patent. The state went after him, and the dispute made its way all the way to the U.S. Supreme Court. It illustrates the extent to which the Franchise Tax Board will go to chase down tax dodgers.

Census data is used to apportion the number of House members to which each state is entitled every 10 years. Congressional seats equal more power, and California currently holds 53 of the 435 seats and as previously mentioned California is expected to lose one seat based on the 2020 census. Census data also determines the population figures that in turn help determine the distribution of federal funding. A higher population generally means more federal money for a state.

This is why then California's Secretary of State Alex Padilla was pushing to ensure an accurate population count through his 2020 census initiative. It's also why there has been debate around whether to include a citizenship question on surveys—a move that critics say would discourage immigrant participation and thus risk an artificially low headcount in this state.

Democratic state legislators already complain that Californians pay more in federal taxes than the state gets back in federal spending. The difference isn't much: For every dollar of taxes paid in 2017, California received $0.99 in federal expenditures, according to a report by the California Legislative Analyst's Office (LAO). But the national average is $1.22, and a smaller headcount could widen this disparity.

What's Happening to the State's Birth Rate?

California's birth rate has fallen to 11.7 per 1,000 people. Birth rates usually pick up after a recession, but California's hasn't yet.

Lower birth rates can herald welcome social trends: fewer teen pregnancies, smaller families among people too poor to afford them, or more people attending college before becoming parents. But for local and state governments, they also have financial implications.

For example, public school districts receive money based on the number of students they serve; fewer school children in a community mean less school funding. If birth rates drop and enrollment declines, a district's budget might shrink, even though costs remain the same for maintaining school infrastructure.

It's one of a host of reasons for financial stress in Los Angeles, Sacramento, and Oakland school districts. For instance, Los Angeles County is projected to be down 19,624 births over the next two decades. At $17,423 per pupil, that translates to $342 million in less revenue for the county's schools.

What About Seniors?

California is quickly becoming the new Florida, thanks to a "silver tsunami" of older Californians as the population ages. According to state projections, by 2030 more than 9 million Californians will be over the age of 65. That is 3 million more than there are today.

Within a decade, one out of every five of the state's residents will be seniors. And despite increased cost of living, baby boomers don't seem to be leaving California. While some are fleeing to lower-cost states, the vast majority are spending their retirement in the Golden State. In 2017, California lost about 20,000 seniors to other states—less than 1% of the total senior population.

The graying of California means changes from health care to transportation and housing for which the state isn't all that prepared. Gov. Gavin Newsom has called for a Master Plan on Aging to better coordinate the current patchwork of often-underfunded senior service programs, particularly long-term health care.

Legal Immigration Compared to Illegal Immigration

California is home to a quarter of the nation's immigrants. That's 11 million people—more than the entire population of Georgia.

More than half (52%) of California's immigrants are naturalized US citizens, and another 34% have some other legal status, including green cards and visas. According to the Center for Migration Studies, only about 14% of immigrants in California are undocumented.

Half of the state's immigrants were born in Latin America and four out of 10 are from Asia, according to the PPIC. The leading countries of origin: Mexico (4.1 million), China (969,000), the Philippines (857,000), Vietnam (524,000) and India (507,000). Among recent immigrants, Asia has surpassed Latin America.

Californians tend to be supportive of immigration. Nearly three residents in four believe immigrants are a benefit to the state for their hard work and job skills, compared to 23% who believe they are a burden, according to a public opinion poll conducted by PPIC. The polling found bipartisan support for letting undocumented immigrants stay in the country.

This translates to governmental support. In 2020, Gov. Newsom took a trip to El Salvador to explore why Central Americans are fleeing their home countries and how California can help. And under the new state budget, California embraced extending health care to young adults ages 19-26, regardless of immigration status.

As debate continues over whether to add a citizenship question to the census, nearly two-thirds of Californians are worried that the federal government won't keep their responses confidential. The concern is highest among Latinos.

Cali's Struggling Middle Class, Minorities and Generation X Y Z Households

This *City Journal* April 2017 "California Squashes Its Young" report is from Joel Kotkin and Wendell Cox:

Many progressives see California as a model of enlightenment. The Golden State's post-2010 recovery has won plaudits in the progressive press from the *New York Times'* Paul Krugman, among others.

Yet if one looks at the effects of the state's policies on key Democratic constituencies—millennials, minorities, and the poor—the picture is dismal. A recent United Way study found that close to one-third of state residents can barely pay their bills, largely due to housing costs. When adjusted for these costs, California leads all states—even historically poor Mississippi—in the percentage of its people living in poverty.

California is home to 77 of the country's 297 most "economically challenged" cities, based on poverty and unemployment levels. The population of these cities totals more than 12 million. In his new book on the nation's urban crisis, author Richard Florida ranks three California metropolitan areas—Los Angeles, San Francisco, and San Diego—among the five most unequal in the nation. California, with housing prices 230 percent above the national average, is home to many of the nation's most unaffordable urban areas, including not only the predictably expensive large metros but also smaller cities such as Santa Cruz, Santa Barbara, and San Luis Obispo. Unsurprisingly, the state's middle class is disappearing the fastest of any state.

California's young population is particularly challenged. As we spell out in our new report from Chapman University and the California Association of Realtors, California has the third-lowest percentage of people aged 25 to 34 who own their own homes—only New York and Hawaii's are lower. In San Francisco, Los Angeles, and San Diego, the 25-to-34 home ownership rates range from 19.6 percent to 22.6 percent—40 percent or more below the national average.

California's young families face an increasingly toxic combination of high costs and relatively low salaries; California millennials earn about the same wages as their counterparts in states such as Texas, Minnesota, and Washington, where the cost of living is far lower. Not surprisingly, California millennials suffer homeownership rates that are diminishing more quickly than elsewhere in the country.

As a result, many young Californians fail to 'launch' well into adulthood. Nearly two in five Californians aged 18 to 34 live with their parents, one of the highest rates in the nation. Nearly 45% of Hispanic youngsters do the same. Nationwide the percentage is under 30%.

We can already see the dangers ahead. Today California's demographics resemble the pattern of out-migration long associated with northeastern and midwestern states. Since 2000, more than 2.4 million net domestic migrants, a population larger than the Sacramento metropolitan area, have moved to other parts of the nation from California. This trend has been growing: between 2014 and 2019, net domestic out-migration has grown from 46,000 to 203,000.

Calculating the 'Californication'

This *City Journal* Winter 2020 "Calculating the Californication: Will migrating Golden State residents bring left-wing politics to their new homes? Maybe not" report is from Steven Malanga:

Figure 2: Net Domestic Migration by Age of Filer
California: 2011/12 to 2018/19

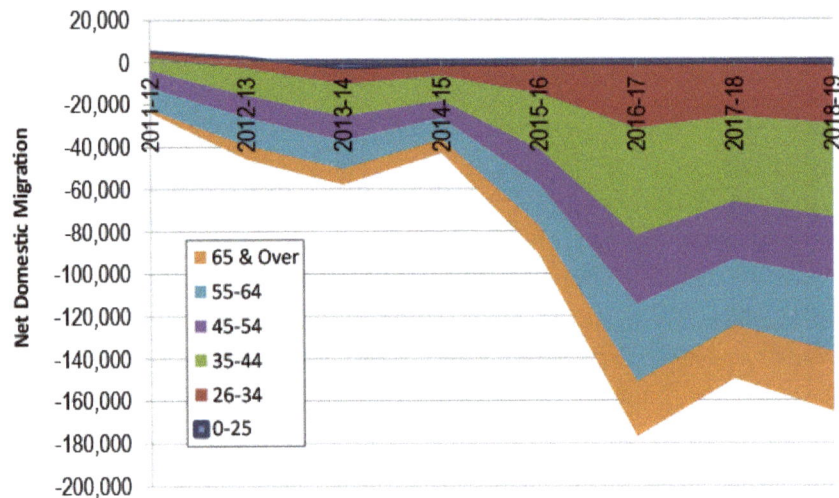

Credit: IRS data.

Beset by high housing costs, crippling taxes, astronomical gas prices, wildfires, and rolling blackouts, Californians are heading for the exits. That's sparking anxiety in places where these Golden State migrants are relocating. A mayoral candidate in Boise, Idaho, recently suggested building a wall to keep out Californians, who account for 60 percent of domestic migration into the growing state. The election of increasingly progressive candidates in Colorado sparked talk there of the "Californication" of the Centennial State.

Early last year, the *Dallas News* described the "California-ing" of North Texas, citing a study showing that 8,300 Californians move to the area yearly. Texas governor Greg Abbott launched a petition titled "Don't California My Texas."

Much of this anxiety revolves around fears that the migrants will transform the politics and culture of the places that they're moving to—bringing an appetite for big, intrusive government. But a new survey suggests that, while plenty of people are looking to leave California, many are fleeing the state's high costs and politics and may not be interested in voting for the same things in their new homes.

The poll, by the Berkeley Institute of Governmental Studies, found that 52 percent of California residents are considering migrating. As these polls go, that's exceptionally high, putting California in the same category as some other states with very unhappy residents. A recent poll in New Jersey, for instance, found that about 44 percent of its people are looking to depart, while 50 percent of Connecticut residents indicated a desire to leave the state in a 2014 Gallup poll, the highest figure among any state at that time.

Politicians in high-tax states claim that taxes don't drive people out, but their constituents disagree: in the Berkeley poll, 58 percent of those considering leaving California said that high taxes were one reason—second only to the 71 percent pointing to the state's astronomical housing costs. Also high on the list of reasons to go was the state's political culture, which nearly half of those thinking of getting out cited as a consideration. Though the poll didn't define "political culture," Gallup ranks California—where the state legislature and elected officials in many of the state's cities have turned increasingly progressive—as among the most liberal of states.

Out-Migration Polls in California

What set the Berkeley poll apart is that it also asked residents their party affiliation and how they characterized themselves politically—revealing a sharp divide. Conservatives and moderates are the most unhappy with the state and most anxious to leave. Liberals, by contrast, are mostly staying put, and some think life in California is just great. Only 38 percent of Democrats said that they were considering leaving, compared with 55 percent of independents and 71 percent of Republicans.

Similarly, those characterizing themselves as "somewhat liberal" were least likely to say that they want to go—fewer than four in ten are considering leaving. But 53 percent of moderates, 66 percent of the "somewhat conservative," and 74 percent of the "very conservative" would like to migrate.

Political affiliation, in fact, was more of a predictor of who wants to go or stay than other demographic information, such as race. The poll found, for instance, that 56 percent of white residents and 58 percent of African-Americans would like to leave; and 54 percent of men, compared with 50 percent of women, are thinking of going.

The results also suggest, however, that a political revolution that reverses the direction of California government is becoming increasingly difficult because it's experiencing the state version of the Curley Effect.

That phrase, coined by economists Edward Glaeser and Andrei Shleifer, describes how big-city mayors like James Michael Curley in Boston in the early twentieth century and Coleman Young in Detroit in the mid-to-late twentieth century managed to solidify their political dominance, even as their cities deteriorated because their policies drove out the people most likely to vote against them.

That may explain why, despite California facing rising homelessness, increasing drug use, outbreaks of infectious diseases, blackouts, soaring housing costs, and high energy prices, voters and elected officials endorse still-higher taxes and fees, lighter penalties for crimes like drug use and shoplifting, and a government takeover of bankrupt power company Pacific Gas & Electric (PG&E).

In a much-quoted interview in the summer of 2020, California governor Gavin Newsom called his state a positive example of where America was heading—proof, he said, that multiculturalism and progressive social values can produce prosperity. "California is America's coming attraction," he said. About half of California begs to differ.

Overall: "Legal" Immigrants Benefit California—"Illegal" Ones Don't

This section comes from the March 2021 "Immigrants in California" report by the Public Policy Institute of California (PPIC):

California has more immigrants than any other state, and 22% of those, possible more, are illegal aliens (undocumented immigrants).

California is home to almost 11 million immigrants—about a quarter of the foreign-born population nationwide. In 2019, the most current year of data, 27% of California's population was foreign born, more than double the percentage in the rest of the country. Foreign-born residents represented at least one-third of the population in five California counties: Santa Clara (39%), San Mateo (35%), Los Angeles (34%), San Francisco (34%), and Alameda (33%). Half of California children have at least one immigrant parent.

Most immigrants in California are documented residents.

More than half (53%) of California's immigrants are naturalized US citizens, and another 25% have some other legal status (including green cards and visas). According to the Center for Migration Studies, about 22% of immigrants in California are undocumented. From 2010 to 2019, the number of undocumented immigrants in the state declined from 2.9 million to 2.3 million.

After decades of rapid growth, the number of immigrants has leveled off.

In the 1990s, California's immigrant population grew by 2.4 million people, a 37% increase. But in the first decade of the 2000s, growth slowed to 15% (1.3 million), and in the past 10 years, the increase was only 6% (about 600,000). The decline in international immigration has contributed to the slowdown of California's overall population growth.

The majority of recent arrivals are from Asia.

The vast majority of California's immigrants were born in Latin America (50%) or Asia (39%). California has sizable populations of immigrants from dozens of countries; the leading countries of origin are Mexico (3.9 million), the Philippines (859,000), China (796,000), Vietnam (539,000), and India (513,000). However, among immigrants who arrived between 2010 and 2019, more than half (53%) were born in Asia, while 31% were born in Latin America.

Most of California's immigrants are bilingual.

More than two-thirds (70%) of immigrants in California report speaking English proficiently, while 10% speak no English. Even among recent immigrants, those in the US for five years or less, 66% report proficiency in English, while 12% speak no English. At home, most immigrants speak a language other than English, with Spanish and Chinese (including Mandarin and Cantonese) being the most common.

California's immigrants have varying levels of education.

Among working-age Californians (age 25–64), foreign-born residents accounted for 70% of those without a high school diploma and 32% of those with at least a bachelor's degree. But recent immigrants and immigrants from Asia tend to have high levels of educational attainment versus the opposite scenario from Mexico and Central America.

Half of foreign-born residents who have come to the state since 2010—and 61% of those who have come from Asia—have at least a bachelor's degree. Overall, 29% of California's immigrants have not completed high school, compared with 7% of US-born California residents. Thirty-two percent of California's foreign-born residents have a bachelor's degree, compared to 38% of US-born residents.

Californians have positive views of immigrants.

Nearly four in five Californians (78%) believe immigrants are a benefit to the state because of their hard work and job skills, compared to only 18% who believe they are a burden. An even larger share (87%) believe there should be a way for undocumented immigrants to stay in the country legally, and a majority (61%) favor state and local governments making their own policies and taking actions, separate from the federal government, to protect the legal rights of undocumented immigrants in California.

The Brown-Becerra-Newsom Axis For Illegal Aliens

This FrontPage Magazine December 2016 article "The Brown-Becerra Axis For Illegals" comes from Lloyd Billingsley:

On November 8, 2016, Kamala Harris gained election to the U.S. Senate and California Governor Jerry Brown has selected Rep. Xavier Becerra to take her place as state attorney general. "I'm confident he will be a champion for all Californians and help our state aggressively combat climate change," said Brown in a statement.

For his part, Becerra made it clear he had other priorities and this radical new California Attorney General's intent is to violate and or defy federal laws regarding illegal immigration.

On his watch, MS-13 has inflicted a reign of terror in Mendota, near Fresno. The gang has murdered 14, hacking victims to death with machetes and leaving the mutilated bodies on display. Becerra took no action against MS-13 until the feds stepped in, and even then the attorney general made it clear that he was not concerned with the gang's "status." That too is business as usual for Becerra.

Like governor Jerry Brown, Becerra supports the sanctuary state policies that protect false-documented illegals, even violent criminals. Becerra has backed laws that would punish employers for cooperating with federal officials. In a way, Becerra is also a beneficiary of the sanctuary policy.

As head of the Democratic Caucus, Becerra controlled the server where Pakistan-born IT man Imran Awan, who worked for DNC boss Debbie Wasserman Schultz, stashed the data he lifted from House Democrats on the intelligence and foreign affairs committees. When capitol police requested the data, they got only a fake image. After the scandal broke, Becerra abandoned his seat and Jerry Brown promptly appointed him attorney general of California.

As the *Sacramento Bee* noted, Becerra "appeared to back California's efforts to prevent removal of unauthorized immigrants who pose no threat to public safety." And as Brown's attorney general pick explained, "If you want to take on a forward-leaning state that is prepared to defend its rights and interests, then come at us." For the task of defending all "unauthorized immigrants," Becerra is well qualified.

At Stanford, where he earned his bachelor and law degrees, Becerra was a member of MEChA, the Movimiento Estudiantil Chicano De Aztlan. MEChA calls the southwest portion of the United States "Aztlan" and seeks to regain the territory for Mexico. The MEChA slogan is "Entre la raza todo, fuera de la raza, nada," and the "raza" is not the human race.

"I was a member of MEChA when I was in college," Becerra told Sean Hannity in 2003. The eleven-year congressman would not respond to Hannity's questions about the group's racist slogans and irredentist campaign.

Becerra was a possible running mate for Hillary Clinton, but apparently had trouble pronouncing his name. The MEChA veteran remained in Congress, where he faithfully supported amnesty for those in the country illegally. His passion, however, remains the defense of illegals and he is a perfect fit for Governor Jerry Brown, uncritical of sanctuary cities that shelter violent criminals.

Juan Francisco Lopez-Sanchez, also known as José Inez García Zarate, was a felon who had been deported five times. He duly found refuge in San Francisco, Jerry Brown's home town, where he gunned down Kathryn Steinle, 32, in July of 2015. That killing did not prompt the governor to challenge sanctuary cities, and Becerra told reporters "I don't believe we should be trying to ascribe blame based on a designation as a sanctuary city."

Becerra also joined Loretta Sanchez, recipient of 748 illegal votes by non-citizens in 1996, in attacking a GOP measure to deny federal funding to sanctuary cities. Becerra and Sanchez called it the "Donald Trump Act," despite the horrific crimes committed by illegals.

8 – Fixing California's Many Obstacles to Fast & Affordable Suburban Housing

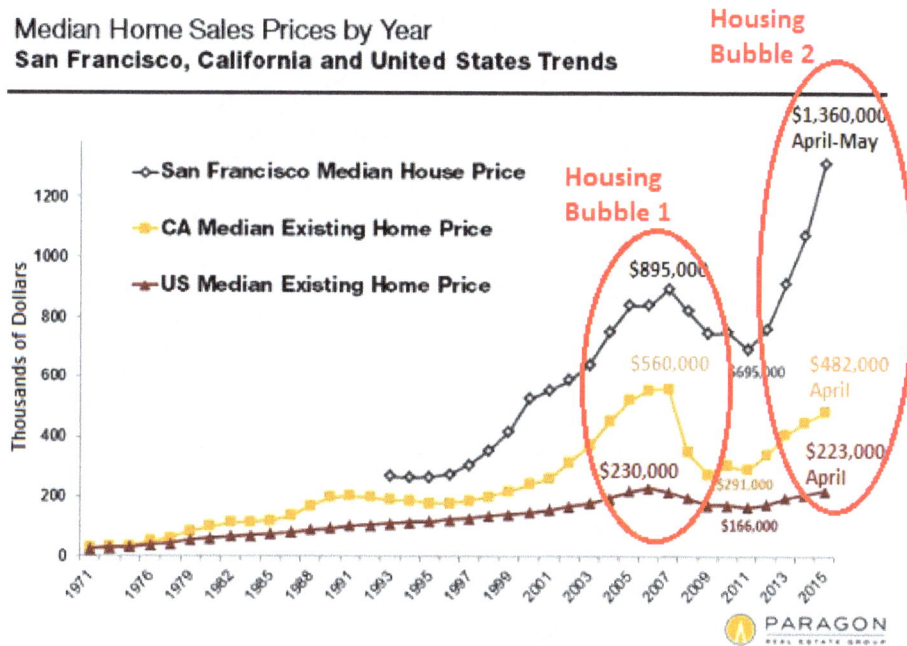

Median Home Sales Prices by Year
San Francisco, California and United States Trends

Once upon a time in California, entrepreneurs would see an unmet housing need and build homes, apartments, or convert buildings to accommodate that need. They would buy the land and build the units that consumers wanted in the locations they desired and at the price points consumers could afford. Today, if an entrepreneur in California did that, they would be violating numerous zoning, permitting, and environmental laws, and be forced to stop.

Housing development is no longer an economic freedom in California. Instead, it is a criminal act without proper paperwork and government approvals. Today, Californians, especially established homeowners, are generally hostile toward housing construction, which is reflected in deliberate state and local policies that have created an artificial housing scarcity.

Many state and local regulations work to delay or stop residential construction projects, or to increase the cost of new construction, the rehabilitation of older buildings, or the conversion of existing buildings into residential housing. These regulations should be eliminated or radically downsized in order to welcome developers, builders, and landlords into the California market to provide housing at all price points. Because of government policies, housing entrepreneurs are not allowed to build the housing demanded by California consumers. This must change if people are to have sufficient access to affordable housing once again.

More housing would obviously ease the supply shortage, but it would also tame, and could potentially lower, ever-rising costs due to the laws of supply and demand. To achieve these outcomes, an array of impediments to housing development must be removed. State and local governments must also reject price controls. And private entrepreneurs should be welcomed into markets to provide creative solutions. Finally, two visionary approaches would quickly cut through the regulatory thicket by reestablishing private property rights to land use and housing development, while favoring local decision making.

It is necessary for state and local officials to avoid the temptation to overregulate the housing market to please self-interested homeowners, and to overregulate entrepreneurs who are trying to fix the problem. As we have seen, pressures to overregulate are prevalent and the consequences severe. Combating this government-created crisis requires fewer entrepreneurial impediments.

The only solution to the housing problem is to rapidly build our way out of the problem, and as noted by San Diego Mayor Kevin Faulconer, "To actually move the needle in a significant way, you have to get government less involved in the production of housing, and take away the barriers." An increased housing stock will ease the upward price trend, improve access, ease homelessness, and speed-up wildfire recovery for tens of thousands of Californians who desperately need relief.

In Defense of Houses

This *City Journal* July 20197 "In Defense of Houses" report is from Joel Kotkin and Wendell Cox:

A critical component in the rise of market-oriented democracy in the modern era has been the dispersion of property ownership among middle-income households—not just in the United States but also in countries like Holland, Canada, and Australia, where it was closely linked with greater civil and economic freedom.

In its early days, this dispersion was largely rural, but after the Second World War, it took on a largely suburban emphasis in the U.S., including within the extended metro regions of traditional cities like New York and Los Angeles. American homeownership soared between 1940 and 1962, from 44 percent to 63 percent.

Today, the aspiration of regular people to own homes—arguably one of the greatest achievements of postwar democracy—is fading. But the dilution of this key aspect of the American dream is not the result of market conditions or changing preferences, but rather the concerted effort of planners and pundits. California offers the most striking example.

Housing affordability was once a hallmark of life in the Golden State, but over the past three decades, and particularly since the imposition of draconian climate policies, stringent land-use regulations have driven up land prices so much that middle-income, single-family housing is now virtually impossible to build, helping make prices of existing homes prohibitive.

Median house prices in the state's coastal metropolitan areas (Los Angeles, San Francisco, San Diego, and San Jose) have risen to nearly 250 percent above the national average, according to the 2017 American Community Survey. Median gross rents, which tend to follow house prices, are more than 75 percent higher than the national average. According to the National Association of Realtors, it takes a household income of $273,000—almost five times the national average—to qualify for the median-priced house in the San Jose metropolitan area. In San Francisco, an income of $208,000 is needed. In San Diego, it's $138,000, and in Los Angeles, $122,000—both more than double the national average.

Single-Family Homes Are the Backbone of American Aspiration: Why Not in California?

Many younger people, wanting to live and work in the wealthy metros, have little choice but to become permanent renters, usually in smaller apartments.

Without owning a home, however, younger people face major obstacles to boosting their net worth, because property remains crucial to long-term financial security. Homes today account for roughly two-thirds of the wealth of middle-income Americans, and homeowners have a median net worth more than 85 times that of renters, according to the Census Bureau.

In California's San Jose metropolitan area (Silicon Valley), homeownership among post-college millennials (aged 25 to 34) dropped by 40 percent in 25 years, compared with a less than 20 percent national drop during that same period. Few are saving sufficiently to make homeownership a reality. Millennials with college debt would need up to 27 years to accumulate enough for a down payment in the San Francisco metro area, according to one study.

Lower homeownership rates are a major reason why (according to 2014 Census numbers) black households had a median net worth of just $10,000 and Hispanic households just $18,000. By contrast, white, non-Hispanic households had a median net worth of $130,000. Asians were even more affluent, at $157,000.

Nearly three-quarters of millennials want single-family detached houses, according to a 2019 report on homebuyer preferences by the National Association of Homebuilders. A 2018 Apartment List survey found that 80 percent of millennials aspire to homeownership.

These preferences can be seen in the marketplace. In America, among those under 35 who buy homes, four-fifths choose single-family detached houses. Since 2010, a net 1.8 million people have moved away from the urban-core counties of major metropolitan areas, largely to lower-density counties, where single-family houses predominate.

Today, often through deliberate policy, we are undermining this critical property-owning middle class—and impeding not only the economic future and family prospects of a young generation but also the wellsprings of liberal democracy. If the trend persists, America will become increasingly feudal in its economic and social form.

The California Housing Crisis

These sections below are from the 2020 research brief by Joel Kotkin and Alicia Kurimska *Beyond Feudalism: A Strategy to Restore California's Middle Class at the* Chapman University Center for Demographics & Policy:

The principle economic cause for the declining fortunes of California's middle class is the high cost of housing. It accounts for more than 85% of the difference in the cost of living between high-cost metropolitan areas and the national average. Unless the housing regulation issues are successfully addressed and a competitive supply of land is restored, housing affordability will likely continue to deteriorate, making life more difficult for the shrinking middle-class and low-er-income households.

California has imposed ever-higher costs on developers and restricted building on the periphery, where land is more affordable. Its housing prices have grown much faster than the national average and those of arch-rival Texas.

Given these extraordinary costs, most new single-family and apartment construction tends to be for the high end market, and often small units that are not family-friendly. Only 7,800 of the new apartments built between 2015 and 2017 in Los Angeles—11%—are affordable, with rents of around $1,842 a month. In contrast, rent on the 66,000 "market rate" apartments exceeds $2,800 a month.

Despite the best of intentions, the state's principal housing strategy, Regional Housing Needs Assessment (RHNA), has not restored housing affordability. RHNA requires metropolitan planning agencies, counties, and cities to zone sufficient land for housing production targets. It faces insurmountable barriers. Land and regulatory costs in the state are so high that builders can earn a competitive return on investment only on houses that are unaffordable for nearly all middle-income households.

The situation for home buyers is even bleaker as unaffordability has risen dramatically, particularly along the coast. Furthermore, California has imposed ever-higher costs on developers and restricted building on the periphery, where land is more affordable.

To qualify for a mortgage on a median-priced house in the San Jose metropolitan area requires an annual income of about $250,000. In the San Francisco metropolitan area, it is $200,000. In Orange County $167,000 is required, in Los Angeles County $125,000, and in the San Diego metropolitan area more than $130,000. The overall national average, including these California metropolitan areas, is $55,000.

Overall, far fewer Californians can afford to buy a median-priced home today than in 2000 even though nationally the percentage of people who can afford homes has actually increased.

The High Cost of Housing In the 'Can't Afford' State

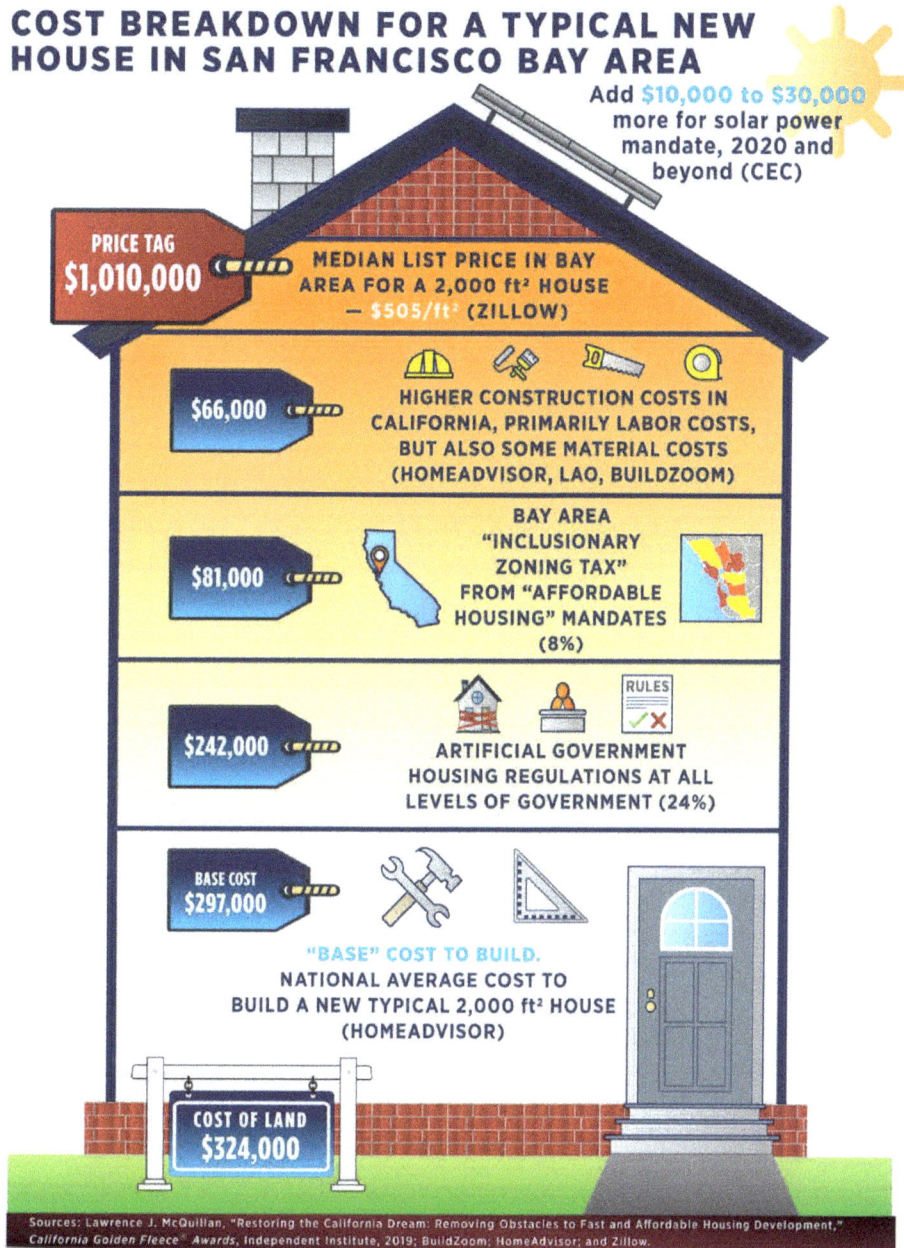

COST BREAKDOWN FOR A TYPICAL NEW HOUSE IN SAN FRANCISCO BAY AREA

Add $10,000 to $30,000 more for solar power mandate, 2020 and beyond (CEC)

PRICE TAG $1,010,000

MEDIAN LIST PRICE IN BAY AREA FOR A 2,000 ft² HOUSE — $505/ft² (ZILLOW)

$66,000 — HIGHER CONSTRUCTION COSTS IN CALIFORNIA, PRIMARILY LABOR COSTS, BUT ALSO SOME MATERIAL COSTS (HOMEADVISOR, LAO, BUILDZOOM)

$81,000 — BAY AREA "INCLUSIONARY ZONING TAX" FROM "AFFORDABLE HOUSING" MANDATES (8%)

$242,000 — ARTIFICIAL GOVERNMENT HOUSING REGULATIONS AT ALL LEVELS OF GOVERNMENT (24%)

BASE COST $297,000 — "BASE" COST TO BUILD. NATIONAL AVERAGE COST TO BUILD A NEW TYPICAL 2,000 ft² HOUSE (HOMEADVISOR)

COST OF LAND $324,000

Sources: Lawrence J. McQuillan, "Restoring the California Dream: Removing Obstacles to Fast and Affordable Housing Development," California Golden Fleece® Awards, Independent Institute, 2019; BuildZoom; HomeAdvisor; and Zillow.

Credit: Lawrence J. McQuillan at Independent Institute.

California is the world's fifth largest economy, recently surpassing the United Kingdom in annual gross domestic product. Unemployment in the state is at a record low rate of 4 percent. By these measures of economic health, California is doing well. Yet housing statistics provide a contrasting story about the quality of life in the Golden State.

Between the late 1980s and 2006, California home-ownership rates steadily trended upward. But during most of the past decade, home-ownership rates have declined in the state. The most recent data from the US Census Bureau estimates that 56 percent of California households own the residence they live in, which is down from 60.2 percent in 2006, and well below the current national average of 64.1 percent. Only New York and Washington, DC, have lower rates of home ownership. California's low home-ownership rate is partially driven by the high cost of housing.

In 2015, California's nonpartisan Legislative Analyst's Office (LAO) issued a report on the state's high housing costs, in which it discussed several underlying causes. The agency reported that California's home prices were about 30 percent higher than the national average in 1970 and rose to 80 percent above national levels by 1980. Today, its home prices are 250 percent above the national average, while average monthly housing rents are about 50 percent above the national average.

According to the most recent data available from the California Department of Finance, the median price for a home in the Golden State was $611,420 in June 2019, a new record price. Housing prices hit record highs despite a "weak" California housing market—home sales statewide were down nearly 6 percent in the first half of 2019 compared to the year earlier. Transactions monitored by online real estate database Zillow show that, over the past 10 years, median home sale prices in California have increased by 72 percent, from $291,000, adjusted for inflation, to about $501,000. They estimate that the median home listing price is currently $549,000. And the median monthly rent has increased, too.

The median monthly rent paid for a one-bedroom apartment was $1,679, adjusted for inflation, in November 2010. Currently, median rent paid for a one-bedroom unit is $1,906. But rent is much higher in certain locations. According to apartment rental platform Zumper, the median monthly rent for a one-bedroom apartment in San Francisco is $3,720, a record high and the highest rent in the nation.

Meanwhile, the average household income in California has not kept pace. In 2009, the median California household income was $70,300 per year in 2019 dollars. By 2017, the most recent year for which data are available, median household annual income only increased about 6.5 percent, to $75,000 (adjusted), while home prices increased 72 percent. A third of California renters and 16 percent of homeowners spend more than half their income on housing.

In the nine-county San Francisco Bay Area, a typical home buyer pays nearly nine times the area's median annual household income to purchase a home, according to a study by Clever Real Estate. In 1960, a home buyer paid about twice the median annual income for a home. The recommended price-to-income ratio is 2.6. Eight of the 10 least-affordable cities nationwide, as measured by the price-to-income ratio, are in California.

Only 30 percent of households in the state can afford a median-priced home in the county in which they live, according to the California Association of Realtors. The national average is 54 percent. Elliot Eisenberg, partner economist at MLS Listings, sums up California's housing market, "This is truly a housing market that's a complete wreck."

California's High Housing Costs are Especially Burdensome for Low-Income Households

Many people have responded to the high housing costs by leaving California. The US Census Bureau's American Community Survey has shown a consistently negative net domestic migration for California during the past several years: more people left California for other states than came to California from other states. On net, from 2007 to 2018, California lost nearly 1.3 million residents to domestic migration (see here and here). And since 2016, overall net migration (including international migration) has been negative in California.

The outward-migration has been concentrated among lower-income and middle-class residents and the less educated, who are increasingly stretched thin in California. Testimonials and patterns of movement reveal a lack of affordable housing to be a driving factor among people increasingly looking elsewhere to achieve the American dream. The exodus is likely to continue.

A July 2019 Quinnipiac University poll found that 45 percent of Californians believe they cannot afford to live in the Golden State, and nearly 80 percent of Californians think the state has a housing crisis. In August 2019, California Gov. Gavin Newsom (D) bluntly acknowledged, "The California dream is in real peril if we don't address the housing crisis."

Sky-High Housing Prices in California Cities

California's largest metropolitan areas best illustrate the dysfunction in the state's housing markets. They also highlight how state and local officials have failed to provide real solutions to the problem.

The prosperity of America's technology sector has dramatically transformed the San Francisco Bay Area, bringing scores of new jobs and workers to fill those jobs. But coalitions of San Franciscans and members of many other Bay Area communities have ferociously fought the construction of new housing to meet the demands brought about by the tech boom. In 2018, San Francisco netted only 2,579 new housing units, a 42 percent decrease from 2017 and the lowest gain in five years. The result is increasingly unattainable housing prices and unaffordable rents, contributing to a growing homelessness problem plaguing the Bay Area.

According to California Employment and Development Department (EDD) statistics compiled by University of California, Berkeley, economist Enrico Moretti, San Francisco County added about 38,000 new jobs between 2016 and the end of 2018. But over that time period, only 4,500 new housing units were permitted. As he notes, the resulting surge in housing prices has been profitable to existing homeowners, who benefit from a shortage, but renters have suffered mightily.

According to research company CoreLogic, the median price paid for a new or existing home or condo in the Bay Area was $810,000 in August 2019. Bay Area communities have experienced surges in rental prices in recent years with some communities experiencing double-digit percentage increases in rental prices in just one year.

Extreme housing costs have also hit Los Angeles County, where the median home price now hovers above $600,000, and about half of all renters report spending more than 30 percent of their income on housing. With rents on a one-bedroom apartment averaging $2,500 per month on the low end, and as much as $3,500 per month in places like Santa Monica, a renter would need to earn more than three times the minimum wage to cover housing costs, according to estimates from the California Housing Partnership. So it is unsurprising that halfway through 2018 Los Angeles County had a net 13,000 fewer residents than it had a year earlier.

Adding new housing in Los Angeles is extraordinarily difficult due to zoning laws that explicitly prevent certain types of much-needed housing. The city currently bans anything other than detached single-family homes on about 75 percent of its residential land. As the *New York Times* notes, "In 1960, Los Angeles had the zoned capacity for about 10 million people.... By 1990, Los Angeles had downzoned to a capacity of about 3.9 million, a number that is only slightly higher today."

Efforts to "upzone," or to rezone certain areas to allow construction of denser multifamily housing, have until now been defeated in the California legislature. These efforts include Senate Bill (SB) 827 and SB 50. In their place, one Los Angeles area state senator who opposed the upzoning bills instead introduced a bill favoring another approach: a special license plate designed to bring awareness to the housing crisis. Money raised through the sale of the "California Housing Crisis Awareness" license plates would go into an existing program that helps moderate-income people purchase homes. This "solution" would be laughable if the problem were not so serious.

A recent poll by the University of California, Berkeley, of registered California voters found that 86 percent in Los Angeles County and 92 percent in the Bay Area consider affordable housing either a "somewhat serious" or "extremely serious" issue in their area. Statewide, 56 percent of voters, including majorities in both metropolitan areas, said they have considered moving due to rising housing costs. Of course, for those who are unable or unwilling to move, being priced out of their homes and apartments, or regulated out of their residences, makes homelessness a real possibility.

Government-Created Roadblocks

The delay or blocking of much-needed housing is a problem that the entire state has failed to confront for decades. Groups—primarily current homeowners and established residents— that oppose the construction of new homeless shelters and other housing often invoke the

California Environmental Quality Act (CEQA), claiming insufficient review of a project's environmental impacts. CEQA has been used to slow or stop housing development in the Golden State since it was signed into law in 1970.

CEQA requires state and local governments to analyze and publish the impacts of development projects on the environment and mitigate impacts if necessary. The law was intended to protect California's natural environment from harm, but its scope has greatly expanded to include a project's impacts on line-of-sight views and traffic patterns, among other things. CEQA requires local governments to hear CEQA-based appeals against projects, and these are often grounds for challenges in court that can drag on for years.

"Without CEQA approvals, no new housing can be built in California, so it's very integral to everything we do," said Katia Kamangar, executive vice president and managing director of SummerHill Housing Group. "While well intentioned, unfortunately, in nearly all of the cases we've been involved in, CEQA was used as a vehicle for stalling a project already approved by the local jurisdiction," Kamangar said. Even just one person can delay or stop a project through court action. "We see these situations largely as a loss for the region and one of the reasons why delivering new housing in California takes years and why housing costs are significantly higher here than in other parts of the country," Kamangar concluded.

Timothy Coyle, a former director of the California Department of Housing and Community Development, has seen CEQA's implementation from the inside and concludes that it is "the mother of all government-sponsored obstacles to development." Business rivals, environmental activists, and neighborhood groups use CEQA to delay, and whenever possible, stop development projects. Unfortunately, CEQA and other regulations that are discussed below prevent an effective response by entrepreneurs to the housing shortage.

Clearly, despite multiple attempts over many decades at the federal, state, and local levels, the housing and homelessness issue has not been "solved" by governments; in fact, it has become worse. Rather than arguing over which government program would best alleviate the suffering, a better question to ask is why have solutions led by housing entrepreneurs not emerged. Housing is a fundamental part of life that was provided by entrepreneurs at every price point for centuries. But today government policy prevents housing entrepreneurs from satisfying the housing demands of Californians.

How to Restore the California Dream

This January 2020 article "How to Restore the California Dream: Removing Obstacles to Fast and Affordable Housing Development" comes from the Independent Institute's Lawrence J. McQuillan:

California has become the national poster child for high housing costs and homelessness. Although no single lawmaker or regulator is to blame for California's housing crisis, a complex array of regulatory obstacles enacted by politicians at various levels of government and pushed by special interests over decades have made California ill-equipped to accommodate the state's growth.

The effect has been a supply of housing that does not keep up with demand, resulting in skyrocketing housing costs, strained budgets, homelessness, and an outflow of people from the Golden State. Housing prices and accessibility are determined by the interaction of supply and demand, and government regulations have constrained the supply side of the equation, exacerbating California's housing and homelessness crises.

Bureaucratic red tape impacts every stage of the development process, and there is no shortage of actors trying to maintain the status quo because they benefit from it financially or in other ways. Despite much hand-wringing and pronouncements by politicians to "fix the problem," state and local governments have made the problem worse, especially for lower-income residents.

In July 2019, San Francisco Mayor London Breed asked, "Why does it take so damn long to get housing built?" Fixing the problem requires a multipronged approach.

California legislators must ease state regulations that impose huge costs on housing construction, stop or delay projects, and disincentivize more rental properties. Local officials need to liberalize zoning and other building regulations, especially in high-demand areas, that prevent much-needed construction of new housing or that prevent the conversion of old buildings into residential housing. Entrepreneurs should be encouraged to enter housing markets across the state to provide creative and low-cost solutions to meet consumer demands for housing, thereby eliminating the government-created shortage.

Housing is a fundamental part of life. The link between consumers and housing entrepreneurs has been severed by government policies, and this link must be reestablished to restore civil society for all Californians. The need for fast and affordable housing construction is especially critical today because of California's horrific wildfires have destroyed tens of thousands of homes, businesses, and schools across the state.

A New Suburbanism–Smart Alternative to "Smart Growth"

This concluding section is from the June 2019 article "New Suburbanism–A Smart Alternative to 'Smart Growth'" comes from the California Policy Center's Edward Ring:

Solutions to California's housing shortage invariably focus on increasing the density of preexisting cities and suburbs. Legislative solutions include SB 375, passed in 2008, which "incentivizes" cities and counties to approve high density land developments, and the failed (this time) SB 50, which would have forced cities and counties to approve high density development proposals.

One cannot ignore the fact that high density land development benefits special interests. Politically connected developers enjoy windfall profits by selling overpriced homes crowded onto smaller parcels of land. Existing cities collect higher taxes from property owners and shoppers who would otherwise have moved into new cities. Government at all levels can spend more money on pay and benefits, and less on infrastructure. Investors harvest higher returns thanks to the real estate bubble.

In front of the hidden agenda of special interests, however, are moral arguments for so-called "smart growth." The crux of these moral arguments for high density "smart growth" are that regional ecosystems bordering urban areas should not be sullied by new growth, and that high density development reduces emissions of greenhouse gasses, which furthers global ecosystem health.

Both of these moral arguments are flawed. As documented in an earlier analysis "Grand Bargains to Make California Affordable," if 10 million new residents moved into homes on half-acre lots, three persons per home (with an equal amount of space allocated for new roads, retail, commercial, and industrial development), it would only use up 3.2 percent of California's land.

If all this growth was concentrated onto grazing land, much which is being taken out of production anyway, it would only consume 21 percent of it. If all this growth were to fall onto non-irrigated cropland, which is not prime agricultural land, it would only use up 19 percent. Much growth, of course, could be in the 58 percent of California not used for either farming or ranching of this.

California's ecosystems can easily withstand significant urban expansion. Even this extreme low density growth scenario—as if there wouldn't still be parallel development within existing urban areas—only consumes 3.2 percent of the land in this vast state.

Similar concerns about greenhouse gasses are unfounded because they rest on the assumption that higher greenhouse gas emissions are correlated with low density development. But correlation does not mean causation. Telecommuting, dispersion of jobs into new suburban nodes, clean energy, and clean vehicles, are all examples of future trends that prove growth does not need to be confined to existing cities.

It is unlikely, if not impossible, for high-density development alone to ever deliver a supply of homes that meets demand, lowering prices to affordable levels.

Part of the reason for this is the understandable resistance high-density proposals arouse from existing residents who don't want to see the ambiance of their neighborhoods destroyed. Equally significant is the extraordinary cost of construction in California. But evidence from around the nation is clear—in areas such as the San Francisco Bay Area where urban containment is practiced, home prices are unaffordable, and in areas such as Houston where urban growth is permitted, home prices are affordable.

If you accept these premises—that urban expansion will not cause unacceptable harm to the environment, and that urban expansion is the only way to deliver enough new homes to lower prices, "smart growth" starts to take on a different meaning. "Special interest growth" might be more descriptive.

New Suburbanism Offers An Alternative to Smart Growth

First expressed in 2005 by urban geographer Joel Kotkin, New Suburbanism is a complement to New Urbanism, a movement initially devoted to the twin principles of architectural and landscape design that celebrates local history and traditions, along with promoting accessible, pedestrian friendly, aesthetically engaging public spaces.

Over time, New Urbanism and New Suburbanism have been taken over by the smart growth crowd, with high-density neighborhood design now the overwhelming priority of these movements. But consider these quotes from Kotkin, written in 2006:

"One critical aspect of New Suburbanism lies in its pragmatism. One cannot always assume, for example, that building a new town center, constructing denser housing, or introducing mixed-use development would automatically improve quality of life."

Kotkin goes on to explain how "sprawling, multipolar" cities that permit suburban growth are creating more jobs and have more affordable homes, how most people starting families prefer single family detached homes, and average commutes in these cities are actually less because "jobs move to the suburban periphery." He writes:

"We instead should follow a pragmatic, market-oriented approach to improving the areas in which people increasingly choose to live. For example, in a low-density suburban community that seeks to retain its single-family character, it may be more appropriate to introduce single-family detached housing, rather than assume multi-family apartments and lofts must be part of the solution."

New Suburbanism is a necessary alternative to Smart Growth because Smart Growth is failing. It not only delivers an inadequate supply of homes, it delivers the wrong mixture of homes, because it delivers apartments, condominiums, townhouses, and "detached" homes with yards barely big enough for an outdoor grill, but it does not deliver what people want, which is a home with a yard.

New Urbanism has become an intellectual movement indistinguishable from the Smart Growth policies that mandate high-density development. Here, from the website "New Urbanism" is an accurate representation of the principles of New Urbanism:

1. Walkability,

2. Connectivity,

3. Mixed-Use & Diversity,

4. Mixed Housing,

5. Quality Architecture & Urban Design,

6. Traditional Neighborhood Structure,

7. Increased Density,

8. Smart Transportation,

9. Sustainability, and,

10. Quality of Life.

And here is a summary of why New Urbanism, or "Smart Growth," is not so smart:

1. Artificially and selectively inflates land values, making housing less affordable,

2. Emphasizes public space over private space,

3. Makes war on the car,

4. Promotes high-density infill in low density neighborhoods,

5. Prefers open space to homes, but not to biofuel crops, solar fields, or wind farms,

6. Presumes that social problems will be alleviated through forcing everyone to live in ultra-high density, mixed neighborhoods,

7. Incorrectly claims there is a shortage of open space and farmland, and,

8. Presumes to have the final answer; that its precepts are beyond debate.

New Suburbanism offers an alternative ideology–one that embraces much of New Urbanist concepts, but from an entirely different perspective. These "Principles of New Suburbanism," are not intended to refute the virtues of high density, but to extol the virtues of low density.

The Principles of New Suburbanism

Embodied in these principles is the idea that human stewardship and private land ownership, combined with 21st century clean technologies, can enable a suburban and exurban landscape to host bucolic and utterly clean low density communities across thousands of square miles.

(1) Embraces Aesthetic Values:

Suburbs can be beautiful. Spacious, forested, with architectural character. New suburban communities can be built with an emphasis on aesthetics, as well as towards creating a sense of place, especially when high density isn't the prevailing mandate.

(2) Low and High Density Are Not Mutually Exclusive:

New Suburbanists support high density zoning in the urban core of large cities. New Suburbanites enthusiastically support building 21st century cities, with high-rises and plentiful car-independent transit options and everything else inimical to the central cores of megacities.

(3) Land is Abundant:

There is abundant available land for low density suburban and exurban development. New Suburbanists encourage zoning that recognizes the importance of progressively lower density zoning from urban cores, instead of draconian "urban service boundaries" that arbitrarily restrict development, especially low density development.

(4) Car Friendly:

Cars are the future, not the past. Personal transportation devices are tantalizingly close to becoming ultra-safe conveyances that can drive on full autopilot and have zero environmental footprint, and we are within a few decades at most of having abundant clean energy. The age of the personal driving machine has just begun.

(5) Road Friendly:

Roads are the most versatile of all mass transit corridors since people, bicycles, cars, busses, and trucks can all travel on or alongside roads. Commercial areas should be car-friendly as well as bike and pedestrian friendly. Since land is abundant, this is not all that difficult.

(6) Decentralized & Off-Grid Friendly:

New communities can have neighborhood-scale groundwater extraction, distribution, and recharge systems. Using new off-grid technologies, sustainable and cost-effective energy and even water independence can be achieved at a household or neighborhood basis, often enabling lower taxes through avoiding more expensive larger public infrastructure.

(7) Farm & Ecosystem Friendly:

Via the economic pluralism fostered by permitting flexible and low density residential zoning, i.e., small independently owned, often independently constructed homes on large lots of .5 to 20 acres, you create the potential for a vibrant market in small property leases for specialty farming. Through zoning (or protecting) vast tracts of outer suburb and exurban lands according to New Suburbanist precepts where low density home building and road building is encouraged instead of discouraged, you create a market for relatively cheap abundant land, making more affordable acquisition of land set-asides for agriculture or nature conservancies.

New Suburbanism embraces the inspiring original vision of New Urbanism, its call to create the 21st century's version of cities and buildings that are welcoming spaces. But New Suburbanism rejects the ideological stridency, the coercion, and the porcine corruption of the powerful high density coalition.

At its heart, New Suburbanism is the necessary counterpart to New Urbanism and Smart Growth, because they are constrained by an imbalanced, unnecessary bias towards high density. New Suburbanism gives back to our cities and towns their freedom; gives us abundant land; gives us affordable homes; gives our cities turned suburbs turned exurbs the unforced, organic, natural, and easy transition from dense to sparse.

9 – California's Earth, Wind, Fire & Water Crises vs. Climate Change & Environmental Madness

Credit: Josh Edelson/AFP via Getty Images.

The first part of this chapter is courtesy of the March 2016 article "Investing in Infrastructure to Lower the Cost of Living" from the California Policy Center's Edward Ring:

State political leaders have committed California to phasing out nuclear and hydrocarbon-powered generation in favor of "renewables—primarily solar panels and windmills—in the name of battling climate change, but have failed to ensure we have enough juice to meet demands during the transition.

One nuclear plant, San Onofre, has been shuttered and the other, Diablo Canyon, is scheduled to shut down in a few years. We have shunned imported power generated by coal and one by one, natural gas-fired plants have been ticketed for closure.

The new political alternative to infrastructure development is conservation. By zoning ultra-high density infill in urban areas, transit villages, light rail, by mandating energy efficiency and subsidizing decentralized renewable energy sources such as rooftop photovoltaics, by mandating water conservation and subsidizing retrofits such as low-flow faucets and toilets, California's political leadership hopes to avoid massive new investments in civil infrastructure.

However, state energy policies have made California gas and electricity prices among the highest in the nation, since 2011 electricity prices have increased five times as fast as the national average. In 2017 alone, they increased at three times the national rate. These prices have been devastating to poorer Californians, particularly in the less temperate interior where "energy poverty" has grown rapidly.

California currently buys 20% to 30% of its daily supplemental energy from other states. We do not produce enough of our own energy to support the state's needs. And with the overwhelming push by the left to rid the state of natural gas production, oil, nuclear and hydro power, intermittent renewable energy cannot provide steady, reliable power for the state's 40 million resident.

The Department of the Interior estimated that the 2018 wildfire season produced 68 million tons of carbon dioxide. "This number equates to about 15 percent of all California emissions, and it is on par with the annual emissions produced by generating enough electricity to power the entire state for a year," the press release noted.

These policies, and not "extreme weather," are leading to rolling blackouts during summers in California. The weather in the Golden "Brown" State is typical–hot dry summers are normal, but power outages didn't used to be the norm.

Cali's Anti-Climate-Change Regime Exacerbates Economic, Regional & Racial Inequality

An analysis by the Chapman Center for Demographics and Policy details how California's draconian anti-climate-change regime has exacerbated economic, geographic, and racial inequality.

One primary impact of climate regulations has been to chase away historically well-paying jobs in manufacturing, energy, and home building, all key employers for working and middle-class Californians. Over time, those high prices will impact not just these industries, but the tech sector; artificial intelligence and live-streaming providers are among the largest and fastest growing consumers of electricity.

State officials refuse to focus on these impacts. There's a well-developed sense that anyone who dissents, even a scientist or respected economist, is a heretic not worth listening to. This treatment is facilitated by a media that tends to embrace the most apocalyptic projections of, for example, coastal erosion, with little attempt to actually ascertain the actual facts or look at alternative analyses.

Governor Jerry Brown is a convenient boogeyman for climate realists since his climate alarmism is as unrelenting as it is hyperbolic. But Brown is just one of the stars in an out-of-control environmental movement that is institutionalized in California's legislature, courts, mass media, schools, and corporations.

As a recent Massachusetts Institute of Technology (MIT) report suggests, over-reliance on renewables will continue to impose costs and threaten reliability, particularly without energy from other sources, such as nuclear plants. Virtually every place that has tried to base its energy on a short-term shift to renewables—Germany, Demark, even resource-rich Australia—has experienced huge spikes in energy prices. In Europe, notes one recent study, reliance on renewables both reduces incomes and boosts rates of household poverty.

Fighting climate change is the imperative, beyond debate, that justified the Golden State passing laws and regulations such as California Environmental Quality Act, the Global Warming Solutions Act of 2006, the Sustainable Communities and Climate Protection Act of 2008, and numerous others at the state and local level. However, they now make it nearly impossible to build affordable homes, develop energy, or construct reservoirs, aqueducts, desalination plants, nuclear power plants, pipelines, freeways, or any other essential infrastructure that requires so much as a scratch in the ground.

Instead, California's environmentalists only redouble their nonsense arguments. Expect these fires to justify even more "climate change" legislation that does nothing to clear the forests of overgrown tinder, and everything to clear the forests, and the chaparral, of people and towns.

If an honest history of California in the early 21st century is ever written, the verdict will be unequivocal. Forests that thrived in California for over 20 million years were allowed to become overgrown tinderboxes. And then, with stupefying ferocity, within the span of a few decades, they burned to the ground. Many of them never recovered.

Special Interests Put Their Agenda Ahead of the Interests of Ordinary Californians

Nobody wants to turn back the clock on an environmental cleanup that has been heroic. But today, environmentalism has gone too far. Regulations and litigation have stopped development in its tracks. More than anything else, environmentalism run amok is the reason Californians live with scarcity and high prices.

The extent and complexity of environmental regulations have allowed special interests to put their agenda ahead of the interests of ordinary Californians. Public employee unions, which didn't even exist when Pat Brown was California's governor 60 years ago, now exercise almost complete control over California's state and local government agencies. Freezing infrastructure spending allows government funds to be redirected to pay and benefits for state bureaucrats, instead of to freeways and water projects. And tying development up in knots with more regulations always means more government hiring.

Also benefiting from extreme environmentalism are California's high-tech billionaires, who now have a lucrative mandate to create an "internet of things" to monitor the consumption of resources. Public utilities benefit because their profits (which are regulated by law at a fixed percentage of revenues) soar when the per-unit costs for electricity and water go way up to pay for renewables and to cope with artificially imposed scarcity. This imposed scarcity keeps housing unaffordable, locking out homebuyers but yielding high returns to real estate speculators.

Electricity Prices in California Rose 5x More Than Rest of USA

From a July 2020 LinkedIn article by Corey Lee Wilson titled "Electricity Prices in California Rose 5x More Than Rest of the USA":

Between 2011 and 2017, California's electricity prices rose five times faster than they did nationally. Today, Californians pay 60 percent more, on average, than the rest of the nation, for residential, commercial, and industrial electricity.

California's high penetration of intermittent renewables such as solar and wind are likely a key factor in higher prices. Economists agree that "the dominant policy driver in the electricity sector [in California] has unquestionably been a focus on developing renewable sources of electricity generation."

High levels of renewable energy penetration make electricity expensive around the world, not just in California. As Germany deployed high levels of renewables over the last 10 years it saw its electricity prices rise 34 percent. Today, German electricity costs twice as much as that in neighboring France.

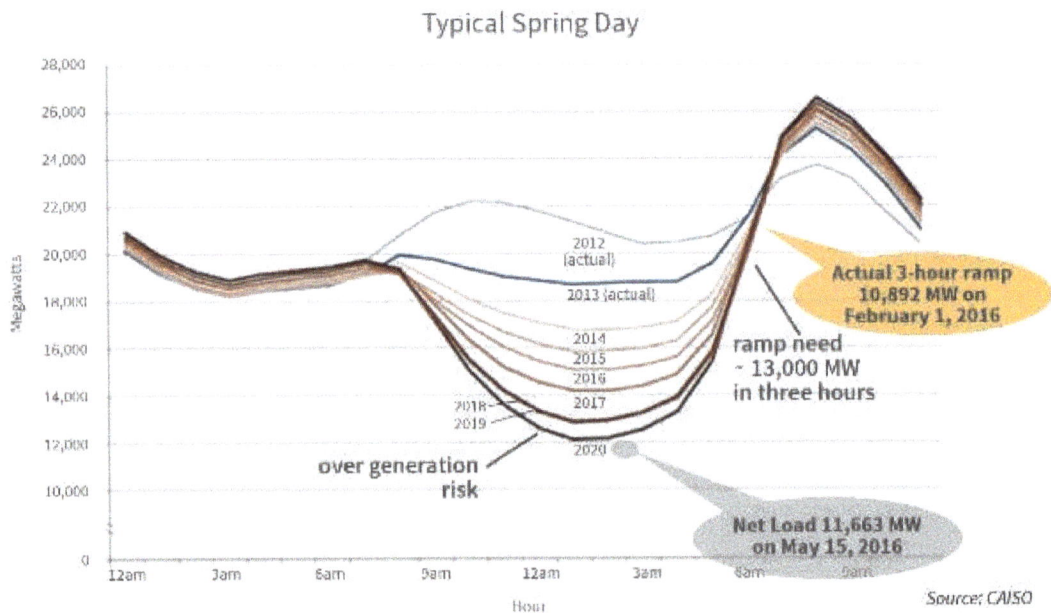

Typical Spring Day

California's Renewable Portfolio Standard (RPS) Increases Electricity Costs

California's renewable portfolio standard (RPS) increases electricity costs in part by requiring the purchase of renewables even when they cannot be relied on to power the grid, requiring undiminished capacity from the combination of natural gas, hydro, and nuclear power.

RPS, also referred to as renewable electricity standards (RES), are policies designed to increase the use of renewable energy sources for electricity generation. These policies require or encourage electricity suppliers to provide their customers with a stated minimum share of electricity from eligible renewable resources. Although national RPS or other clean energy policies have been proposed, no federal RPS or similar policy is currently in place. However, most states have enacted their own RPS programs.

As a result, California today has a large amount of excess electricity generating capacity (known as the 'Duck Curve' shown below) without being able to know if much of it will be available from day to day and week to week.

As Wind and Solar Capacity Climbs, Returns of Usable Power Diminish

As wind and solar capacity climbs, the returns of usable power diminish because of increasing curtailment during surges that the grid cannot absorb. More and more intermittent capacity has to be pushed onto the grid to get less and less additional renewable electricity. The dynamic of soaring overcapacity and falling prices is the inevitable result of the fundamental inability of intermittent wind and solar generators to efficiently match supply to demand.

Where will the power come from with solar power offline and not producing in the evening? When renewables aren't available, natural gas kicks in. It's not only a reliable energy source, natural gas is the always-ready backup for intermittent solar and wind renewable energy—because the sun doesn't always shine and goes down at night, and the wind doesn't always blow.

The burden of higher cost electricity and benefits of renewable energy subsidies fall unevenly on Californians. Between 2007 and 2014, the highest-income 40 percent of California households received three times more in solar subsidies—valued between $10,000 and $20,000 per household—as the lowest-income 40 percent. California households with over $100,000 in annual income benefitted from energy efficiency subsidies at twice the rate of households whose income was under $50,000.

Regressive Energy Policies

Gas-powered vehicles, and natural gas are endangered species in California. Gov. Gavin Newsom issued an executive order in September 2020 requiring sales of all new passenger vehicles to be zero-emission by 2035 and "additional measures to eliminate harmful emissions from the transportation sector," the Globe reported. Newsom also called for an end to Hydraulic Fracturing, commonly referred to as "fracking" for natural gas in California.

Cities are banning the use of natural gas. The California Energy Commission rolled out new building code drafts in May 2020, proposing building standards to require new homes have all-electric appliances instead of natural gas appliances.

Perhaps nowhere will the pain be worse than in Bakersfield, the capital of the California's once vibrant oil industry. That industry is now slated for extinction by policy-makers, even as the state has emerged as the largest US importer of energy and oil, much of it from Saudi Arabia. This ultimate effort at 'virtue signaling' will cost California as many of 300,000 generally high paying jobs, roughly half held by minorities, and will devastate, in particular, the San Joaquin Valley where 40,000 jobs depend on the industry.

"Imagine that the state dictated that the entertainment industry be eliminated from Los Angeles, or the tech industry be eliminated from Silicon Valley. That is what removing the oil and agriculture industries from Bakersfield is like. It is an existential threat to the entire area," says Rob Ball of the Kern County Council of Governments.

Environmentalists Destroyed California's Forests

This September 2020 article "Environmentalists Destroyed California's Forests" comes from the California Policy Center's Edward Ring:

Millions of acres of California forest have been blackened by recent summer wildfires, leading to the usual angry denunciations from the usual quarters about climate change. But in 1999, the *Associated Press* reported that forestry experts had long agreed that "clearing undergrowth would save trees," and that "years of aggressive firefighting have allowed brush to flourish that would have been cleared away by wildfires." But very little was done. And now fires of unprecedented size are raging across the Western United States.

"Sen. Feinstein blames Sierra Club for blocking wildfire bill," reads the provocative headline on a 2002 story in California's *Napa Valley Register*. Feinstein had brokered a congressional consensus on legislation to thin "overstocked" forests close to homes and communities, but could not overcome the environmental lobby's disagreement over expediting the permit process to thin forests everywhere else.

Year after year, environmentalists litigated and lobbied to stop efforts to clear the forests through timber harvesting, underbrush removal, and controlled burns. Meanwhile, natural fires were suppressed, and the forests became more and more overgrown. The excessive biomass competed for the same water, soil, and light a healthier forest would have used, rendering all of the trees and underbrush unhealthy. It wasn't just excess biomass that accumulated, but dried out and dead biomass.

What happened among California's tall stands of Redwood and Ponderosa Pine also happened in its extensive chaparral. Fire suppression along with too many environmentalist-inspired bureaucratic barriers to controlled burns and undergrowth removal turned the hillsides and canyons of Southern California into tinderboxes.

A Green Conundrum for the Golden State

This August 2021 American Greatness article "A Green Conundrum for the Golden State" comes from the California Policy Center's Edward Ring:

In 2006, California Governor Arnold Schwarzenegger signed the landmark AB 32, the "Global

Warming Solutions Act." Determined to leave a legacy that would ensure he remained welcome among the glitterati of Hollywood and Manhattan, Schwarzenegger may not have fully comprehended the forces he unleashed.

Under AB 32, California was required to "reduce its [greenhouse gas] emissions to 1990 levels by 2020." Now, according to the "scoping plan" updated in 2017, California must "further reduce its GHG emissions by 40 percent below 1990 levels by 2030."

The problem with such an ambitious plan is that achieving it will preclude ordinary Californians ever enjoying the lifestyle that people living in developed nations have earned and have come to expect. It will condemn Californians to chronic scarcity of energy, with repercussions that remain poorly understood by voters.

It isn't merely that Californians will experience unreliable energy, as the percentage of energy generated from "renewable" sources continues to increase. That will eventually get sorted out, although at a stupendous cost. Battery farms will replace natural gas plants to fill in those times of day when there is no sun and insufficient wind, and over time, the entire solar, wind, battery, and "smart grid" infrastructure will get overbuilt enough to cope even with those months in the year when days are short and there isn't much wind. It will cost trillions and despoil thousands of square miles of supposedly sacred open space, but it will get done.

The Scorching of California

This June 2019 report "California Wildfires: Key Recommendations to Prevent Future Disasters" comes from a joint effort from Independent Institute researchers Lawrence J. McQuillan, Hayeon Carol Park, Adam B. Summers, and Katherine Dwyer:

During the 2018 wildfires, Californians repeatedly were told that "climate change" was the primary cause, and that as a consequence, these fires would become a fact of life from then on. It's true that fire danger is elevated during droughts and heatwaves—and therefore "climate change" can be connected to more severe wildfires. But there are other, bigger factors. The most significant of these is decades of aggressive fire suppression.

In the natural forest and chaparral that defines most of California's fire-prone regions, natural fires sparked by lightning had been a part of the ecosystem for millennia. In mature forests, these fires periodically would sweep through to burn out the smaller trees and vegetation. This not only would reduce tinder that otherwise would accumulate, but the removal of these smaller trees and shrubs that competed with mature trees for water and nutrients would ensure the health of the larger trees.

When ecologists claim California's trees are stressed, they're right, but when California's politicians echo these concerns, they opportunistically focus on climate change, instead of telling the truth about the role that aggressive fire suppression has played in undermining the health of these trees.

Left unsaid is that more than 130 million trees died throughout the state's foothills and mountain ranges during the drought of 2011–2016 and were not removed from the forest floor, providing an immensity of natural kindling for fires.

To walk in a Sierra Nevada forest during summers requires navigating not just over fallen limbs and branches, but also rotting trees—all amid dead brush and dead but still-towering brown pines. Gone are the periodic meadows and open spaces of the 1960s and 1970s, when logging companies harvested trees, thinned out the forests, replanted what was cut, and cleaned up the forest floor.

Opinions vary regarding how much of the conflagrations of 2018 could have been avoided, but nobody disputes that more could have been done. Everyone agrees, for example, that aggressive fire "suppression" has been a mistake. Most everyone agrees that good "prevention" measures include forest thinning (especially around power lines), selective logging, controlled burns, and power line upgrades. And everyone agrees that residents in fire-prone areas need to create defensible space and fire-harden their homes.

Opinions also vary as to whether or not environmentalists stood in the way of these prevention measures. In a blistering critique published in the aftermath of the fires of 2018, investigative journalist Katy Grimes cataloged the negligence resulting from environmentalist overreach.

"For decades," Grimes wrote, "traditional forest management was scientific and successful— that is until ideological, preservationist zealots wormed their way into government and began the overhaul of sound federal forest management through abuse of the Endangered Species Act and the 're-wilding, no-use movement.'"

Why Were California's Wildfires So Devastating?

U.S. Representative Tom McClintock, whose Northern California district includes the Yosemite Valley and the Tahoe National Forest, told Grimes that the U.S. Forest Service 40 years ago departed from "well-established and time-tested forest management practices."

"We replaced these sound management practices with what can only be described as a doctrine of benign neglect," McClintock explained. "Ponderous, byzantine laws and regulations administered by a growing cadre of ideological zealots in our land management agencies promised to 'save the environment.' The advocates of this doctrine have dominated our law, our policies, our courts, and our federal agencies ever since."

Critics had warned for many years that worsening conditions across the state were increasing the risk of a "perfect storm" of cataclysmic wildfires. Multiple government officials and agencies contributed to the unprecedented destructiveness of the recent wildfire seasons by pursuing, for decades, misguided priorities and perverse incentives. This includes impeding sensible and effective fire-prevention policies.

Along with Cal Fire, these blameworthy parties include past California governors and state legislators, the U.S. Forest Service, U.S. Bureau of Land Management, National Park Service, state and federal Environmental Protection Agencies, California Natural Resources Agency, California Air Resources Board (CARB) and its 35 local air-quality management districts, and various environmental organizations. While all share blame to varying degrees for the flawed public policies and their disastrous outcomes, Cal Fire and the U.S. Forest Service bear special responsibility, given their mandates to protect Californians from wildfires.

The deadly cumulative errors of the responsible parties are numerous, but some mistakes played an especially harmful role in California's recent megafires. One fundamental cause is that public agencies and officials succumbed to pressure by environmental groups who pushed for fire-management policies that take a reactive posture (fire suppression), rather than a proactive stance (fire prevention and active management).

Although the hope was to preserve land in its "natural state," this approach set the stage for horrific wildfires by allowing excessive growth of fuels. Another fundamental policy failure that encouraged deadly megafires was the shifting of decision-making authority for wildfire management away from the local communities at risk. This resulted in delays and inaction, which helped fuel the megafires. At a more operational level, public agencies have failed to proactively adopt cutting-edge fire prevention and detection technologies as early as possible.

Recommendations for Prevention, Early Detection, and Rapid Suppression of California Wildfires

This June 2019 follow-up report "California Wildfires: Key Recommendations to Prevent Future Disasters" comes from a joint effort from Independent Institute researchers Lawrence J. McQuillan, Hayeon Carol Park, Adam B. Summers, and Katherine Dwyer:

Under normal (non-emergency) circumstances, the top priority of any sustainable firefighting strategy is to prevent an unplanned major fire from ever beginning. The next highest priority should be the early detection of an unplanned fire in order to assess its threat and extinguish it quickly, if necessary. Another high priority should be the rapid suppression of any wildfire that grows into a significant threat.

Once a fire reaches the scale of the 2018 Camp Fire, for example, firefighters have few tools to successfully combat it. Thankfully, there are many preventive measures that can be implemented or expanded in California that would reduce the probability and severity of wildfires.

In February 2019, Cal Fire released its Community Wildfire Prevention and Mitigation Report. As the title implies, the bulk of the 19 recommendations contained in the report focus on preventing future wildfires through fuel reduction, forest management, prescribed burns, and local action.

Cal Fire wrote that multiple agencies must "begin systematically addressing community vulnerability and wildfire fuel buildup through rapid deployment of resources. Implementing several of these recommended actions is necessary to execute the priority fuel reduction projects referenced above. Other recommendations are intended to put the state on a path toward long-term community protection, wildfire prevention, and forest health."

In April 2019, Governor Newsom's Strike Force released a 52-page report titled Wildfires and Climate Change: California's Energy Future. The report recommends the steps that California needs to take in order to reduce the incidence and severity of wildfires while renewing its commitment to "clean energy" and holding utilities accountable for their role in past wildfires.

The Strike Force recommends expanding fire prevention activity, making communities more resilient, investing in fire suppression and response, and calling on the federal government to better manage its forestlands. Further, it states, "The growing risk of catastrophic wildfires has created an imperative for the state to act urgently and swiftly to expand preemptive fire prevention and bolster wildfire response efforts to help protect vulnerable communities and reduce the severity of wildfires in our state. All levels of government, communities, utilities, and residents must share in this responsibility in order to better defend California from this devastating threat."

As outlined in the Independent Institute's California Golden Fleece® Award report: Cal Fire, the U.S. Forest Service, and Other Government Agencies there are many actions that need to be taken in order to get ahead of the wildfire problem. Most of these actions require a change in culture to embrace innovation, new technology, new procedures, a focus on prevention, and vastly more local control.

Simply Throwing More Taxpayer Money at Current Practices is Not the Answer

Nor is the answer a temporary reallocation of resources that will revert back to old ways of doing things once politicians shift their focus away from fires to the next issue of the day. California must get beyond the status quo permanently. If not, more Californians will needlessly die, more homes will be destroyed, and more lives will be upended by out-of-control wildfires. Worst of all, much of this future destruction will have been preventable.

Here are 26 recommendations from the Independent Institute that incorporate the Cal Fire Community Wildfire Prevention and Mitigation and Governor Newsom's Strike Force reports with additional measures added:

1. Emphasize proactive forest management and forest restoration.

2. Conduct more prescribed or controlled burns.

3. Allow low-intensity natural fires to burn.

4. Encourage more use of "fire breaks" and "fuel breaks."

5. Allow private-property owners to remove trees and provide active forest management through forest thinning and the creation of breaks, especially near communities more easily.

6. Hire more private firefighters.

7. Inject competition and market discipline into electricity markets by ending the monopoly protections of utility companies, encouraging utilities to focus more on customer safety and less on the pet projects of politicians and regulators.

8. End California housing policies that encourage more people to live in fire-prone areas.

9. Stop government interference in the home insurance market in California.

10. Review investigative procedures and budgets to ensure legal accountability for people and companies who start wildfires.

11. Deploy more early-detection systems to quickly identify fires in California forests and in wildland-urban interfaces.

12. Deploy Internet of Things-connected sensors.

13. Use more artificial intelligence to analyze data and improve firefighting.

14. Improve wildfire alert systems.

15. Use steel poles to hold electricity lines.

16. Use new and improved fire retardant.

17. Deploy more firefighting robots such as Thermite.

18. Replicate Israel's Matash system in California.

19. Encourage "home hardening" through the installation of exterior fire sprinklers and fireproofing of buildings.

20. Encourage the undergrounding of electrical lines in high-risk areas.

21. Enable fast, targeted cutoff of power lines during high-risk incidents to prevent electrical arcs or downed power lines from sparking wildfires.

22. Insulate power lines.

23. Use innovative technology on aircraft and satellites.

24. Invest in an overwhelming strike force to rapidly suppress large fires.

25. Use virtual reality simulations to improve firefighter training.

26. Encourage more private stewardship of California land.

Reforming California's Water Policies to Survive Droughts

This April 2021 *National Review* article "Reform California's Water Policies" comes from Steven Greenhut, author of the new Pacific Research Institute book *Winning the Water Wars*:

The current California water apocalypse is helpful to study for two reasons—it's a cautionary tale of environmentalist-induced disaster, and second, lesser versions of the same disaster could be coming to other Western states soon. While former Governor Brown surely was right that California needed to address its water shortages even in non-drought years, he was wrong to suggest that the solution is more government mandates for conservation among urban and commercial water-users.

Lake Mead, the reservoir created by the Hoover Dam on the Colorado River, which supplies water to 20 million Californians, has hit its lowest water levels since 1935, the year the dam was built. "The Colorado River supplies water to 40 million people, while the Hoover Dam generates electricity to about 25 million people," ABC reported. Northern California's Lake Oroville is already so low we won't have any hydro power from it. And the Colorado River Basin told California to expect water cutbacks.

Around 50 percent of the state's available water flows unimpeded to the Pacific Ocean. Agriculture uses 40 percent and urban users (commercial and residential) account for the final 10 percent. State officials fixate on eking out additional savings from residences, which use only 5.7 percent of available water resources.

Many agricultural subsidies are a vestige from the past, when the agricultural industry was more powerful than it is today. These days, the environmentalist lobby is in the driver's seat—and it sees conservation and rationing as ends in themselves. The state hasn't built significant water infrastructure since the 1970s, when the population was half its current 40 million.

Today's Environmental Groups Operate as Litigation Machines

They fight almost every proposal to expand the state's water resources—from slightly boosting the height of existing dams to building reservoir projects that have been in the planning stages for decades. More prominently, California water policy has devolved largely into an insane battle over fish habitats.

In his new Pacific Research Institute book *Winning the Water Wars*, journalist and R Street Institute western region director Steven Greenhut writes that California can end its decades-long battles over water and meet the needs of its current and future population by promoting abundance rather than managing scarcity.

Most proposals run up against the usual cast of bureaucratic and environmental characters. The environmental movement and its friends in state government are using water policy as a means to achieve broader goals. For instance, the California Coastal Commission, which advocates slow growth, for years has delayed the approval of a Huntington Beach desalination plant at a shuttered energy facility over worries about the impact on—get this—plankton. A concern about depleting a small amount of drifting whale food in the massive Pacific Ocean seems like a red herring to stop the plant.

Despite years of inaction, California can still avoid taking draconian steps. It needs to do what previous generations have done: Tap new water resources and build sufficient infrastructure to capture and store water during rainy years so that it has enough during dry ones. It needs to plan, rather than live at the mercy of Mother Nature.

In 1987, former Democratic governor Pat Brown recalled his approach toward the state's water shortages. "If we had not built the Oroville Dam, the Edmund G. Brown Aqueduct and the San Luis Reservoir, California would be facing a tremendous water shortage," he wrote. It's a straightforward idea that used to be widely shared even by environmentalists.

"Californians have only to see to it that the forests on which the regular and manageable flood of the rivers depend[s] are preserved, that storage reservoirs are made at the foot of the range and all the bounty of the mountains may be put to use," wrote John Muir, the Sierra Club founder. The problem isn't a lack of rain but a lack of political will to assure that.

Electricity and Ideology–Competing Priorities in California

From the August 2020 article "We Have a Power Supply Problem" by CalMatters' Dan Walters:

Solar production is by nature intermittent, sometimes so much so that energy has to be shipped, at low prices, out of the producing state. At other times the producer must bring energy in from elsewhere.

Last summer, the August 14-15, 2020 power blackouts happened when the state was short 400 Megawatts of energy. According to our energy expert, California is currently short 1,300 Megawatts of hydroelectric power. The other significant factor in California's power shortages is unreliable, yet mandated, "renewable energy" and specifically solar power.

The recent blackouts that hit California during wildfire summer months are a warning that the state has a serious electrical power shortage on its energy sustainability goal of achieving 100% renewable supply by 2045. The rolling electrical blackouts that hit California in mid-August 2020 were—or should have been—a wakeup call about power supply deficits that have been building for years.

Furthermore, this October 2019 article "Electricity and Ideology–Competing Priorities in California" comes from the California Policy Center's Edward Ring:

The only potential upside of 2045 renewables mandates is the possibility that if cost-effective power storage is developed at scale—i.e., cheap, and affordable battery systems with capacities measured in hundreds of megawatt-hours per unit, then grid electricity can be distributed and stored. This would permit uninterrupted power whenever transmission lines delivering power into an area is cut off, since the power stored in these batteries would pick up the slack.

Consider this, renewables mandates in California redirect utility resources away from safety, and into technologies that may soon be obsolete. Do we really want to construct a 2.3 gigawatt-hour electricity storage facility at Moss Landing, on California's Central Coast, using lithium-ion technology, when solid-state batteries may be a reality within the next 10 years?

Should we really carpet the Mojave Desert with photovoltaic panels, when safe and cost-effective fission reactors are being constructed all over the world, and commercially viable fusion power could be here within the next 20 to 30 years?

California's determination to pour hundreds of billions into implementing renewables needs to be examined not only against the obvious pitfall of likely obsolescence but against the costs and benefits of that course versus building a safe and reliable power grid that can meet the needs and expectations of residents in the 21st century.

Californians Are Being Penalized by Environmental Mandates

This Winter 2021 *City Journal* article "The Other California" is from Joel Kotkin and Karla López del Río:

Fighting climate change by limiting the supply of housing to already-expensive areas seems an inefficient and regressive way to cut emissions. The call for more density is unlikely to get people out of their cars, given California's spatial configuration.

Much of the problem, suggests Ron Loveridge, a former county supervisor and former mayor of Riverside, lies in California's one-party political system, largely dominated by the Bay Area's urban and green progressives, as well as the public-employee unions. As one recent study demonstrates, the San Francisco metropolitan area, with 12 percent of the state population, has dominated housing policy, while representatives from places like the Inland Empire, the Central Valley, and Orange County have been notably ineffective in getting legislation passed.

"We were left behind politically for so many years," says former Eastvale city manager Michele Nissen, now chief of staff to Riverside County Supervisor Karen Spiegel. "Northern California gets what it wants and needs, and the Inland Empire is seen as, 'Oh, you are cute, now go sit over there and be quiet.'"

Rather than trying to re-create San Francisco on a statewide basis, it would make more sense to allow development in those inland areas where working and middle-class households are more likely to be able to afford to rent or buy homes. Encouraging the growth and success of the Inland Empire represents the most compelling way to resuscitate Southern California.

The state's current approach, wherein highly unaffordable coastal areas get most of the high-end jobs, forcing huge numbers of commuters onto the freeways, is not sustainable economically, socially, or environmentally. The state should seek to promote more job growth in areas where people can afford to live.

10 – Mexifornia: Why the State's Largest Ethnic Group is Falling Behind the Others

Illegal Immigrant Population Falls To Decade Low

Estimated number of unauthorized immigrants living in the U.S.

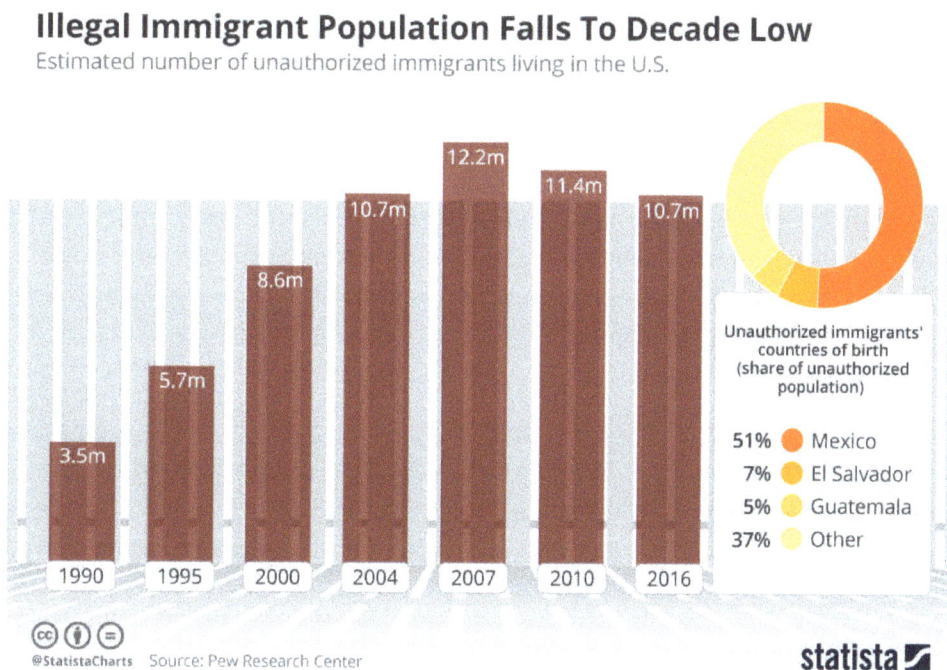

3.5m	5.7m	8.6m	10.7m	12.2m	11.4m	10.7m
1990	1995	2000	2004	2007	2010	2016

Unauthorized immigrants' countries of birth (share of unauthorized population)

51% Mexico
7% El Salvador
5% Guatemala
37% Other

@StatistaCharts Source: Pew Research Center

statista

Per Victor Davis Hanson, renowned author of *Mexifornia: A State of Becoming (third 2021 edition)*:

As I write in mid-March 2021,the southern border of the United States is porous. Traffic across it is fluid and unchecked to a degree not seen in the recent forty-year history of massive illegal immigration.

Tens of thousands of immigrants, most from Central America and Mexico, many of them unaccompanied minors, some of them members or cartels or gangs are crossing illegally every day. They arrive in the country unvetted and unimpeded. Panicked Biden administration officials suddenly assert that the visibly permeable border is "closed."

Millions of would-be immigrants boast of renewed hopes of entering the United States without legal permission. They express relief at the end of the restrictionist Trump administration. They have been incentivized through the celebration of Trump's departure by many of the loudest and most influential people in the U.S. government, popular culture, and academia. Messaging that the new Biden administration is mostly against whatever Trump was for has provided encouragement to make the trek northward, as many border crossers unapologetically admit.

More specifically, illegal immigrants claim they were emboldened by Joe Biden's widely reported executive orders stopping further bordar wall construction. They were heartened by news of an imminent relaxing of border enforcement, a return to "catch and release" policies in the detaining of illegal aliens, promises to allow would-be refugees to have their claims adjudicated inside the United States, and Washington's backing off from agreements in which Mexico was to patrol its borders to prevent Central Americans in transit from entering the U.S. illegally. Many had heard rumors of serial multimillion-person amnesties that would soon make the facts of illegal entry and unlawful residency irrelevant. Optimistic phone texts from friends and relatives who had successfully crossed the border inspired thousands more to try.

Officials in the new Biden administration seem shocked at the public unease with their open-border agenda. They had assumed that the public was more evenly divided over immigration enforcement, given the controversies of the restrictionist Trump years. But polls in March already showed that over 57 percent of Americans were opposed to President Biden's nonenforcement policies.

Apparently the idea of allowing unvetted foreign nationals to enter the United States-and without any testing for Covid-19 when American citizens are still locked down, restricted in their travel, and not yet fully vaccinated--does not win majority support. Yet the Democratic Party's progressive base has persisted in pushing radical changes in immigration policy, despite their increasing unpopularity.

Mexifornia: A State of Becoming

The following issues affecting primarily the Mexican and Central American illegal alien component, are not unique to these ethnic groups, but they are at their worst by degree and shear volume with these ethnic groups. For these reasons, an open U.S. border appears to be losing favor even among Mexicans and Central Americans.

Perhaps they have learned that illegal immigration is ultimately as harmful to their own societies as to America. It breaks families apart. Breadwinners vanish and are unlikely to return permanently. Thousands become ill or fall victim to predation on their way north. Emboldened cartels and criminals profit from the migrations. Some expatriates in the United States grow hostile to their homeland, as the remittances they send back out of their hard-won earnings remind them just how inept and callous are the social services there.

After years of acrimonious negotiations with the Trump administration, Latin American leaders had finally hammered out agreements to keep their own citizens from crossing borders unlawfully. They did so in part to avoid consequences such as trade penalties and U.S. taxes on some $100 billion in remittances sent annually to Central America and Mexico, an astronomical figure four to five times higher than when I first wrote Mexifornia (in 2003).

A few Latin American governments have even shown surprise that the Americans now seem to have broken their Trump-era agreements. They wonder at the logic of encouraging mass migrations at precisely the time they were dramatically waning.

The president of Mexico, Andres Manuel Lopez Obrador frustrated at the thousands crossing through his country from Central America, the manipulation of these masses of humanity by Mexican cartels and smugglers, and the end of carefully negotiated protocols with the Trump administration- seemed to dismiss President Biden as "the Migrant President," a transparently backhanded compliment.

As the numbers of illegal aliens climbed, as American entry -level wages stagnated, and as crime increased in many places, immigration became more politicized and weaponized. The official government response would shift, but there was a fixed theme to America's attitude toward open borders: both poll-driven parties voiced increased concern that immigration laws were "broken."

Securing America's Southern Border With Mexico

Back in the 1990s, the astute, pragmatic, but also cynical President Bill Clinton had been keenly aware of growing political unease with the huge numbers of people crossing the border from the south. In his 1995 State of the Union address with an eye to his reelection bid Clinton spoke of illegal immigration in terms that today would be condemned by his party as nativist and indeed racist:

All Americans, not only in the States most heavily affected but in every place in this country, are rightly disturbed by the large numbers of illegal aliens entering our country. The jobs they hold might otherwise be held by citizens or legal immigrants. The public service they use impose burdens on our tax payers.

That's why our administration has moved aggressively to secure our borders more by hiring a record number of new border guards, by deporting twice as many criminal aliens as ever before, by cracking down on illegal hiring, by barring welfare benefits to illegal aliens. ... We are a nation of immigrants. But we are also a nation of laws so it is wrong and ultimately self-defeating for a nation of immigrants to permit the kind of abuse of our immigration laws, and we must do more to stop it!

Later, President George W. Bush signed into law the bipartisan "Secure Fence Act of 2006," which promised a 700-mile fence from California through parts of Texas. But the barrier was never fully completed. It was also porous and unimpressive in size. Studies showed that it had almost no effect in reducing unlawful entry. Open-borders advocates disingenuously cited the failure of that poorly constructed fence as proof that border walls are futile.

The numbers of people residing illegally in the United States and of those entering unlawfully grew year by year. So did the pool of American citizens born to illegal aliens on U.S. soil. After decades of immigration nonenforcement, first-generation voters and supporters of undocumented aliens were becoming a potent electoral force in the American Southwest, especially as progressives after 2008 began to recalibrate the Democratic Party leftward.

By 2014, not surprisingly, the Obama administration was offering "amnesty" to nearly five million illegal aliens. A series of executive actions encouraged more illegal immigration by sharply reducing the ability of immigration authorities to control the border. In response to a perceived lack of deterrence, so-called "caravans" of illegal immigrants began to swarm the border, creating a human melodrama as thousands of unaccompanied minors-often prompted by their parents crossed without hindrance.

If Latino's Upward Mobility Doesn't Improve—California Will Suffer

This Winter 2012 *City Journal* article "California's Demographic Revolution: If the upward mobility of the impending Hispanic majority doesn't improve, the state's economic future is in peril" is by Heather Mac Donald:

Unless Hispanics' upward mobility improves, the state risks becoming more polarized economically and more reliant on a large government safety net. And as California goes, so goes the nation, whose own Hispanic population shift is just a generation or two behind.

The scale and speed of the Golden State's ethnic transformation are unprecedented. In the 1960s, Los Angeles was the most Anglo-Saxon of the nation's ten largest cities; today, Latinos make up nearly half of the county's residents and one-third of its voting-age population.

A full 55 percent of Los Angeles County's child population has immigrant parents. California's schools have the nation's largest concentration of "English learners," students from homes where a language other than English is regularly spoken. From 2000 to 2010, the state's Hispanic population grew 28 percent, to reach 37.6 percent of all residents, almost equal to the shrinking white population's 40 percent.

Nearly half of all California births today are Hispanic. The signs of the change are everywhere—from the commercial strips throughout the state catering to Spanish-speaking customers, to the flea markets and illegal vendors in such areas as MacArthur Park in Los Angeles, to the growing reach of the Spanish-language media.

The poor Mexican immigrants who have fueled the transformation—84 percent of the state's Hispanics have Mexican origins—bring an admirable work ethic and a respect for authority too often lacking in America's native-born population. Many of their children and grandchildren have started thriving businesses and assumed positions of civic and economic leadership.

California's English Learner students are a diverse group. Of the more than 60 languages spoken, Spanish is by far the most common: 83 percent of ELs in California schools speak it at home. The next most common languages are Vietnamese and Mandarin, spoken by 2 percent and 1.6 percent of EL students, respectively. Arabic, Filipino, and Cantonese each make up about 1 percent of languages spoken.

But a sizable portion of Mexican, as well as Central American, immigrants, however hardworking, lack the social capital to inoculate their children reliably against America's contagious underclass culture.

Furthermore, the *New York Times*, in 2006, wrote an editorial called "Young Latinas and a Cry for Help": "About one-quarter of Latina teens drop out, a figure surpassed only by Hispanic young men, one-third of whom do not complete high school. Latinas, especially those in recently arrived families, often live in poverty and without health insurance.

"Another piece of the puzzle is how to address the complication of very early, usually unmarried motherhood. Religious beliefs in Hispanic families often limit sex education and rule out abortion. Federal statistics show that about 24 percent of Latinas are mothers by the age of 20—three times the rate of non-Hispanic white teens. ... One in four women in the United States will be Hispanic by the middle of the century. The time to help is now."

City Journal's Heather Mac Donald quotes Anita Berry, a case manager who works at Casa Teresa, a California program for homeless single mothers. Berry says: "There's nothing shameful about having multiple children that you can't care for, and to be pregnant again, because then you can blame the system. ... The problems are deeper and wider. Now you're getting the second generation of foster care and group home residents. The dysfunction is multigenerational."

Whether this can be turned around remains to be seen. But it certainly casts doubt on the *Times*' blissful assertion that "a young Latino workforce (will help) the economy."

The Resulting Dysfunction is Holding Latinos Back and California as Well

The complicated reality of Hispanic family life in California—often straddling the legitimate and the criminal worlds, displaying both a dogged determination to work and poor decision making that interferes with upward mobility—helps explain why the state's Hispanic population has made only modest progress up the educational ladder.

Most parents want their children to flourish, yet they may not grasp the study habits necessary for academic success or may view an eighth-grade education as sufficient for finding work. Julian Rodriguez, a Santa Ana gang detective, recalls a case several years ago in which two parents had taken their 14-year-old daughter out of school to care for their new baby—a classic display of "Old World values," he says.

Many of California's Hispanic students who have been schooled in the U.S. for all their lives and are orally fluent in English remain classified as English learners in high school because they have made so little academic progress. In the Long Beach Unified School District, for example, nearly nine-tenths of English learners entering high school have been in a U.S. school at least since first grade.

The lack of progress isn't due to bilingual education: Long Beach got rid of its last bilingual program in 1998, and the current ninth-grade English learners have been in English-only classrooms all their lives. Some come from families that immigrated to the U.S. two or three generations ago.

True, Hispanics' cognitive skills have been improving over the last decade; the percentage of Hispanic eighth-graders deemed proficient in math and reading on the California Standards Tests doubled from 2004 to 2010.

But the gap between Hispanics' performance and that of whites and Asians narrowed only modestly, since white and Asian scores rose as well. Latino students' rate of B.A. completion from the University of California and California State University is the lowest of all student groups, reports the Institute for Higher Education Leadership and Policy at California State University, Sacramento.

The state spends vast sums each year trying to get more Hispanics into college and to keep them there—$100 million in 2009, for instance, on the education of full-time community-college students who dropped out after their first year, according to the American Institutes for Research. (Facilitating transfers from community college is a favored strategy for increasing Hispanic enrollment in four-year colleges.)

Latino Student Underperformance Contributes to California's Dismal Educational Statistics

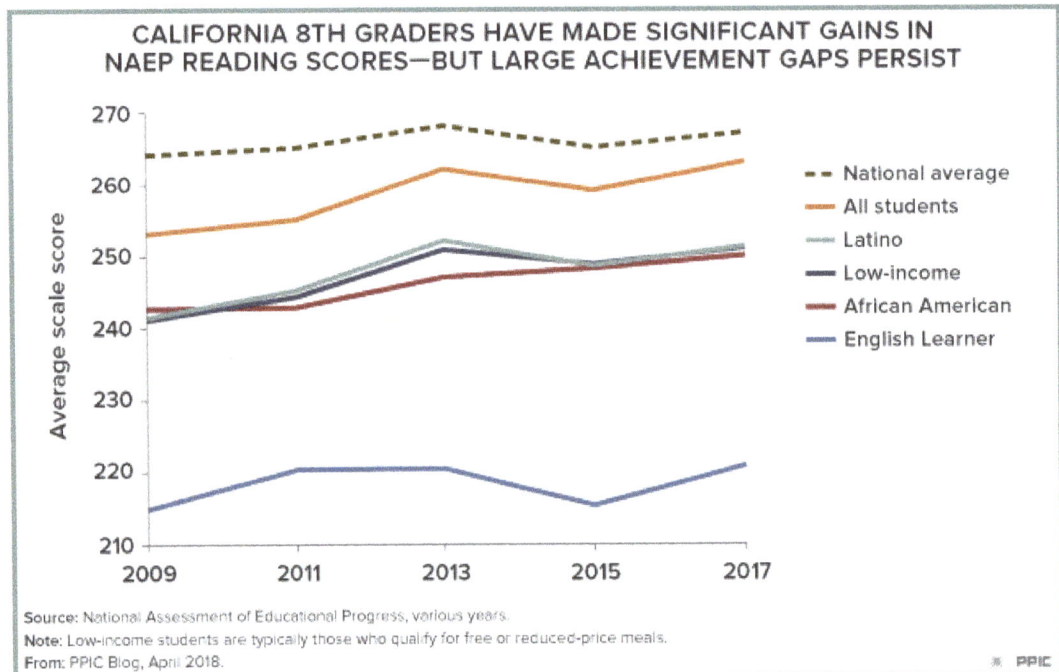

Credit: Public Policy Institute of California (PPIC).

Heather Mac Donald continues:

More from the "California's Demographic Revolution: If the upward mobility of the impending Hispanic majority doesn't improve, the state's economic future is in peril" is by Heather Mac Donald:

Only Mississippi had as large a percentage of its eighth-grade students reading at the "below basic" level on the 2011 National Assessment of Educational Progress (NAEP); in eighth-grade math, California came in third, after Alabama and Mississippi, in the percentage of students scoring "below basic." Only 56 percent of ninth-graders graduate in four years in Los Angeles; statewide, only two-thirds do.

Since the 1980s, California's economic growth has been powered by skilled labor. Silicon Valley, for example, added jobs at a rate of 3.2 percent for the year beginning in November 2010, despite the continuing economic slump. If current labor-market trends continue, 41 percent of California's workers will need a B.A. by 2025, according to the Public Policy Institute of California (PPIC).

California already has trouble finding skilled employees

Because it can't produce all the skilled workers that it needs, it imports them: in 2006, for example, 33 percent of all college-educated California workers had been born in other states and 31 percent had been born abroad, PPIC says. Moreover, since 2000, more college graduates have been exiting California than entering. California will need to attract almost 160,000 college-educated workers annually for 20 years in a row to meet the projected demand, PPIC estimates—three times the number who have been arriving from elsewhere since 2000.

Unfortunately, though Hispanics will make up 40 percent of the state's working-age population by 2020, just 12 percent of them are projected to have bachelor's degrees by then, up from 10 percent in 2006.

Moreover, their fields of academic concentration are not where the most economically fertile growth will probably occur. At California State University in 2008, just 1.7 percent of master's degree students in computer science were Mexican-American, as were just 3.6 percent of students in engineering master's programs. The largest percentage of Mexican-American enrollment in M.A. programs was in education—40 percent—despite (or perhaps because of) Mexican-Americans' low test scores.

The future mismatch between labor supply and demand is likely to raise wages for college-educated workers, while a glut of workers with a high school diploma or less will depress wages on the low end and contribute to an increased demand for government services, especially among the less educated Hispanic population.

U.S.-born Hispanic households in California already use welfare programs (such as cash welfare, food stamps, and housing assistance) at twice the rate of U.S.-born non-Hispanic households, according to an analysis of the March 2011 Current Population Survey by the Center for Immigration Studies. Welfare use by immigrants is higher still. In 2008–09, the fraction of households using some form of welfare was 82 percent for households headed by an illegal immigrant and 61 percent for households headed by a legal immigrant.

Higher rates of Hispanic poverty drive this disparity in welfare consumption. Hispanics made up nearly 60 percent of California's poor in 2010, despite being less than 38 percent of the population. Nearly one-quarter of all Hispanics in California are poor, compared with a little over one-tenth of non-Hispanics.

Nationally, the poverty rate of Hispanic adults drops from 25.5 percent in the first generation—the immigrant generation, that is—to 17 percent in the second but rises to 19 percent in the third, according to a Center for Immigration Studies analysis. (The poverty rate for white adults is 9 percent.) That frustrating third-generation economic stall repeats the pattern in high school graduation and college completion rates as well.

Latino's Lack of Assimilation Has Depressed Their 'Per-Capita' Political Influence

More from the "California's Demographic Revolution: If the upward mobility of the impending Hispanic majority doesn't improve, the state's economic future is in peril" is by Heather Mac Donald:

Nearly 40 percent of Latino adults are ineligible to vote, according to Lisa Garcia Bedolla, an education professor at UC Berkeley. But Hispanics' representation in the state legislature has been growing even faster than their population numbers, and a string of recent speakers in the state assembly have been Hispanic.

Even as Hispanics are gathering clout in Sacramento, the immigrant populations of some small, almost entirely Latino cities in the Los Angeles basin have been politically passive toward local governance. As a result, the city councils and managers of Bell, Maywood, La Puente, and other localities, unchecked by their residents, have engaged in rampant self-dealing, virtually bankrupting those cities' governments.

Such extreme civic miscarriages will diminish as Latinos become further integrated into American society. And there may be advantages to an increasingly Latino-populated state legislature, which may prove less prone to job-killing regulation than one led by white liberals.

But the cost of government services for the Hispanic poor is not likely to abate soon—a serious problem for a state suffering budget woes. The most expensive of those services is education, which is increasingly dominated by enormous programs to try to close the achievement gap; Santa Ana's Willard Intermediate School, for example, where Pastor Pederson once taught, is on the receiving end of a $35 million state transformation grant.

California's Poor Latinos Don't Pay in Taxes What They Cost in State Expenditures

And with rising Latino political power, California's welfare policies will probably become even more redistributionist, predicts CSU San Jose's Larry N. Gerston—at least if Latinos remain poor, their drop-out rates don't improve, and they don't feel they can climb the economic ladder. A 1996 study for Pepperdine University found that Latinos in Southern California achieved middle-class status by pooling wages from three or more workers in a single household, rather than through an "education-based meritocratic formula—as is more common with Asians and Jews." While such a collective work ethic is praiseworthy, it is limited as a strategy for further upward mobility.

And Washington should institute an immigration pause for low-skilled immigrants. In 1970, the average Southern California Latino spoke only English and had assimilated to Anglo culture, according to the Pepperdine study. Since then, even though California's Hispanic population has expanded outside its traditional enclaves and spread across the state and nation, the acculturation process has slowed.

In 1988, when accountant and entrepreneur Martha de la Torre began *El Clasificado*, a free Spanish classified-advertising newspaper, she assumed that the demand for Spanish-language publications would last only a few decades; instead, the market for *El Clasificado* has grown far beyond its original base in Los Angeles, even as similar English-language publications have gone bankrupt. "I'm surprised by how people in some communities try not to change," she observes. Teachers, service employees, police officers, and ordinary private-sector workers report that many California residents now expect to be addressed in Spanish.

The reason for this assimilation reversal is our de facto open-borders policy, argues Michael Saragosa, a public-relations consultant who oversaw Latino outreach for Meg Whitman's 2010 gubernatorial campaign. "We need to allow people who are already here to grow into the American Dream over generations," he says. "That can't happen when they have a steady flow of people behind them." Illegal immigration, which did not drop in California during the recession, should be reduced, and legal immigration should be reoriented toward high-skilled immigrants rather than the family members of existing immigrants.

How Unskilled Immigrants Hurt Our Economy

This *City Journal* Summer 2006 "How Unskilled Immigrants Hurt Our Economy: A handful of industries get low-cost labor, and the taxpayers foot the bill" report from Steven Malanga covers the sections below:

Since the mid-1960s, America has welcomed nearly 30 million legal immigrants and received perhaps another 15 million illegals, numbers unprecedented in our history. These immigrants have picked our fruit, cleaned our homes, cut our grass, worked in our factories, and washed our cars. But they have also crowded into our hospital emergency rooms, schools, and government-subsidized aid programs, sparking a fierce debate about their contributions to our society and the costs they impose on it.

Advocates of open borders immigration argue that welcoming illegal immigrants, versus skilled based immigrants, is essential for our American economy because our businesses need them due to a shortage of people willing to do low-wage work. Moreover, the free movement of labor in a global economy pays off for the United States because immigrants bring skills and capital that expand our economy and offset immigration's costs. Like tax cuts, supporters argue, immigration pays for itself.

As many sapient Americans sense and so much research has demonstrated—America does not have a vast labor shortage that requires waves of low-wage immigrants to alleviate; in fact, unemployment among unskilled workers is high—about 30 percent. Moreover, many of the unskilled, uneducated workers now journeying here labor, in shrinking industries, where they force out native workers, and many others work in industries where the availability of cheap workers has led businesses to suspend investment in new technologies that would make them less labor-intensive.

Yet while these workers add little to our economy, they come at great cost, because they are not economic abstractions but human beings, with their own culture and ideas—often at odds with our own. Increasing numbers of them arrive with little education and none of the skills necessary to succeed in a modern economy. Many may wind up stuck on our lowest economic rungs, where they will rely on something that immigrants of other generations didn't have: a vast U.S. welfare and social-services apparatus that has enormously amplified the cost of immigration.

California Sets a Bad Example With the Largest Share of America's Illegal Immigrants

Just as welfare reform and other policies are helping to shrink America's underclass by weaning people off such social programs, we are importing a new, foreign-born underclass. As famed free-market economist Milton Friedman puts it: "It's just obvious that you can't have free immigration and a welfare state."

The flood of immigrants, both legal and illegal, from countries with poor, ill-educated populations, has yielded a mismatch between today's immigrants and the American economy and has left many workers poorly positioned to succeed for the long term. Unlike the immigrants of 100 years ago, whose skills reflected or surpassed those of the native workforce at the time, many of today's arrivals, particularly the more than half who now come from Central and South America, are farmworkers in their home countries who come here with little education or even basic training in blue-collar occupations like carpentry or machinery. (A century ago, farmworkers made up 35 percent of the U.S. labor force, compared with the under 2 percent who produce a surplus of food today.)

Nearly two-thirds of Mexican immigrants, for instance, are high school dropouts, and most wind up doing either unskilled factory work or small-scale construction projects, or they work in service industries, where they compete for entry-level jobs against one another, against the adult children of other immigrants, and against native-born high school dropouts.

Of the 15 industries employing the greatest percentage of foreign-born workers, half are low-wage service industries, including gardening, domestic household work, car washes, shoe repair, and janitorial work. To take one stark example: whereas 100 years ago, immigrants were half as likely as native-born workers to be employed in household service, today immigrants account for 27 percent of all domestic workers in the United States.

Although open-borders advocates say that these workers are simply taking jobs Americans don't want, studies show that the immigrants drive down wages of native-born workers and squeeze them out of certain industries.

Harvard economists George Borjas and Lawrence Katz, for instance, estimate that low-wage immigration cuts the wages for the average native-born high school dropout by some 8 percent, or more than $1,200 a year. Other economists find that the new workers also push down wages significantly for immigrants already here and native-born Hispanics.

Consequently, as the waves of immigration continue, the sheer number of those competing for low-skilled service jobs makes economic progress difficult.

Low-Skilled Immigrants Are Likely to Wind Up Farther on the Margins of Our Economy

As foreign competition and mechanization shrink manufacturing and farmworker jobs, low-skilled immigrants are likely to wind up farther on the margins of our economy, where many already operate. For example, although only about 12 percent of construction workers are foreign-born, 100,000 to 300,000 illegal immigrants have carved a place for themselves as temporary workers on the fringes of the industry. In urban areas like New York and Los Angeles, these mostly male illegal immigrants gather on street corners, in empty lots, or in Home Depot parking lots to sell their labor by the hour or the day, for $7 to $11 an hour.

That's far below what full-time construction workers earn, and for good reason. Unlike the previous generations of immigrants who built America's railroads or great infrastructure projects like New York's bridges and tunnels, these day laborers mostly do home-improvement projects.

A New York study, for instance, found that four in ten employers who hire day laborers are private homeowners or renters wanting help with cleanup chores, moving, or landscaping. Another 56 percent were contractors, mostly small, nonunion shops, some owned by immigrants themselves, doing short-term, mostly residential work. The day laborer's market, in other words, has turned out to be a boon for homeowners and small contractors offering their residential clients a rock-bottom price, but a big chunk of the savings comes because low-wage immigration has produced such a labor surplus that many of these workers are willing to take jobs without benefits and with salaries far below industry norms.

Because so much of our legal and illegal immigrant labor is concentrated in such fringe, low-wage employment, its overall impact on our economy is extremely small.

A 1997 National Academy of Sciences study estimated that immigration's net benefit to the

American economy raises the average income of the native-born by only some $10 billion a year—about $120 per household. And that meager contribution is not the result of immigrants helping to build our essential industries or making us more competitive globally but instead merely delivering our pizzas and cutting our grass.

Estimates by pro-immigration forces that foreign workers contribute much more to the economy, boosting annual gross domestic product by hundreds of billions of dollars, generally just tally what immigrants earn here, while ignoring the offsetting effect they have on the wages of native-born workers.

If the Benefits of the Current Generation of Migrants Are Small, the Costs Are Large

If the benefits of the current generation of migrants are small, the costs are large and growing because of America's vast range of social programs and the wide advocacy network that strives to hook low-earning legal and illegal immigrants into these programs. A 1998 National Academy of Sciences study found that more than 30 percent of California's foreign-born were on Medicaid—including 37 percent of all Hispanic households—compared with 14 percent of native-born households.

The foreign-born were more than twice as likely as the native-born to be on welfare, and their children were nearly five times as likely to be in means-tested government lunch programs. Native-born households pay for much of this, the study found, because they earn more and pay higher taxes—and are more likely to comply with tax laws. Recent immigrants, by contrast, have much lower levels of income and tax compliance (another study estimated that only 56 percent of illegals in California have taxes deducted from their earnings, for instance). The study's conclusion: immigrant families cost each native-born household in California an additional $1,200 a year in taxes.

Immigration's bottom line has shifted so sharply that in a high-immigration state like California, native-born residents are paying up to ten times more in state and local taxes than immigrants generate in economic benefits. Moreover, the cost is only likely to grow as the foreign-born population—which has already mushroomed from about 9 percent of the U.S. population when the NAS studies were done in the late 1990s to about 12 percent today—keeps growing. And citizens in more and more places will feel the bite, as immigrants move beyond their traditional settling places.

Almost certainly, immigrants' participation in our social welfare programs will increase over time, because so many are destined to struggle in our workforce. Despite our cherished view of immigrants as rapidly climbing the economic ladder, more and more of the new arrivals and their children face a lifetime of economic disadvantage, because they arrive here with low levels of education and with few work skills—shortcomings not easily overcome.

Mexican Immigrants Are Six Times More Likely to be High School Dropouts Than Native-Born Americans

Mexican immigrants, who are up to six times more likely to be high school dropouts than native-born Americans, not only earn substantially less than the native-born median, but the wage gap persists for decades after they've arrived.

A study of the 2000 census data, for instance, shows that the cohort of Mexican immigrants between 25 and 34 who entered the United States in the late 1970s were earning 40 to 50 percent less than similarly aged native-born Americans in 1980, but 20 years later they had fallen even further behind their native-born counterparts.

Today's Mexican immigrants between 25 and 34 have an even larger wage gap relative to the native-born population. Adjusting for other socioeconomic factors, Harvard's Borjas and Katz estimate that virtually this entire wage gap is attributable to low levels of education.

Meanwhile, because their parents start off so far behind, the American-born children of Mexican immigrants also make slow progress.

First-generation adult Americans of Mexican descent studied in the 2000 census, for instance, earned 14 percent less than native-born Americans. By contrast, first-generation Portuguese Americans earned slightly more than the average native-born worker—a reminder of how quickly immigrants once succeeded in America and how some still do.

One reason some ethnic groups make up so little ground concerns the transmission of what economists call "ethnic capital," or what we might call the influence of culture. More than previous generations, immigrants today tend to live concentrated in ethnic enclaves, and their children find their role models among their own group.

Thus the children of today's Mexican immigrants are likely to live in a neighborhood where about 60 percent of men dropped out of high school and now do low-wage work, and where less than half of the population speak English fluently, which might explain why high school dropout rates among Americans of Mexican ancestry are two and a half times higher than dropout rates for all other native-born Americans, and why first-generation Mexican Americans do not move up the economic ladder nearly as quickly as the children of other immigrant groups.

There is a Huge Difference in Asian Immigrant Success vs. Latino Immigrant Success

In sharp contrast is the cultural capital transmitted by Asian immigrants to children growing up in predominantly Asian-American neighborhoods. More than 75 percent of Chinese immigrants and 98 percent of South Asian immigrants to the U.S. speak English fluently, while a mid-1990s study of immigrant households in California found that 37 percent of Asian immigrants were college graduates, compared with only 3.4 percent of Mexican immigrants.

Thus, even an Asian-American child whose parents are high school dropouts is more likely to grow up in an environment that encourages him to stay in school and learn to speak English well, attributes that will serve him well in the job market. Not surprisingly, several studies have shown that Asian immigrants and their children earn substantially more than Mexican immigrants and their children.

At the same time, legalization will only spur new problems, as our experience with the 1986 immigration act should remind us. At the time, then-congressman Charles Schumer, who worked on the legislation, acknowledged that it was "a riverboat gamble," with no certainty that it would slow down the waves of illegals.

Now, of course, we know that the legislation had the opposite effect, creating the bigger problem we now have (which hasn't stopped Senator Schumer from supporting the current legalization proposals). The legislation also swamped the Immigration and Naturalization Service with masses of fraudulent, black-market documents, so that it eventually rubber-stamped tens of thousands of dubious applications.

If We Do Not Legalize Them, What Can We Do With 11 to 22 Million Illegals?

Ship them back home? Their presence here is a fait accompli, the argument goes, and only legalization can bring them above ground, where they can assimilate.

But that argument assumes that we have only two choices: to decriminalize or deport. But what happened after the first great migration suggests a third way: to end the economic incentives that keep them here. We could prompt a great remigration home if, first off, state, and local governments in jurisdictions like New York and California would stop using their vast resources to aid illegal immigrants.

Second, the federal government can take the tougher approach that it failed to take after the 1986 act. It can require employers to verify Social Security numbers and immigration status before hiring, so that we bar illegals from many jobs. It can deport those caught here. And it can refuse to give those who remain the same benefits as U.S. citizens. Such tough measures do work: as a recent Center for Immigration Studies report points out, when the federal government began deporting illegal Muslims after 9/11, many more illegals who knew they were likely to face more scrutiny voluntarily returned home.

If America is ever to make immigration work for our economy again, it must reject policies shaped by advocacy groups trying to turn immigration into the next civil rights cause or by a tiny minority of businesses seeking cheap labor subsidized by the taxpayers. Instead, we must look to other developed nations that have focused on luring workers who have skills that are in demand and who have the best chance of assimilating.

Australia, for instance, gives preferences to workers grouped into four skilled categories: managers, professionals, associates of professionals, and skilled laborers. Using a straightforward "points calculator" to determine who gets in, Australia favors immigrants between the ages of 18 and 45 who speak English, have a post–high school degree or training in a trade, and have at least six months' work experience as everything from laboratory technicians to architects and surveyors to information-technology workers.

Such an immigration policy goes far beyond America's employment-based immigration categories, like the H1-B visas, which account for about 10 percent of our legal immigration and essentially serve the needs of a few Silicon Valley industries.

Immigration Reform Must Also Tackle Our Failing Family-Preference Visa Program

Immigration reform must also tackle our family-preference visa program, which today accounts for two-thirds of all legal immigration and has helped create a 40-year waiting list. Lawmakers should narrow the family-preference visa program down to spouses and minor children of U.S. citizens and should exclude adult siblings and parents

America benefits even today from many of its immigrants, from the Asian entrepreneurs who have helped revive inner-city Los Angeles business districts to Haitians and Jamaicans who have stabilized neighborhoods in Queens and Brooklyn to Indian programmers who have spurred so much innovation in places like Silicon Valley and Boston's Route 128. But increasingly over the last 25 years, such immigration has become the exception vs. Mexican and Central American immigration. It needs once again to become the rule.

'Illegal' Aliens Commit Crime at a Far Higher Rate Than Citizens and 'Legal' Immigrants

When making immigration policy, it is important that we be honest about the facts. In this case, the available facts appear to show that illegal aliens (primarily Mexican and Central American) commit crimes at a much higher rate than the rest of the population. But, as noted above, much of the research on illegal aliens and crimes is marked by a deliberate attempt to ignore such data.

As noted in the January 2019 *City Journal* article by Barry Latzer titled "Do Illegal Aliens Have High Crime Rates?" Per Latzer: No amount of crime by those who enter this country unlawfully should be acceptable because it is "extra" crime that wouldn't occur if our border security were effective. Crime by illegal aliens is costly.

The real issue underlying the current public debate is whether the crimes of illegal immigrants are so numerous that they provide a compelling reason, or at least a powerful supporting argument, for urgent spending to secure our southern border. To answer that question, the simple fact of the matter is that an examination of SCAAP reporting that relies on tested methods of statistical analysis clearly demonstrates that:

- In states with significant illegal alien populations, illegal aliens are incarcerated at a much higher rate than citizens and lawfully-present aliens.

- Illegal aliens commit crimes at a higher rate than U.S. citizens and lawfully-present aliens.

Until lawmakers in the United States are able to review accurate, transparent data regarding the rate at which illegal aliens commit criminal offenses, they will, inevitably, continue making bad immigration policy. As a result, too many Americans will continue becoming victims of preventable crimes, and the terrible stories that occupy our news cycles all too often will remain a regular part of daily life in this country.

Hopefully, this study (and chapter content and conclusions) represents a step in the right direction, and will encourage legislators, the media, and academic researchers to demand better information on illegal aliens and crime.

Non-Citizens Committed a Disproportionate Share of Federal Crimes

The Center for Immigration Studies is an independent, non-partisan, non-profit research organization founded in 1985, and per Steven A. Camarota's January 2018 report from The Center for Immigration Studies titled "Non-Citizens Committed a Disproportionate Share of Federal Crimes, 2011-16" the findings show that in 2018, 21% of those convicted of non-immigration crimes were non-citizens—2.5 times their share of the population. Among the findings of the new data:

Areas where non-citizens account for a much larger share of convictions than their 8.4 percent share of the adult population include:

- 42.4 percent of kidnapping convictions.

- 31.5 percent of drug convictions.

- 22.9 percent of money laundering convictions.

- 13.4 percent of administration of justice offenses (e.g. witness tampering, obstruction, and contempt).

- 17.8 percent of economic crimes (e.g. larceny, embezzlement, and fraud).

- 13 percent of other convictions (e.g. bribery, civil rights, environmental, and prison offenses); and

- 12.8 percent of auto thefts.

Areas where non-citizens account for a share of convictions roughly equal to their share of the adult population include:

- 9.6 percent of assaults.

- 8.9 percent of homicides; and

- 7.5 percent of firearm crimes.

Areas where non-citizens account for a share of convictions lower than their share of the adult population include:

- 4.1 percent of sex crimes.

- 3.3 percent of robberies.

- 4.5 percent of arsons; and

- 0 percent of burglaries.

11 – Unbalanced Budgets, Prop Madness, Stolen Stimulus, Voter Fraud & Boondoggles

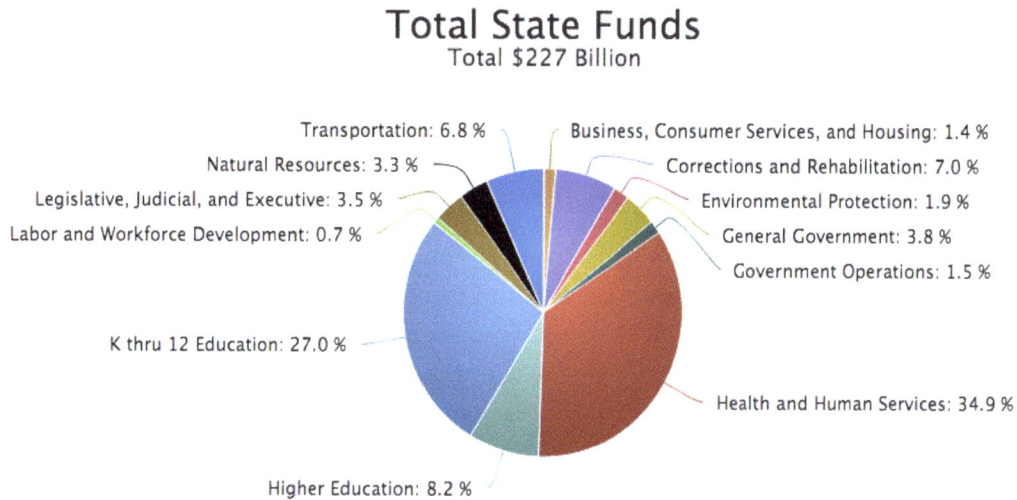

Total State Funds
Total $227 Billion

Transportation: 6.8 %

Natural Resources: 3.3 %

Legislative, Judicial, and Executive: 3.5 %

Labor and Workforce Development: 0.7 %

K thru 12 Education: 27.0 %

Higher Education: 8.2 %

Business, Consumer Services, and Housing: 1.4 %

Corrections and Rehabilitation: 7.0 %

Environmental Protection: 1.9 %

General Government: 3.8 %

Government Operations: 1.5 %

Health and Human Services: 34.9 %

Credit: StreetsblogCalifornia - General categories of spending from Governor Newsom's proposed budget.

From the 2020 research brief by Joel Kotkin and Marshall Toplansky *Beyond Feudalism: A Strategy to Restore California's Middle Class at the* Chapman University Center for Demographics & Policy:

Back in the 1950s and 1960s, Californians paid relatively high taxes (for the time), but got plenty for their money. Californians saw their taxes used to build a massive, statewide system of water storage and distribution, beautiful freeways to tie together the growing cities, and the finest public university in the world.

The late historian and one-time state librarian Kevin Starr observed that, under the governorship of Pat Brown, California enjoyed "… a golden age of consensus and achievement, a founding era in which California fashioned and celebrated itself as an emergent nation-state." In 1971, the economist John Kenneth Galbraith described the state government as run by "a proud, competent civil service," and enjoying among "the best school systems in the country."

California's advantages in those times lured people and businesses from elsewhere. This is not happening so much today. *Chief Executive Magazine's* 2019 survey found California to be the worst state in which to do business, while arch-rival Texas ranked best, and prime regional competitors Arizona and Nevada placed in the top five.

The Canada-based Fraser Institute ranked the state 49th in economic freedom, largely due to the enormous regulatory burdens imposed on businesses. The Tax Foundation's 2019 State Business Tax Climate Index, which evaluates taxes in five categories, also lists California at number 49, with only New Jersey trailing. Kiplinger Report's summary map confirms those findings.

Remarkably, such rankings do not seem to bother Sacramento's political elites. California's legislature is now made up largely of people with virtually no business experience. Among the Democrats— the party that dominates California's 2019-2020 state senate—79% do not have any private sector experience. In contrast, Democrats in the Texas legislature are more than twice as likely to claim private-sector experience outside the field of law, while 75% of Texas Republicans earn a living in business, farming, or medicine.

California's Democrat supermajority do a poor job of assessing the costs and benefits of capital-investment projects since politicians do not personally bear the costs and benefits of the projects or of their calculation errors. In fact, politicians have an incentive to exaggerate the benefits and hide true costs, as was done with the bullet train, to build support for these projects.

In contrast, private investors and private operators generally have an incentive to develop accurate projections of capital projects because, if they are wrong, they will typically bear the costs, and, if they are right, they can reap any profits from the wise stewardship of resources.

California's General Fund Relies on Bailouts and Billionaires

This January 2021 article "California's General Fund Relies on Bailouts and Billionaires" comes from the California Policy Center's Edward Ring:

The Governor's Budget for 2019-2020 projected 69 percent of all general fund revenue to come from personal income taxes. Another 20 percent came from sales taxes and 9 percent from corporation taxes. The other 3 percent came from a variety of sources, mostly insurance tax. While property tax is a significant source of revenue, it is a local revenue source and only impacts the state budget insofar as when property taxes go up, it relieves pressure on the state to allocate more out of the general fund to support local schools and other local agencies.

Bearing in mind that nearly seven out of every ten dollars going into California's general fund comes from personal income taxes, the following chart shows who is paying those taxes. Using Franchise Tax Board data from 2018, and sorted by the reported taxable income of the 16.8 million Californians filing returns, it is immediately apparent that nearly everyone paying taxes made under $100,000. That is, 13.2 million Californians, or 78 percent of the people filing state income tax returns, contributed only $7.8 billion or 9 percent of the total personal income taxes collected.

On the other side of this chart below, to the right, the flipside of this top-heavy equation is presented. There were 89,000 Californians in 2018 that reported taxable income of over $1.0 million. At one-half of one percent of the total filers, their numbers don't even register on the chart. But the orange column, representing the $34.5 billion they paid in taxes, dwarfs the contributions from the other brackets. One-half of one percent of California's taxpayers paid 40 percent of all personal income taxes.

**California State Government
Income Tax Revenue by Bracket**

Data for Calendar Year 2018: filers (blue), collections (orange)
Vertical axis: filers (millions), revenue (billions)

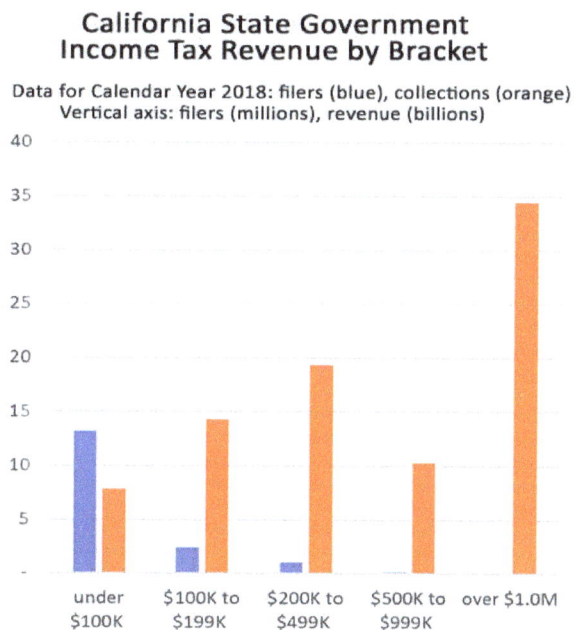

Credit: California Policy Center.

Moving one notch to the left to incorporate the filers who reported taxable income in excess of $500,000 in 2018 yields further evidence of just how top-heavy California's reliance is on the wealthy to fund state government operations: Only 275,000 individuals, representing 1.6 percent of tax filers, paid 56 percent of all personal income tax revenue, which in turn is 40 percent of all general fund revenue in the State of California.

It is easy enough to scoff at the prospect of extremely wealthy people having to pay more. But one way or another, California's state government needs more money. Governor Newsom's proposed 2021-2022 state budget proposes record spending. He does this in the face of structural deficits that existed before COVID-19 trashed California's economy.

The pandemic drove the global economy online, disproportionately helping California's tech industry, that contributed evening more to California's tax revenues—but how much higher can tech stocks soar, and how much more will the tech billionaires continue to pay?

California's Budget "Surplus" Ignores Crushing Debt Burden

This January 2019 article "California's Budget "Surplus" Ignores Crushing Debt Burden" comes from the California Policy Center's Edward Ring:

When new governor, Gavin Newsom, delivered an inaugural address in January 2019, it accurately reflected the mentality of his supporters. Triumphalist, defiant, and filled with grand plans. But are these plans grand, or grandiose?

Will Governor Newsom try to deliver everything he promised during his campaign, and if so, can California's state government really deliver to 40 million residents universal preschool, free community college, and single payer health care for everyone? It's reasonable to assume that to execute all of these projects would cost hundreds—plural—of billions per year. Where will this money come from?

While California's 2021-22 budget outlook currently offers a unique surplus in excess of $76 billion, that is an order of magnitude less than what it will cost to do what Newsom is planning to do in the long run. And this surplus, while genuine, is the result of an extraordinary, unsustainable surge in income tax payments by wealthy people.

California's tax revenues are highly dependent on collections from the top one-percent of earners, and over the past few years, the top one-percent has been doing very, very well. Can this go on?

To illustrate just how unusually swollen California's current state tax revenues have gotten, compare state tax collections in fiscal-year-end (FYE) 6/30/2017 (our most recent available data) to seven years earlier, in 2010. Back in 2010, California was in the grip of the great recession. Total state tax revenue was $94 billion, and $44 billion of that was from personal income taxes.

Skip to FYE 6/30/2017, and total state tax revenue was $148 billion, and $86 billion was from personal income taxes. This means that 80 percent of the increase in state tax revenue over the seven years through 6/30/2017 was represented by the increase is collections from individual taxpayers, which doubled.

It isn't hard to figure out why this happened. Between 2010 and 2017 the tech heavy NASDAQ tripled in value, from 2,092 to 6,153. In that same period, Silicon Valley's big three tech stocks all quadrupled. Adjusting for splits, Apple shares went from $35 to $144, Facebook opened in May 2012 at $38, and went up to $150, Google moved from $216 to $908.

While California's tech industry was booming over the past decade, California real estate boomed in parallel. In June 2010 the median home price in California was $335,000; by June 2017 it had jumped to $502,000. Along the California coast, median home prices have gone much higher. Santa Clara County now has a median home price of $1.3 million, double what it was less than a decade ago.

As people sell their overpriced homes to move inland or out-of-state, and as tech workers cash out their burgeoning stock options, hundreds of billions of capital gains generate tens of billions in state tax revenue.

But can homes continue to double in value every six or seven years? Can tech stocks continue to quadruple in value every six or seven years? Apparently Gavin Newsom thinks they can. Reality may beg to differ.

Just a Slowdown in Capital Gains Will Cause Tax Revenue to Crash

The problem with Gavin Newsom's grand plans is that it won't take a downturn in asset values to sink them. All that has to happen to throw California's state budget into the red is for these asset values to stop going up. Just a plateauing of their value–will wreak havoc on state and local government budgets in California.

The reasons for this are clear enough. Wealthy people, making a lot of money, pay the lion's share of state income taxes, and state income taxes constitute the lion's share of state revenues.

Returning to the 2017 fiscal year, of the $86 billion collected in state income taxes, $28 billion was from only 70,437 filers, all of them making over $1.0 million in that year. Another $7.3 billion came from 131,120 filers who made between a half-million and one million in that year. And since making over $200,000 in income in one year is still considered doing very, very well, it's noteworthy that another 807,000 of those filers ponied up another $15.1 billion in FYE 6/30/2017.

There is an obvious conclusion here: if people are no longer making killings in capital gains on their sales of stock and real estate, California's tax revenues will instantly decline by $20 billion, if not much more. And it won't even take a slump in asset prices to cause this, just a leveling off.

Debt, Unfunded Pension Liabilities, Neglected Infrastructure

When considering how weakening tax revenues in California will impact the ability of the state and local governments to cope with existing debt, it's hard to know where to begin.

To get an idea of the scope of this problem, the California Policy Center released an analysis of California's total state and local government debt. California's total state and local government debt as of 6/30/2017 is over $1.5 trillion. More than half of it, $846 billion, is in the form of unfunded pension liabilities.

Calculating pension liabilities is a complex process, with controversy surrounding what assumptions are valid. In basic terms, a pension liability is the amount of money that must be on hand today, in order for withdrawals on that amount–plus investment earnings on that amount as it declines–to eventually pay all future pensions earned to-date for all active and retired participants in the fund. Put another way, a pension liability is the present value of all pension benefits–earned so far–that must be paid out in the future. The amount by which the total pension liability exceeds the actual amount of assets invested in a fund is referred to as the unfunded liability.

The controversy over what is an accurate estimate of a pension liability arises due to the extreme sensitivity that number has to how much the fund managers think they can earn. Using the official projection, which is typically around 7.0 percent per year, the official pension liability for all of California's government pension funds is "only" $316 billion.

But Moody's, the credit rating agency, discounts pension liabilities with the Citigroup Pension Liability Index (CPLI), which is based on high grade corporate bond yields. In June 2017, it was 3.87 percent, and using that rate, CPC analysts estimated the unfunded liability for California's state and local employee pension systems at $846 billion. Using the methodology offered by the prestigious Stanford Institute for Economic Policy Research, California's unfunded pension debt is even higher, at $1.26 trillion!

Where pension liabilities move from controversial theories to decidedly non-academic real world consequences, however, is in the budget busting realm of how much California's government agencies have to pay these funds each year.

California's state budget is extraordinarily vulnerable to economic downturns

California's public sector employers contributed an estimated $31 billion to the pension systems in 2018. Extrapolating from officially announced pension rate hikes from CalPERS, California's largest pension system, by 2024 those payments are projected to increase to $59 billion. And these aggressive increases the pension systems are requiring are a reflection more of their crackdown on the terms of the "catch up" payments employers must make to reduce the unfunded liability than on a reduction to their expected real rate of return.

Huge unfunded pension liabilities are another reason, equally significant, as to why California's state budget is extraordinarily vulnerable to economic downturns. If assets stop appreciating, not only will income tax revenue plummet—at the same time, expenses will go up, because pension funds will demand far higher annual contributions to make up the shortfall in investment earnings.

A cautionary overview of the economic challenges facing California's state government would not be complete without mentioning the neglected infrastructure in the state. For decades, this vast state, with nearly 40 million residents, has been falling behind in infrastructure maintenance. The American Society of Civil Engineers assigns poor grades to California's infrastructure. They rate over 1,300 bridges in California as "structurally deficient," and 678 of California's dams are "high hazard."

They estimate $44 billion needs to be spent to bring drinking water infrastructure up to modern standards, and $26 billion on wastewater infrastructure. They estimate over 50 percent of California's roads are in "poor condition." In every category–aviation, bridges, dams, drinking water, wastewater, hazardous waste, the energy grid, inland waterways, levees, ports, public parks, roads, rail, transit, and schools, California is behind. The fix? Literally hundreds of additional billions.

What Governor Newsom might consider is refocusing California's state budget priorities on areas where the state already faces daunting financial challenges, rather than acquiescing to the utopian fever dreams of his constituency and his colleagues.

Facing Recall, California's Governor Blows Out the State Budget

This section is from the May 2021 report "Facing Recall, California's Governor Blows Out The State Budget" by the Hoover Institution's Lee Ohanian:

Santa has already arrived in California for 2021, dressed as Governor Gavin Newsom, who is awash in new cash arising from much higher tax revenues than anticipated, plus bailout funds from the federal Santa Clauses in Washington, DC.

Newsom's new budget proposal will be throwing dollars to most everyone and everything on the Democratic party's wish list, including billions on expenditures that never came close to making the cut when resources were scarcer, largely because they were so far down any sensible priority list that they never were going to see the light of day.

Newsom is calling this record $267 billion budget, which is 28 percent more than the pre-COVID 2019–20 budget a "historic, transformational budget. This is not a budget that plays small ball. We're not playing in the margins. We are not trying to fail more efficiently."

Do you know what "efficient failure" means? I don't, but no matter, this budget is destined to fail on a grand scale. Not small-ball failure. Really big, beach-ball failure.

Santa's elves didn't create this largesse. They can't print money that fast. What was feared to be a $5 billion deficit by budget analysts last year turned into a $74 billion surplus, thanks to those vilified one-percenters who really stepped up and delivered for everyone else in the state by paying a ton of taxes last year, reflecting capital gains on the sale of stocks, homes, and other assets, all of which are taxed as ordinary income in California, with some paying a tax rate as high as 13.3 percent.

Add on another $26 billion from the feds, who also know a thing or two about how to blow out a budget, and this provides the $100-plus billion that Newsom refers to as helping fund "a transformational budget that doesn't play small ball." Put another way, $100 billion is close to half of the GDP of Portugal.

Listening to Newsom's speech, you would think that his proposal for doling out this $100 billion is entirely his. But it is far from that. Roughly half of the state surplus—around $38 billion—must be spent on public schools, used to pay off state debt, and deposited in the state's reserve account.

What California Could Have Done With the $31 Billion Lost by the EDD

Per the July 2021 California Globe article "What California Could Have Done With the $30 Billion Lost by the EDD: All 40 million Californians could dine at the French Laundry with Gavin Newsom" by Thomas Buckley:

The financial loss to pandemic economic stimulus fraud in the estimated amount of $30+ billion by the California Employment Development Department (EDD) has no comparison.

While estimates of the actual amount–an exact amount will never be known–range from $12 billion to more than $40 billion, experts in the field tend to coalesce around the $30+ billion figure. It must be noted that this enormous EDD fraud did not have to happen, that the EDD's systems could have been fixed quickly and cheaply 15 months ago, preventing the vast majority of the loss.

Sadly, it must also be noted that that money is never coming back; while law enforcement may occasionally tout the seizure and re-sale of the Ferrari a person bought with the ill-gotten gains from filing 147 fraudulent claims, an overwhelming percentage of the funds were stolen by organized international criminal syndicates and has disappeared permanently into the ether.

To put the scale of the problem into perspective, it may be helpful to consider what else, besides giving every California resident $750 directly, could have been done with that $30+ billion. First, if the state hadn't lost it to fraud California would not currently owe the federal government the $24 billion it borrowed to keep its system solvent. That would mean that businesses across the state would not be faced–as they are currently–with paying additional money into the unemployment system to cover the debt.

While the issue is not completely settled, it now stands that each employer will have to pay an extra $21 per year per employee, with that number expected to grow each year until it reaches $420 per year per employee in 10 years. This extra fee will damage already struggling small businesses in particular and definitely put a kink in California's overall economic climate and at a competitive disadvantage compared to other states (at this point, the much-touted state budget surplus is not being touched to repay the funds).

California's Ongoing Campaign, Voting & Election Irregularities

California's November 3, 2020, election was marred by significant voting and registration irregularities, according to Election Integrity Project® California, Inc. (EIPCa), a nonpartisan IRC 501(c)(3) charity and watchdog seeking answers on over 2 million documented registration and voting anomalies.

EIPCa analyzed the state's official voter list of February 9, 2021; and reported its findings to California's Secretary of State (SOS) Shirley Weber on June 17, 2021. This followed EIPCa reports of 2020 cross-state voting on April 30 and May 18, 2021, that the Secretary has ignored. EIPCa's June report cites California's election code that requires officials to provide timely answers to citizens' questions.

Secretary of State's (SOS) Office Awards Questionable $35M Contract to Firm Linked to Biden Campaign

As per the Fox News December 2020 report "Republicans demand probe into Padilla's $35M grant to Biden-linked firm, claim 'misuse' of taxpayer funds" by Brooke Singman:

The lawmakers say the California Secretary of State's (SOS) office used CARES Act grant money to fund a contract for a consulting firm working for the Democratic Party.

Republicans on the House Oversight and House Administration Committees are demanding answers from then California Secretary of State Alex Padilla about a "highly questionable" $35 million contract his office awarded to a firm linked to the Biden campaign, claiming it was a "misuse of taxpayer money and a violation of the law."

Padilla's office, according to House Oversight Committee Ranking Member James Comer, R-Ky., Administration Committee Ranking Member Rodney Davis, R-Ill., and Rep. Jody Hice, R-Ga., allegedly used Help America Vote Act (HAVA) grant money from the coronavirus stimulus package, known as the CARES Act, to fund a voter contract with SKD Knickerbocker— a public affairs and political consulting firm the Republican lawmakers described as "Joe Biden's main election campaign advisory firm."

Padilla was the identify politics frontrunner to be appointed to Vice President-elect Kamala Harris' Senate seat and as anticipated, Governor Newsom appointed him to this position. In a domino effect, Shirley Weber succeeded him as SOS when Padilla filled Senator Harris' vacancy when she became Vice-President.

The Republican lawmakers wrote that they provided documents to the office of the inspector general which "appear to show that the California Secretary of State's Office planned to use HAVA money for voter contact. As you know, the use of HAVA funds for voter contact is a violation of the law," they wrote. "According to the U.S. Election Assistance Commission, HAVA grants cannot be used to get out the vote or encourage voting."

They added that the CARES Act "is very specific about the use of these funds, which must be used to 'prevent, prepare for, and respond to coronavirus, domestically or internationally, for the 2020 Federal election cycle. The lawmakers claimed that the $35 million contract was "apparently intended to provide a partisan firm the opportunity to use taxpayer money to influence the federal election."

The *Sacramento Bee*, first reported on the contract, which was awarded on Aug. 13, 2020, after an "expedited approval process." SKD Knickerbocker employs a number of former Obama communications officials and others who have worked with Democrats in the past. On the firm's website, it states: "Joe Biden, Kamala Harris and all of our clients who fought for the soul of the nation….Thank you."

The firm's website also lists its "2020 Clients," which include Biden for President and other

Democratic candidates for public office. Biden senior campaign adviser Anita Dunn is a partner and founding member of SKD Knickerbocker. She returned to the firm after Election Day.

New Lawsuit Alleges State of California Violated National Voter Registration Act

The section below per the California Globe October 2019 report "New Lawsuit Alleges State of California Violated National Voter Registration Act: California failing to verify citizenship before placing voters on the voter rolls" by Katy Grimes:

California is violating federal law by failing to verify citizenship before placing voters on the voter rolls, according to attorneys Harmeet Dhillon and Mark Meuser. They say this compromises the integrity of our election system.

Calling this "Judicial Watch 2.0," Dhillon and Meuser filed a federal lawsuit on behalf of Plaintiffs Roxanne Beckford Hoge, Ali Mazarei, and Corrin Rankin against then Alex Padilla, California Secretary of State, and Steve Gordon, Director of California Department of Motor Vehicles for violations of the National Voter Registration Act of 1993.

The lawsuit alleges that the state is neglecting two of its three duties as outlined by the voter act. Judicial Watch already filed a federal lawsuit against Los Angeles County and the State of California over their failure to clean their voter rolls and to produce election-related records as required by the federal National Voter Registration Act.

"Eleven of California's 58 counties have registration rates exceeding 100% of the age-eligible citizenry," Judicial Watch said. "California has the highest rate of inactive registrations of any state in the country. Los Angeles County has the highest number of inactive registrations of any single county in the country."

"The National Voter Registration Act says three things," attorney Meuser said in an interview. "Number 1 is that the state shall determine eligibility. Eligibility and citizenship go hand in hand," Meuser said. "All they are doing is looking at state records for felons or duplicate registrations." Meuser said the United States Supreme Court says state records can be used for citizenship verification. But California is picking and choosing which records to use, rather than using all three qualifying issues.

"Number two is to notify the voter(s) of the determination," Meuser said. "The NVRA requires Padilla to guarantee that only eligible citizens are registered to vote. Since citizenship is at the core of voter eligibility, Padilla is violating the NVRA by omitting a citizenship verification as a part of the eligibility verification process.

California DMV's "Motor Voter" Program

A 2018 state audit found the California DMV's "motor voter" program only recently implemented, was riddled with technical problems that led to hundreds of thousands of discrepancies in voter registrations. Last September, the DMV sent out 23,000 "erroneous" voter registrations they blamed on "technical errors." In September 2019, the DMV sent out

23,000 "erroneous" voter registrations they blamed on 'technical errors,'" California Globe reported. "Padilla proclaimed himself 'extremely disappointed and deeply frustrated,'" but nothing changed.

The lawsuit alleges the Secretary of State's office has "forsaken his duty to ensure that non-citizens" are kept off voter rolls. "In direct violation of his duties to ensure that only eligible voters are placed on the voter rolls, then California Secretary of State Alex Padilla has established a pattern and practice of doing nothing to verify that a potential voter is a United States citizen, thus causing non-citizens to be placed on the voter rolls," the lawsuit says

"The Secretary of State has forsaken his duty to ensure that non-citizens are never placed on the voter rolls, and has relegated his office to that of a glorified clerk simply transmitting the data from the voter registration application to the counties for data entry purposes," the lawsuit alleges.

Meuser said two of the plaintiffs–Roxanne Hoge and Ali Mazarei–are immigrants who earned their citizenship, and are passionate about ensuring the integrity of the voting rolls to ensure that only citizens are registered to vote. The attorneys sent SOS Padilla a Notice of Violations Letter which revealed how Padilla was violating the NVRA by failing to ensure eligibility of voters prior to putting their names on the voter rolls.

The Padilla Notice Letter made four demands:

a. Start receiving from the DMV documentation regarding an individual's citizenship, so that you may fulfill your NVRA requirements to ensure eligibility prior to placing a registrant on the voter rolls;

b. Begin reviewing all voter registrations and compare the voter registration with databases maintained by the state of California to ensure that all registrants are eligible to vote before you place them on the California voter rolls;

c. Review all current California registered voters to determine eligibility and send notices to all non-citizens who happen to be on the voter rolls; and

d. Update the California NVRA Manual to specifically lay out the responsibilities of the registrar of voters in verifying eligibility with state and county databases to determine eligibility.

Padilla's response said he does not believe that he is violating the NVRA, and therefore declined to make any changes, the lawsuit says. Yet shortly after the launch of the Motor Voter law, it became clear that some legal non-citizens were placed on the voter rolls. "Padilla had no procedure in place to ensure that an applicant was eligible to vote prior to placing them on the voter rolls."

The lawsuit also notes a crucial piece of the equation: "The DMV does not transfer to the Secretary of State the citizenship information obtained from the Proof of Identity Documents, although it is required by the NVRA to transfer to the Secretary of State "a completed voter registration portion of an application for a State motor vehicle driver's license accepted at a State motor vehicle authority."

EIPCa Seeks Answers From SOS Weber to the Following Questions on Behalf of California Voters

Per the 2020 Election Integrity Project® California (EIPCa) report "Questions Surround Irregularities in California's 2020 Election" by Linda Paine:

"Many in the nation are questioning the validity of the 2020 general election in their states", said EIPCa President Linda Paine. "Mass irregularities in California's registration and voting numbers continue to erode voter confidence here and we are hopeful Secretary Weber will immediately address our questions."

1. Why are there almost 124,000 more votes counted in California's November 3, 2020 election than voters recorded as voting in that election? And why is most of the discrepancy driven by 116,000 vote-by-mail ballots with no apparent voter identified in VoteCal's voting histories? Click here for a list by county.

2. Why do more than 7,700 voters have TWO November 3, 2020, votes credited to their voting histories? These are two votes credited to each of 7,700 unique (non-duplicated) registration ID numbers in the state database. This indicates mass double voting, a significant programming error in the state's registration system, or both.

3. Why does California have 1.8 million more registered voters than eligible citizens and why did this overage rise 72% in the 2020 election cycle?

4. Why did California's on-line and DMV registration systems change 33,000 foreign-born voters' birthplaces of record to "California" or "United States", potentially masking non-citizens unlawfully registered to vote? Similarly, why were 76,000 birthplaces changed from another U.S. state to California?

California's Bullet Train: A Boondoggle in the Making

The section below id from the February 2019 "The California High-Speed Train that Wasn't: The Opportunity Cost of Megaprojects" article by Daniel Herriges of Strong Towns:

Time reported in February 2019 that California Governor Gavin Newsom was abandoning the state's plan to build high-speed rail connecting its major cities, a project which, at last count, had ballooned to an estimated cost of $77 billion and climbing. A number of other outlets also adopted the "it's dead" line. What Gov. Newsom actually said, in his annual State of the State address, was a bit more confusing:

"There's been too little oversight and not enough transparency," Newsom said. "Right now, there simply isn't a path to get from Sacramento to San Diego, let alone from San Francisco to L.A. I wish there were."

But Newsom's administration reiterated the project isn't dead, more like indefinitely on hold.

"Abandoning the high-speed rail entirely will have wasted billions of dollars, with nothing but broken promises and lawsuits to show for it," said Newsom at Tuesday's State of the State Address. "I have no interest in giving $3.5 billion federal dollars allocated for this project back."

Regardless, it's clear a fast train trip between SF and LA isn't becoming a reality any time soon. Instead, we get a train between the mid-size cities of Bakersfield and Merced, only a 2.5-hour drive, and with very little you can do without a car at either end of that trip.

In November 2008, California voters approved Proposition 1A, a $9.95 billion bond measure authorizing construction of a high-speed "bullet train" between downtown San Francisco and the greater Los Angeles area. The vote was 53 percent in favor and 47 percent opposed. The ballot measure contained key details regarding the project's cost, dedicated tracks, trip time, and financing plan. Many of these details have been changed repeatedly since 2008.

The Cost: A Moving Target

This April 2016 report "California's High-Speed Rail Authority Wins Dishonor of the California Golden Fleece® Award" comes from Independent Institute researchers Lawrence J. McQuillan and Hayeon Carol Park:

Before the 2008 vote on the bond measure, the California High-Speed Rail Authority said: "The total cost to develop and construct the entire high-speed train system would be about $45 billion." Proposition 1A also promised voters that the train system would operate without taxpayer subsidies: "The planned passenger service by the authority in the corridor or usable segment thereof will not require a local, state, or federal operating subsidy." Soon after voters approved the project, however, cost projections escalated.

In its original 2012 Business Plan, the CHSRA set the price tag at a staggering $98 billion. Public and political outcry caused rail officials to quickly backtrack. Just five months later, the revised 2012 Business Plan lowered the cost by $30 billion by moving to a "blended" route: one that would share existing rail tracks in urban areas with other train systems, rather than building new dedicated tracks.

Based on this radical redesign, CHSRA said the entire 520-mile system would be completed in 2029 at a cost of $68 billion, but only by eliminating high-speed service between Los Angeles and Anaheim and between San Jose and San Francisco.

Then in 2016, the CHSRA Business Plan lowered the cost by roughly $4 billion net, to $64 billion, through a combination of vaguely specified "design refinements," "system optimization," "value engineering," and "lessons learned from bids."

At this point, the ever-changing cost estimates defy belief. As noted by Dan Walters, *Sacramento Bee* columnist and longtime observer of state government: "Those charged with building California's north-south bullet train system have been more or less making it up as they go along."

But regardless of whether the final cost is $64 billion, $68 billion, $98 billion, or even higher, the reality should be clear: The cost far exceeds the $45 billion approved by voters in 2008 were told the high-speed train would whisk travelers from San Francisco to Los Angeles in a "maximum nonstop service travel time" that "shall not exceed" 2 hours and 40 minutes.

Travel Time: Bait and Switch on Train Speed

This specific trip time was often mentioned by supporters to sell the bond measure to voters. But with the blended approach, the fastest time between these cities is now estimated by the CHSRA to be 3 hours and 8 minutes, with zero nonstop trips planned—another violation of Proposition 1A. But more realistic trip times are expected to be 3 hours and 50 minutes, or more, under real-world travel conditions.

The original 2:40 trip time assumed that trains would operate at peak speeds of 220 mph, and "sustained revenue operating speeds of at least 200 miles per hour." But under the blended approach, high-speed trains must share tracks with commuter trains and freight trains, forcing them to slow down at the urban "bookends." And today's older urban tracks can typically handle maximum speeds of only 125 mph.

In February 2016, officials announced that the first operating leg of the high-speed train system would be built for $21 billion from downtown San Jose to an agricultural field in Shafter, north of Bakersfield, which would begin operating by 2025. The previous plan called for trains to operate first from Merced to Burbank by 2022, three years earlier.

This change in the initial route might appear innocent, but by moving the first leg of construction further north, officials can delay construction on a tunnel through the Tehachapi and San Gabriel Mountains, which is likely to bust the current $64 billion budget according to a *Los Angeles Times* special report.

12 – Illiberal Academia, Failing Public Schools & Critical Race Theory Madness

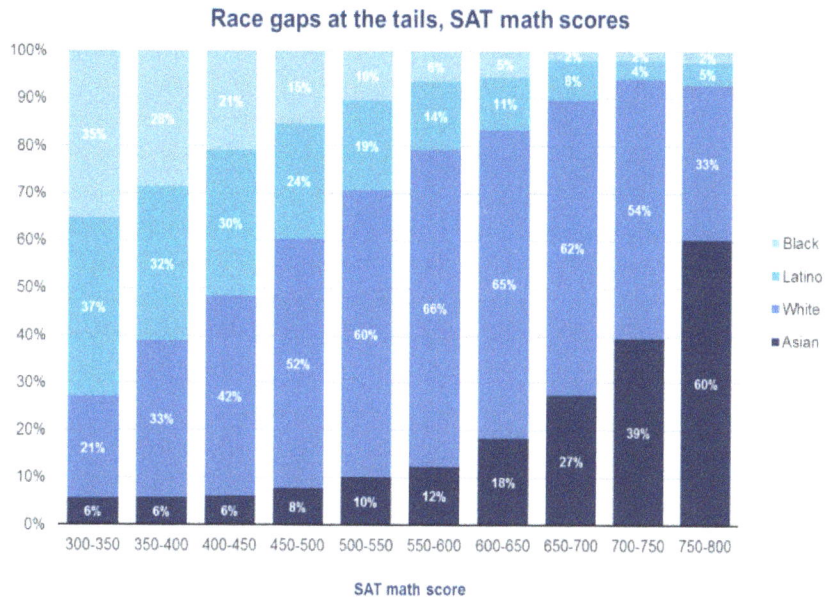

Credit: College Board, SAT Math Percentile Ranks for 2015 College Bound Seniors.

When considering the influence of unions on American society, there are vast differences depending on what type of union one considers. Private sector unions, for all the criticisms they may deserve, have nonetheless played a vital role in securing rights for the American worker. Subject to appropriate regulations, private sector unions have the opportunity to continue to play a vital role in American society.

Public sector unions, on the other hand, should be illegal because they are a monopsony (the labor equivalent of a product monopoly). Why? Because they negotiate with elected officials who they help elect. They negotiate for a share of coerced tax revenue, rather than for a share of profits, meaning there are no competitive checks on how much they can demand.

The agenda of public sector unions is inherently in conflict with the public interest. But given the reality of public sector unions, it is important to recognize that some public sector unions are worse than others.

Public safety unions, for example, have successfully lobbied for pension benefits that are not sustainable. This calls for a difficult but necessary economic discussion that can only end two ways–either these pension benefits are going to be reduced, or cities and counties across California and elsewhere will go bankrupt in the next major recession. But public safety unions have not undermined their profession the way the teachers unions have.

The teachers unions are guilty of all the problems common to all public sector unions. They, too, have negotiated unsustainable rates of pay and benefits. They, too, elect their own bosses, negotiate inefficient work rules, have an insatiable need for more public funds, and protect incompetent members. But the teachers union is worse than all other public sector unions for one reason that eclipses all others: Their agenda is negatively affecting how we socialize and educate our children, the next generation of Americans.

California's children are California's future, and 21st century teachers union leaders have all but destroyed the quality of education these children receive. They oppose charter schools, they oppose school choice, they oppose vouchers, they oppose extending tenure requirements, they oppose reform of work rules governing layoff and dismissal policies, and they support curricula that indoctrinates instead of educates.

Why Teachers Unions Are the Worst of the Worst

This August 2018 article "Why Teachers Unions are the Worst of the Worst California" comes from the California Policy Center's Edward Ring:

One of the most compelling examples of just how much harm the teachers union has done to California's schools was the 2014 case *Vergara v. the State of California*.

In this case, attorneys representing public school students argued that union negotiated work rules harmed their ability to receive a quality education. In particular, they questioned rules governing tenure (too soon), dismissals (too hard), and layoffs (based on seniority instead of merit). In the closing arguments, the plaintiff's lead attorney referenced testimony from the defendant's expert witnesses to show that these and other rules had a negative disproportionate impact on students in disadvantaged communities.

Despite winning in the lower courts, the Vergara case was eventually dismissed by the California Supreme Court. Teachers still get tenure after less than two years of classroom observation. Incompetent teachers are still nearly impossible to fire. And whenever it is necessary to reduce teacher headcount in a district, the senior teachers stay and the new teachers go, regardless of how well or poorly these teachers were doing their jobs. The consequences of these self-serving work rules are more than academic.

The evidence that California's public schools are failing is everywhere. Los Angeles, a city whose residents are–perhaps more than anywhere else–representative of America's future, is home to the Los Angeles Unified School District (LAUSD), with 640,000 K-12 students. And as reported in a 2018 LA School Report, according to the new "California School Dashboard," a ratings system that replaced the Academic Performance Index, LAUSD is failing to educate hundreds of thousands of students. In the most recent year of results, 52 percent of LAUSD's schools earned a D or F in English language arts, and 50 percent earned a D or F in math. Fifty percent of LAUSD's schools are failing or nearly failing to teach their students English or math.

They Attack Innovative Charter Schools

In the face of failure, you would think LAUSD, and other failing school districts would embrace bipartisan, obvious reforms such as those highlighted in the Vergara case. But instead, these unions are relentlessly trying to unionize charter schools, which would force those schools to adhere to the same union work rules. In Los Angeles, the Alliance Network of charter schools has delivered demonstrably better educational outcomes for less money, while serving nearly identical student populations.

How does it help to impose union work rules on charter schools that are succeeding academically? How does that help the children who are America's future?

They Promote a Left-Wing Political Agenda

The other way the teachers union is unique among public sector unions is their hyper-partisanship. Despite and often in defiance of their memberships, nearly all unions are left-wing partisan organizations. Nearly all of them support left-wing causes and Democratic political candidates. But the teachers unions do so with a zeal that dwarfs their counterparts. Larry Sand, a former LAUSD teacher and prolific observer of teachers union antics, has spent years documenting their left wing agenda.

For example, reporting on the annual conventions of the two largest national teachers unions, Sand writes: "The National Education Association (NEA) convention...gave us a clue which theory would become reality when the union passed quite a few über liberal New Business Items, maintained its lopsided leftward political spending, and gave rogue quarterback Colin Kaepernick a human rights award. And here in the Golden State, the California Teachers Association (CTA) continues its one-way spending on progressive initiatives and endorsed 35 state legislators in the 2018 June primary–all Democrats."

A week after the NEA convention, the other national teachers union, the American Federation of Teachers (AFT) held its yearly convention and left absolutely no doubt as to its future political direction. The resolutions passed by the union at the convention would make any socialist proud.

Universal health care–whether single-payer or MediCare for All, full public funding for, and free tuition at all public colleges and universities, and universal, full-day, and cost-free child care are what AFT wants for the country. Additionally, the union resolved to double per-pupil expenditures for low-income K-12 districts and to 'tax the rich' to fully fund Individuals with Disabilities Education Act (IDEA), Title I and state allocations to public colleges and universities.'"

They Support Left-Wing Student Indoctrination

This left-wing political agenda finds its way into the classroom, of course. At the same time as

California's K-12 public school students are not being effectively taught English or math skills, they are being exposed to agenda-driven political and cultural indoctrination.

Again, as documented by Larry Sand: "Nor are textbooks safe. Communist and notorious America-hater Howard Zinn's "A People's History of the United States" is assigned in many high school history classes. Zinn felt that the teaching of history "should serve society in some way" and that "objectivity is impossible, and it is also undesirable." As a Marxist, he'd prefer a society that resembles Stalin's Russia.

Additionally, Pacific Research Institute's Lance Izumi notes that pages and pages of the latest California History, Social Science Framework are devoted to identity politics, and the environmentalist, sexual, and anti-Vietnam War movements, with detailed and extensive bibliographical references. In contrast, the contemporaneous conservative movement, which succeeded in electing Californian Ronald Reagan as president, with its complex mixture of social, economic, and national security sub-movements, is given cursory and passing mention, with no references provided.'"

Public sector unions are going to be with us for a long time. But in the wake of the Janus ruling, members who don't agree with the political agenda of these unions can quit, depriving them of the dues that—to the tune of nearly a billion per year just in California—make them so powerful.

Teachers, in particular, should carefully consider this option. America's future depends on it.

A Failing Education System

From the 2020 research brief by Joel Kotkin and Marshall Toplansky *Beyond Feudalism: A Strategy to Restore California's Middle Class at the* Chapman University Center for Demographics & Policy:

The demand for middle-skill jobs is high and meeting it could prove a crucial challenge. I In 2015 we identified over 50% of all jobs in California as middle-skill, but only 39% of the state's workers were trained at that level. Demand for these skills is expected to continue for years, and will provide benefits for the students who obtain them, as well as for the California business community. The California Employment Development Department (EDD) estimates that by 2026, the state will need 9.5 million mid-skill workers, an increase of 858,000 over 2016 levels.

College educated people face similar challenges. According to the Public Policy Institute of California (PPIC), as boomers age and retire, California is going to need approximately 1.1 million more college graduates by 2030. PPI projects that the demand will then exceed the supply of college graduates by 5.4%, making it even more essential that K-12 institutions do a better job of preparing students for college and careers.

Sadly, our educational system seems ill-prepared to train either mid-skilled or college educated people. Since 1998 California has ranked, on average, 46th in 8th-grade reading and mathematics subject-area performance on the National Assessment for Educational Progress (NAEP), the only comparable assessment between states nation-wide.

It includes comparisons with demographically similar states such as Texas, which spends less money per student, as well as New York. Almost three of five California high schoolers are not prepared for either college or a career; the percentages are far higher for Latinos, African Americans, and the economically disadvantaged. Among the 50 states, California ranked 49th in the performance of poor, largely minority, students. San Francisco, the epicenter of California's woke culture, suffers the worst scores for African-Americans of any county in the state.

The need for remedial courses for approximately 40% of California State University freshmen upon entry to college reveals the low level of preparedness among our high school graduates. Those same deficiencies limit the success of a high school graduate who goes straight into the workplace. Basic reading comprehension, writing and mathematics are necessary for success in life. Remarkably, some educators wish to address this problem by eliminating remedial classes.

Making matters worse is the state's abandonment, in 2015, of the California High School Exit Exam (CAHSEE). There were many critics of the test, but the CAHSEE provided assurance to employers and the community that graduates could meet a certain level of proficiency in grade level work. In California, half of our high school students barely read. The state's solution: a proposal to mandate that each California State University student take an ethnic studies course designed to promote a progressive, and somewhat anti-capitalist, multi-cultural agenda.

With an anything-goes approach, some school districts, Los Angeles Unified School District in particular, have banned "willful defiance" removals and suspensions for behavior that disrupts the learning environment. This is seen as a way of redressing racial issues, as many of the malefactors (like most California students) are from historically disadvantaged minority groups. Under similar criteria, a bill is progressing quickly through the legislature to do the same statewide. Yes, these young people may be getting diplomas—but do they have the skills, academic as well as social, to compete in the real world?

LAUSD Analysis of Charter High School vs. Traditional High School Cost & Academic Performance

This June 2015 article "Analyzing the Cost and Performance of LAUSD Traditional High Schools and LAUSD Alliance Charter High Schools" comes from the California Policy Center's Marc Joffe:

This California Policy Center study examines cost-per-pupil for high school students in the Los Angeles Unified School District), comparing its traditional public schools to those attending its largest charter school network, the Alliance College Ready Public Schools.

It also examines the educational achievement outcomes for traditional and charter high school students, focusing on nine LAUSD traditional schools and nine LAUSD Alliance charter schools. The schools were chosen because of their close proximity to each other and similar demographic makeup, limiting extraneous variables from corrupting the study, and making for as close to an "apples-to-apples" comparison as is possible.

Charter schools have a lower cost per pupil than traditional schools: Based on an analysis of relevant school costs and the number of enrolled high school students, the data shows the per pupil per pupil costs for Alliance charter high school students to be $10,649 per year, compared to $15,372 per year for students at traditional public high schools within LAUSD, that is, we find a per pupil cost differential of 44% in favor of Alliance charter schools.

Charter schools have higher API scores and graduation rates than traditional schools: Academically, comparing LAUSD Alliance charter high schools to LAUSD traditional high schools located in the same neighborhoods, we found the Alliance schools have decisively higher API scores, 762 vs. 701, and higher graduation rates, 91.5% vs. 84.1%.

Charter schools have higher normalized SAT scores than traditional schools: With respect to SAT scores, when we normalized the comparison between the LAUSD Alliance charter and LAUSD traditional schools under consideration to equalize the rate of test participation, we found that the Alliance charter students outperformed the LAUSD traditional students with average scores of 1417 vs. 1299–a significant difference. Among college bound students, an SAT score of 1299 puts the student in the bottom 27% nationally. A score of 1417, by contrast, places the student at 41% nationally.

The academic comparisons the California Policy Center made involve 18 high schools, nine LAUSD Alliance charter high schools, and nine LAUSD traditional high schools. Our financial comparisons are somewhat broader in scope–involving the cost per high school pupil attending one of the largest public school districts in the nation and those attending a large charter school system.

They concluded from this data that an effective charter school operator can better learning outcomes at lower cost than traditional public schools serving a similar population. Ultimately, this finding supports the educational choice concept: by replacing a "one size fits all" solution with an array of educational choices, we can provide better results for California's children and taxpayers.

Now There's an Alternative: Home Schooling

This section below comes from the May 2020 article "Public Education is Changing Forever" comes from the California Policy Center's Edward Ring:

The COVID pandemic has closed public schools for over two months, with no end in sight. This represents a seismic disruption to a system that was already strained. Before the pandemic lockdown, public schools in California faced financial insolvency, woeful failures to educate (especially in low income communities), and a parent uprising that was growing exponentially.

As reported on May 14 in Real Clear Politics:

"A RealClear Opinion Research survey of 2,122 registered voters shows that support for educational choice is strong, and that a significant portion of parents are more likely to pursue homeschooling opportunities after the lockdowns end. The results show that 40% of families are more likely to homeschool or virtual school after lockdowns, and that 64% support school choice and 69% support the federal Education Freedom Scholarships proposal."

If you want to disrupt the public sector union monopoly on public education, the pandemic shutdown is made to order. Up until fall semester in 2020, parent resentment of unionized public education was restricted to relatively small numbers of activists. But that has now changed in two critical ways.

First, the newly mandated practice of "racial equity discipline" had turned many public schools into war zones. These Obama era federal rulings require punishments such as suspensions or expulsions to be meted out to students in equal proportions according to race. Districts that practiced racially proportionate discipline would receive bonus funds, and districts that did not would see federal funds withheld. The practical effect of these laws are to remove effective restraints on the behavior of disruptive students. Parents of students who behave have become outraged, because their children are coming home suffering from traumatic stress because they are not learning in a safe environment.

As an aside, a Google search under "racial equity discipline" yields nothing apart from reports and studies alleging that racial equity is necessary to combat institutional racism. Search results do not show even one article or study that questions this practice. As an author that publishes conservative and contrarian commentary on a variety of issues, I can say with certainty that this happens all the time and on all controversial topics. It is not by accident, and, to put it mildly, it constitutes manipulation of public sentiment with far reaching implications.

Probably the biggest victims of "racial equity discipline" are the students who require discipline. Their behavior is not being checked in the K-12 school environment, and they are subsequently entering the real world without learning to respect authority. They are being done a tragic disservice. But federal money talks, even as young lives are squandered.

Second, parents across California have been put off by the new sex education curriculum. These new guidelines have exposed children to sexually explicit material even in primary grades; it has also added layers of sexual indoctrination to the instruction. Parents, for example, are liable to become concerned when their third graders are taught that gender and sex are distinct, that sex is "assigned" at birth, but "gender" has nothing to do with a child's sexual anatomy.

Even before the pandemic, groups had arisen to spread awareness among parents of these new sex education guidelines and to organize resistance to them. These groups include the "Informed Parents of California," with 43,500 members on Facebook, along with the Capitol

Resource Institute, "advancing parental rights and religious freedom in California." If you peruse these online resources, you may be surprised at just how graphic and agenda-driven public school sex education has become.

Since the Pandemic Lockdown Closed Schools, Resistance to Status Quo in Public Education Has Mushroomed

When parents across California were suddenly forced to assume daily responsibility for their child's at-home education, it was no longer activists or victims who became aware of the new curricula.

Suddenly everybody became aware of what their children were being taught. This awareness extended not only to sex education but to history, English, math, and science. In all cases, an obvious agenda is at work: history that disparages America's legacy, emphasizing the negative. English that ignores classics of Western Civilization. Math that imposes cumbersome new "common core" standards. Science lessons that foment fear of apocalyptic climate change.

If suddenly gaining an intimate understanding of what their children are learning has driven more parents to activism, the response of the teachers union and the school districts has also had an impact. In some large California school districts the teachers union has demanded that teachers only spend four hours per day participating in online instruction, yet their rate of pay is untouched. How does that go over with parents who are shut out of their jobs and ability to make a living?

Henry David Thoreau, a great American writer who is all too often displaced in contemporary high school English classes, had this to say about the good fight: "There are a thousand hacking at the branches of evil to one who is striking at the root."

If these changes in public education, a biased, left-wing agenda infusing literally every classroom discipline, are branches, the root is surely the teachers union. Public education in California is virtually ran by the teachers union. Anyone who doubts this might consider the financial power they wield in the United States, and California in particular.

According to their own websites, there are approximately 3.0 million members of the National Education Association, and around 1.7 million members of the American Federation of Teachers. At roughly $1,000 per year in dues, these two teachers unions combined are collecting $4.7 billion per year.

This is an astonishing sum of money, sufficient to filter down to any political contest, anywhere, and win. From literally every school district board to the battles for the U.S. Senate and the White House, these teachers unions buy politicians via campaign contributions and lobbying. And their support is almost exclusively for Democrats. In California alone, the state chapters of public education unions–CTA, CFT and CSEA–collect nearly a half-billion in dues and fees each year.

Someone who has hacked at the root of education rot for years is the tireless Rebecca Friedrichs, a 28 year veteran of public education who became nationally famous when her case, *Friedrichs v. the CTA*, made it all the way to the U.S. Supreme Court. Friedrichs was fighting for the right for teachers to opt-out of union membership. After the untimely death of justice Antonin Scalia, her case was tabled, and it was left to Mark Janus, a few years later in 2018, to prevail in a similar case.

When asked about unions and public education, Friedrichs didn't mince words. "The founders never had government schools in mind," she said, "the unions and their special interests created the public school industrial complex that doesn't meet the needs of most but allows the government and the unions to indoctrinate us in leftist ideology."

What's coming next in public education is anybody's guess. But the forced and very unexpected transition of millions of Californian parents into homeschoolers is a profound disruption. Virtual private schools, offering affordable educational options to parents who don't want to put their children back into the public schools, now constitute a mortal threat to the teachers union monopoly on public education.

Perhaps that is one silver lining amid this medical crisis that is far from over, and economic challenges that have just begun.

How Public Sector Unions Exploit Identity Politics

This section below comes from the November 2017 article "How Public Sector Unions Exploit Identity Politics" comes from the California Policy Center's Edward Ring:

As the ethnic composition of America changes from mostly white to a kaleidoscope of color within a generation, there is no better way to fracture society than to teach everyone to resent everyone else.

Nurturing tribal resentment is a winning strategy for government unions, because a swollen, authoritarian, unionized government becomes the referee. Government union power increases every time another "person of color" becomes convinced that only government redistribution and racial quotas can mitigate their persecution at the hands of a racist white "patriarchy."

When society fractures, when we face increasing unrest and poverty, government unions win. It is inherently in the interests of government unions for society to fail. If public education fails, hire more teachers and education bureaucrats. If crime goes up, hire more police, and build more prisons. If immigrants fail to assimilate, hire more multilingual bureaucrats and social workers. If poverty increases, hire more welfare administrators.

If you don't think this strategy can work, come to California, America's most multi-ethnic state, and a place where government unions wield absolute power. Their wholly owned subsidiary, the Democratic party in California, has spent the last 20+ years perfecting the art of convincing the electorate that Republicans are racists. The strategy has been devastatingly effective, especially with people of color.

According to the Public Policy Institute of California (PPIC), among California's "likely voters," slightly more whites remain registered as Republicans, 39%, than Democrats, 38%. Among Latinos the registered Democrats, 62%, far outnumber Republicans, 17%, and among Blacks the disparity is even greater, 82% Democrat vs. 6% Republican. Among Asians, where the disparity is less, the Democrats still have a nearly two-to-one advantage, 45% to 24%.

All of this racial perseverating comes at tragic cost. Among the fifty states, California has the highest taxes, the highest state and local government debt, the most welfare recipients, the most people living in poverty, and the highest cost-of-living. The roads and bridges are crumbling, and the water and energy infrastructure hasn't been significantly upgraded in 30 years. But purveyors of identity politics have a strategy that earns votes, so why engage in actual governance? It's all about race, stupid. Hire more bureaucrats.

The worst consequence of choosing identity politics over actual governance is the slow but relentless destruction of California's once great system of public education. There has been negligible improvement in educational achievement for members of California's disadvantaged, despite decades of political control by public sector union funded Democrats who pander incessantly to the voter's lowest common denominator of resentment, race.

Rather than admit that failures of culture, community, and public education are the real reasons some ethnic groups underachieve, the Democrats that run Sacramento attribute every disparity in outcome among races to the pervasiveness of racism. Their solution? Quotas.

Quotas Are Being Used to Discriminate Against California's "Privileged" Youth

Here is an interesting comparison to prove that quotas are being used to discriminate against California's "privileged" youth. All data is for 2017.

The first column shows what percentage of students taking the SAT, by ethnicity, achieved a score at or above the minimum to be considered "college ready." The second column shows the ethnic breakdown of college age students in California. Column three uses a factor calculated from columns one and two, for each ethnicity, the percent of college ready students is multiplied by that ethnicity's percent of the total pool of college age Californians.

	SAT Score "College Ready"	College Age Californians	Merit based Admissions	Actual Admissions
Asian	70%	13%	21%	34%
Black	20%	6%	3%	5%
Latino	31%	50%	35%	33%
White	59%	31%	41%	23%

Credit: California Policy Center - California's UC System–2017 Admissions–Actual vs. SAT Based

Each factor is then divided by the sum of all four factors, to calculate a crude but significant indicator of what percentage of 2017 college admissions would be offered to students of each ethnicity, if admissions were based on merit as expressed by SAT scores. Column four shows the actual admissions to California's UC System in 2017 by ethnicity.

There are a few obvious takeaways from the above chart. Most salient is the fact that white applicants, if SAT scores were the sole basis for admission, are clear victims of discrimination. After all, if based on their college readiness as assessed by their SAT performance combined with their percentage of the population, they should have earned 43% of the admissions to the UC System, why did they only represent 23% of the incoming freshmen in 2017? But there are other disparities that point to an even bigger problem.

Why, for example, do actual Asian admissions, 34%, exceed the merit based admissions percentage, 21%, as indicated based on their percentage of the college age population and the percentage of them achieving the SAT benchmark? Why, for that matter, are the actual Latino admissions, 33%, slightly less than the amount they would theoretically earn, 35%, based that same criteria?

The answer in both cases is the same, and can be best summarized in this quote taken from a report released earlier this year by the Brookings Institution (with the SAT math example graph shown at the beginning of this chapter and as noted below):

"Race gaps on the SATs are especially pronounced at the tails of the distribution. In a perfectly equal distribution, the racial breakdown of scores at every point in the distribution would mirror the composition of test-takers as whole i.e. 51 percent white, 21 percent Latino, 14 percent black, and 14 percent Asian.

But in fact, among top scorers—those scoring between a 750 and 800—60 percent are Asian, and 33 percent are white, compared to 5 percent Latino and 2 percent black. Meanwhile, among those scoring between 300 and 350, 37 percent are Latino, 35 percent are black, 21 percent are white, and 6 percent are Asian."

What Does a Member of Board of Regents at the University of California Has to Say?

To further investigate this evidence, I talked someone who spent over a decade serving on the Board of Regents at the University of California. They did not mince words. Here are a few of the things they had to say:

- SAT scores have become less important because the university has gone to "holistic admissions" instead of SAT based admissions—the SAT is also watered down with a subjective 3rd "essay" section. The subjectivity of the admissions criteria makes it harder to prove discrimination.

- For years now, the UC System has diversified the faculty by taking more professors to fill positions in African American and Latino studies and shielded itself from discrimination because they can say the person hired had strength in the discipline they needed to fill.

- Ethnic studies departments are academically weak and don't provide graduates with anything they can use. Most ethnic studies departments are growing because people are being hired and enrolled in order to fulfill de facto diversity quotas both for faculty and students. The alternative would be to destroy the integrity of the hard sciences with unqualified faculty and students.

- After the passage of Prop. 209, the admission of Asians rose to about 35% because you could not suppress their achievement without admitting you're breaking the law. Latino and Black admissions track at 29% and 6%, respectively, more consistent with their percentage within California's population. To accommodate the Asian over-enrollment and the Black and Latino quotas, qualified white applicants are the victims—Whites represented less than 25% of admissions to the UC system last year.

- California's legislature is controlled by the Latino Caucus, which makes sure that 25% Latino admissions are maintained. Whites don't go out and protest and make noise because that is politically incorrect, and the media doesn't report the data anyway.

Readers are invited to challenge the accuracy of any of the above statements, made by an informed observer. And what is the result of all this mediocrity that hides behind diversity, this discrimination that hides behind achieving quota-driven equality of outcome? A fracturing of society into identity groups, each of them, whether via propaganda or via reality, encouraged to harbor resentment towards every other group.

If one were to identify which of California's public sector unions is the most guilty of fomenting racial disharmony, it would certainly be the ones representing K-12 public school teachers and the ones representing college faculty. Their outlook, which is reflected in their policies, their curricula, and only somewhat camouflaged on their websites, is to blame the academic achievement gap on anything but their own poor performance as the most influential determinant of educational policy in California.

Blame the rich. Blame capitalism. Blame Western Civilization. Blame "white privilege." Blame racist Republicans. But don't look in the mirror.

A rising trope among these neo-racialist purveyors of separatist identity politics is that white people should engage in "allyship," which to them means for well-behaved white people to do whatever they're told by the high priests of the disadvantaged, no matter how disingenuous or ridiculous.

But a true ally would provide tough, genuine love, and tell the truth—the sapient approach. Which is if you want to achieve in America, the most inclusive and tolerant nation in the history of the world, you have to work hard, stay sober, stay out of jail, keep your families intact, be thrifty, and hit the books.

That truth would unify and enrich this nation. And a unified and prosperous nation would mean less government, less government employees, and weaker public employee unions. We can't have that now, can we?

Mandatory Ethnic Indoctrination Approved in California Schools

This March 2021 article from the Editorial Board of the *Wall Street Journal* is titled "California's Ethnic Studies Mandate: A New Curriculum Rejects Merit and Sees Oppression Everywhere":

Conservatives in the 1990s worried about the rise of "critical race theory" in higher education. But at least college students were there by choice, and the Marxist-influenced courses, which indicted American values, were often optional. That's changing fast as the largest U.S. state moves this week toward imposing a radical ethnic studies curriculum as a high-school graduation requirement.

The recent push to mandate ethnic studies in California public schools has met resistance from liberals and conservatives—including a surprise veto last year from Gov. Gavin Newsom. He called for revisions in the model curriculum before the state required it.

So what will California teenagers be taught? A multitude of ethnic groups have shaped the American experience, and some of the material presents that history. But the thrust of the hundreds of pages of course outlines is to enlist students in progressive politics. "One of the main focuses of ethnic studies is translating historical lessons and critical race theory into direct action for social justice," a course outline says.

This requires that students are taught to view the American creed as sinister. One lesson plan introduces students to what it calls "dominant narratives," defined as stories "told in service of the dominant social group's interests and ideologies." A University of Michigan lesson plan that forms the basis for the outline explains that one example of a "dominant narrative" was the antebellum claim that "slavery is necessary for the wellbeing of slaves." A contemporary example, according to the lesson plan? That "America is a meritocracy, and anyone can achieve their ambitions through hard work and perseverance."

Why would California want to teach young people that their dreams of rising through merit are akin to defenses of slavery? Because a core tenet of ethnic studies is that a person's identity is determined first and foremost by group membership. Another teaching resource warns that if we accept meritocracy, then "we would strive to do our best on our own" and "should focus on individual achievement."

Ethnic studies wants to invert traditional American ideas of individual merit, opportunity, and success. It imposes its own dominant narrative that interprets all social interactions through the lens of oppression, including a worksheet on the "four I's of oppression"—ideological, institutional, interpersonal, and internalized, terms repeated throughout.

If America's traditional "narratives" are designed to encourage social mobility and prosperity,

California's proposed Marxist narratives are designed to encourage intergroup conflict and perpetual upheaval in existing institutions. That's explicit in sample assignments, such as drafting a "manifesto" of demands for the Third World Liberation Front or "implementing a systematized campaign for social justice at their school."

"When we encounter dominant narratives," the curriculum says, "we must always ask 'what is the motivation behind this narrative?'" Californians would do well to ask the same question about the radical narrative promoted in this mandatory curriculum. The motivation is a left-wing power grab—and it's not in the interest of ordinary Californians of any ethnicity.

California State University Now Requires Ethnic Studies

Per the August 2020 "California State University now requires ethnic studies" by CalMatters' Mikhail Zinshteyn:

The AB 1460 implementation of mandated ethnic studies began on August 17, 2020 when Governor Gavin Newsom signed into law a new 3-unit Ethnic Studies requirement for the 23-campus California State University system. AB 1460 means students in the CSU system will have to take an ethnic studies course before graduation. The bill overrides a similar but less strict requirement the system imposed earlier this summer.

On October 8, 2020 campuses received a draft Executive Order on CSU General Education Breadth Requirements. This information is being shared so that CSUSM faculty and the campus community will be well informed during this process and able to provide input during the consultation period between the California State University Council on Ethnic Studies, the Academic Senate of the California State University, and the Chancellor's Office.

The Chancellor's Office has created a webpage on the Ethnic Studies Requirement. This page contains the link to the CO response to Frequently Asked Questions which were submitted by the CSU Chairs group.

AB 1460 is the brainchild of then Assemblymember Shirley Weber (now California Secretary of State), a San Diego Democrat and author of the bill, taught Africana Studies, an ethnic studies discipline, at San Diego State University for several decades. She and other backers called the CSU ethnic studies and social justice plan watered-down.

"We've been told that one should move the system, get in front of the system, push the system when the system is being unresponsive," Weber said at a rally in support of the bill, which was three years in the making. "And that's what has happened here with the faculty and staff and students."

The Legislature passed the bill on Aug. 3., 2020.

Ethnic studies courses typically examine the persecutions, contributions and power dynamics affecting four ethnic and racial groups: Native Americans, African Americans, Asian Americans, and Latina and Latino Americans. The four groups combined account for about two-thirds of California's population.

Starting in the 2021–22 academic year, California State University has to provide for courses in ethnic studies at each of its campuses. The graduation requirement of one, 3-unit course begins for students completing their degrees in the 2024–25 academic year.

Sapient Ways to Teach Ethnic Studies

As America turns multi-racial with stunning rapidity, maybe teaching some sort of ethnic studies is a good idea. But the premises that underlie California's proposed version of ethnic studies are all wrong, because it is written by leftist agitators who have taken over virtually all of California's public institutions, certainly including public education.

To properly teach ethnic studies, a small subset of the instruction might deal with significant differences in customs that it would be helpful for members of different communities should know about each other. More practical and less ideological courses offered, for example, to nurses and others who work with the public are careful to include this sort of instruction.

Similarly, another useful portion of an ethnic studies curriculum might do a broad survey of the historical legacies of various parts of the world where students of different backgrounds came from. To the extent something like this isn't already offered in a history class, it could enrich the curriculum in an ethnic studies class.

But the dominant message that should inform an ethnic studies class in California's high schools, and everywhere else in America where these classes may eventually be offered, needs to be positive and uplifting. For that reason, such a class should not pander to the bitter sentiments and careerist pimping of the victim industry, whose mission is to instill destructive self-pity into every member of every race or gender that isn't "cis-hetero-white." Rather, students should be encouraged to take individual responsibility for their success or failure in life, regardless of their race or gender, in the most tolerant, enlightened society in the history of the world.

Moreover, an ethnic studies class aimed at high school students should not be proclaiming capitalism to be an "engine of oppression." It should be examining capitalism, with honesty and balance, as an economic system that has, despite imperfections, proven the best way to deliver prosperity, innovation, and freedom.

An ethnic studies class does not have to be saturated in pseudo-scientific gobbledygook, nor steeped in anti-Western, anti-White, anti American propaganda. As California, and America in due course, transitions to becoming a fully multi-ethnic nation, teaching these falsehoods to a multi-ethnic student body is the worst way to create a harmonious society, whether it's a sweet tasting salad or a savory stew.

The Latino Education Crisis That Won't Go Away

Per the July 2015 "California's Latino Education Crisis" article by Larry Elder in Real Clear

Politics:

Education professors Patricia Gandara of UCLA and Frances Contreras of University of Washington wrote the 2009 book *The Latino Education Crisis: The Consequences of Failed Social Policies*. Heather Mac Donald, a contributing editor of *City Journal*, reviewed the book.

She wrote: "Hispanics are underachieving academically at an alarming rate, the authors report. Though second and third-generation Hispanics make some progress over their first-generation parents, that progress starts from an extremely low base and stalls out at high school completion.

High school drop-out rates—around 50 percent—remain steady across generations. Latinos' grades and test scores are at the bottom of the bell curve. The very low share of college degrees earned by Latinos has not changed for more than two decades. Currently only one in 10 Latinos has a college degree."

Before the book came out, co-author Gandara wrote an article for the National Education Association, where she said: "The most urgent problem for the American education system has a Latino face. Latinos are the largest and most rapidly growing ethnic minority in the country, but, academically, they are lagging dangerously far behind their non-Hispanic peers.

For example, upon entering kindergarten 42 percent of Latino children are found in the lowest quartile of performance on reading readiness compared to just 18 percent of white children. By fourth grade, 16 percent of Latino students are proficient in reading according to the 2005 NAEP, compared to 41 percent of white students. A similar pattern is notable at the eighth grade, where only 15 percent of Latinos are proficient in reading compared to 39 percent of whites.

"With respect to college completion, only 11 percent of Latinos 25 to 29 years of age had a BA or higher compared to 34 percent of whites. Perhaps most distressing, however, is the fact that no progress has been made in the percentage of Latinos gaining college degrees over a 20-year period, while other groups have seen significant increases in degree completion."

The Latino Education Crisis authors Gandara and Contreras fear a "permanent underclass." They write, "With no evidence of an imminent turnaround in the rate at which Latino students are either graduating from high school or obtaining college degrees, it appears that both a regional and national catastrophe are at hand."

13 – Public Sector & Teacher Unions' Pension Madness vs. Fiscal Timebomb

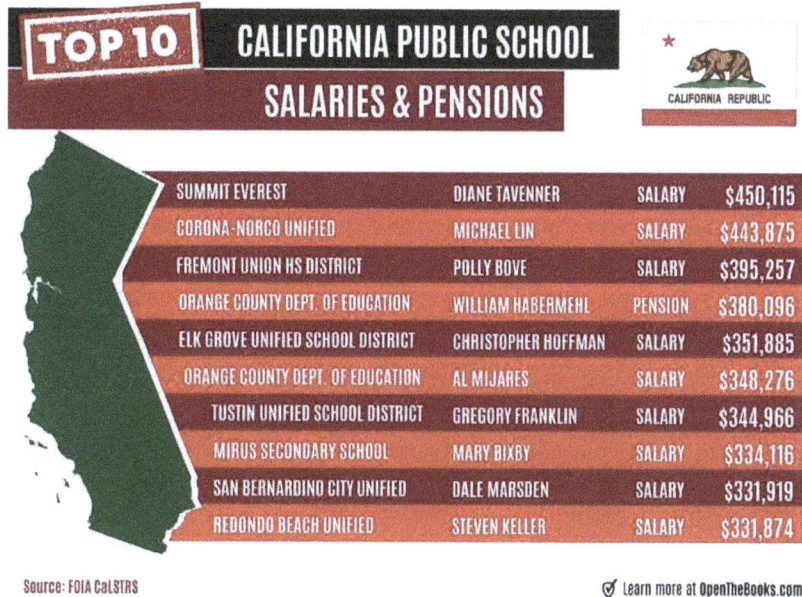

TOP 10	CALIFORNIA PUBLIC SCHOOL SALARIES & PENSIONS		
SUMMIT EVEREST	DIANE TAVENNER	SALARY	$450,115
CORONA-NORCO UNIFIED	MICHAEL LIN	SALARY	$443,875
FREMONT UNION HS DISTRICT	POLLY BOVE	SALARY	$395,257
ORANGE COUNTY DEPT. OF EDUCATION	WILLIAM HABERMEHL	PENSION	$380,096
ELK GROVE UNIFIED SCHOOL DISTRICT	CHRISTOPHER HOFFMAN	SALARY	$351,885
ORANGE COUNTY DEPT. OF EDUCATION	AL MIJARES	SALARY	$348,276
TUSTIN UNIFIED SCHOOL DISTRICT	GREGORY FRANKLIN	SALARY	$344,966
MIRUS SECONDARY SCHOOL	MARY BIXBY	SALARY	$334,116
SAN BERNARDINO CITY UNIFIED	DALE MARSDEN	SALARY	$331,919
REDONDO BEACH UNIFIED	STEVEN KELLER	SALARY	$331,874

Source: FOIA CaLSTRS

Learn more at OpenTheBooks.com

Credit: Forbes - Why California Is In Trouble–340,000
Public Employees With $100,000 + Paychecks Cost Taxpayers $45 Billion.

This section is from the Spring 2010 *City Journal* article "The Beholden State: How public-sector unions broke California" by Steven Malanga:

It is no secret that California has its own myriad of economic issues: high taxes, a bloated government, overly powerful unions, and underfunded pension funds. However, the common denominator for all of these is California's Democratic Party. A popular TV commercial from 2010 below show how:

The camera focuses on an official of the Service Employees International Union (SEIU), California's largest public-employee union, sitting in a legislative chamber and speaking into a microphone. "We helped to get you into office, and we got a good memory," she says matter-of-factly to the elected officials outside the shot. "Come November, if you don't back our program, we'll get you out of office."

The 2010 video become a sensation among California taxpayer groups for its vivid depiction of the audacious power that public-sector unions wield in their state. The unions' political triumphs have molded a California in which government workers thrive at the expense of a struggling private sector. The state's public school teachers are the highest-paid in the nation. Its prison guards can easily earn six-figure salaries. State workers routinely retire at 55 with pensions higher than their base pay for most of their working life.

Meanwhile, what was once the most prosperous state now suffers from an unemployment rate far steeper than the nation's and a flood of firms and jobs escaping high taxes and stifling regulations. This toxic combination—high public-sector employee costs and sagging economic fortunes—has produced recurring budget crises in Sacramento and in virtually every municipality in the state.

How public employees became members of the elite class in a declining California offers a cautionary tale to the rest of the country, where the same process is happening in slower motion. The story starts half a century ago, when California public workers won bargaining rights and quickly learned how to elect their own bosses—that is, sympathetic politicians who would grant them outsize pay and benefits in exchange for their support.

Over Time, the Unions Have Turned the State's Politics Completely in Their Favor

The result: unaffordable benefits for civil servants; fiscal chaos in Sacramento and in cities and towns across the state; and angry taxpayers finally confronting the unionized masters of California's unsustainable government.

A politically created crisis of epic proportions is brewing in California and elsewhere across the United States. For decades, public pension officials and politicians of both parties have promised their employees increasingly generous retirement benefits—while low-balling the contributions from government agencies and employees that are needed to cover these promises—presenting our greatest financial challenge since the Great Depression.

Pushing the pension liability from today and onto our children and grandchildren leaves them with a depleted future and a potentially bankrupt California.

- State and local governments will scramble to find funds, forcing them to raise taxes, slash public services, and/or declare bankruptcy.

- Schools, parks, emergency services, and public-employee retirement benefits will be at risk.

- Politicians will defer until circumstances force them to reckon with a disaster of their own making.

The problem? For far too long, state, and local governments have promised their employees increasingly generous retirement benefits—but without ensuring that sufficient funds will be on hand when the pension payments come due.

California's Immense Pension Dilemma

Per the August 2020 "California's immense pension dilemma" by CalMatters' Dan Walters:

The incessant drive of the unions to increase government workers' pay and benefits has led to a public-pension system that both sides of the political aisle recognize is unsustainable.

Moreover, expansive state-court interpretations of government-worker benefit protections effectively mean that employees' pensions are locked in and cannot be reduced without their permission—not even on a "going forward" basis for future work. This has come to be known as the "California rule."

California's public pension system faces a huge unfunded debt but dealing with it involves increasing risk. California's public employee pension dilemma boils down to this: The California Public Employees Retirement System has scarcely two-thirds of the money it needs to pay benefits that state and local governments have promised their workers.

Moreover, CalPERS' official estimate that it is 70.8% funded is based on an assumption of future investment earnings averaging 7% a year, which probably is at least one or two percentage points too high. In the 2019-20 fiscal year that ended June 30, CalPERS posted a 4.7% return and over the last 20 years it has averaged 5.5% by its own calculation.

Were the earnings assumption dropped to a more realistic level, the system's "unfunded liability"—essentially a multi-billion-dollar debt—would increase sharply from the current $160 billion to at least $200 billion.

There are three ways to resolve the debt dilemma: Earn higher returns, require government employers and employees to pay more, or reduce future benefits. CalPERS is pursuing the first two, but a recent state Supreme Court ruling makes the third virtually impossible.

The court had an opportunity to revisit the "California rule"—an assumption, based on past rulings, that once promised, future pension benefits cannot be revised downward.

Pension Spiking

The case involved pension reform legislation sponsored by former Gov. Jerry Brown, particularly a ban on manipulating benefit calculations. Some unions said that the California rule protected "pension spiking," but the justices, while ruling it doesn't apply, also declared, "we have no jurisprudential reason to undertake a fundamental reexamination of the rule."

So reducing future benefits is now off the table, which leaves improving investment earnings and increasing contributions as the only options for avoiding an eventual meltdown.

CalPERS has been pursuing a more aggressive policy, contending that without it, the system can't achieve its 7% goal. It has proposed to borrow up to $80 billion to expand its investment portfolio and make direct loans to corporations or government entities. However, last week's abrupt resignation of chief investment officer Ben Meng, architect of the strategy, leaves it in limbo.

Basic economics tell us that pursuing higher investment returns means taking higher risks of failure. Direct lending also increases the risk of corruption, which has infected CalPERS in the past.

That's why a pending CalPERS-sponsored bill is troublesome. The measure, Assembly Bill 2473, would exempt details of CalPERS loans from the state's Public Records Act, making it much more difficult for watchdogs and journalists to sniff out insider dealing.

Meanwhile, CalPERS' demands for more money from state and local governments is hitting their budgets even harder these days because tax revenues have been eroded by the COVID-19's recession. They force employers to dip into reserves, shift funds from other services, ask their voters to raise taxes or even borrow money to pay pension debts.

The latter involves what are called "pension bonds," issued on an assumption that their interest rates will be less than the 7% percent rate by which CalPERS inflates unfunded liabilities—a practice known in financial circles as "arbitrage."

Many local governments issue arbitrage bonds, despite the obvious risks, and recently, a hybrid form emerged in Torrance, a small Southern California city.

Torrance is leasing its city streets to a city-controlled entity called the Torrance Joint Powers Financing Authority, which will issue $350 million in bonds to pay for the lease. The city will use the bond money to pay down the city's $500 million pension debt while making payments to the authority so it can service the bonds.

The bottom line: The city is pawning its streets to pay for pensions. That's not healthy by any definition.

The "California Rule"

This December 2019 article "Pension reform waits for California Supreme Court" comes from the California Policy Center's Edward Ring:

With markets fitfully advancing after a nearly two year pause, the need for pension reform again fades from public discussion. And it's easy for pension reformers to forget that even when funds are obviously imperiled, with growing unfunded liabilities and continuously increasing demands from the pension funds, hardly anyone understands what's going on. Unless you are sitting on a city council and facing a 10 percent budget deficit at the same time as your required pension contribution is increasing (again) by 20 percent, pension finance is eye-glazing arcana that is best ignored.

But when your local government has reached the point where it's spending nearly as much on pensions as it spends on base salaries, and pension finance commands your attention, you still can't do much. Pension reforms were approved by voters in San Jose and San Diego, among other places, but their impact was significantly reduced because of court challenges. Similarly, a moderate statewide pension reform passed by California's legislature and signed by Governor Brown in 2013 has been repeatedly challenged in court.

The primary legal dispute is over what is referred to as the "California Rule." According to this interpretation of California contract law, pension benefit accruals–the amount of additional pension benefit an employee earns each year–cannot be reduced, even for future work.

Reformers find this appallingly unfair, based on the fact that when California's public employee pension benefit accruals were enhanced, the enhancement was applied retroactively. Suddenly increasing a pension benefit by 50 percent or more, not only for future work, but for decades of work already performed, is a big part of why California's pension funds are in the precarious shape they're in today.

California's State and Local Liabilities Total $1.5 Trillion

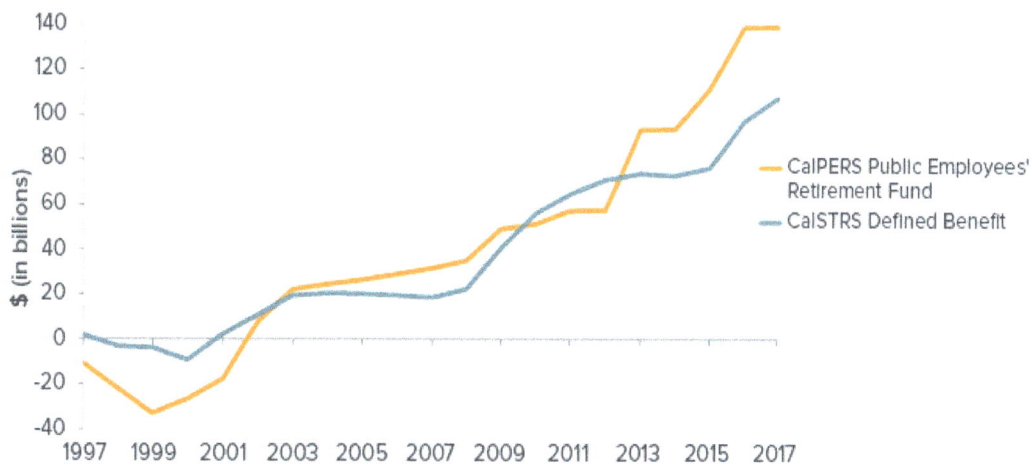

Credit: Public Policy Institute of California (PPIC).

This January 2019 article "California's State and Local Liabilities Total $1.5 Trillion" comes from the California Policy Center's Edward Ring:

California's total state and local government liabilities as of June 30, 2017, the most recent year for which a complete set of financial and actuarial reports are available, totaled just over $1.5 trillion. Over two-thirds of that total consists of unfunded liabilities for pensions and retiree health insurance for California's state and local public employees.

That's the finding of an in-depth analysis released this week by the California Policy Center. In 2019, "California may have a state budget surplus of a few billion," said California Policy Center president Will Swaim, "But California's state and local governments are now carrying debt that amounts to literally hundreds of times more than this surplus."

The new study found that bonds, loans, and other liabilities owed by California's state and local governments amounted to $482 billion. "OPEB," or Other Post-Employment Benefits– primarily retirement health insurance benefits–totaled $187 billion. But the biggest component of state and local debt was pensions.

Study authors Marc Joffe and Edward Ring analyzed hundreds of financial statements from cities, counties, special districts, state agencies, and public sector pension funds. They contend that the officially recognized total unfunded pension liability, $316 billion, is understated by just over a half-trillion dollars.

"When we recalculated the unfunded pension liability using the Citigroup Pension Liability Index discount rate (3.87 percent in June 2017), which is recommended by Moody's, we estimated that the real unfunded actuarial accrued liability (UAAL) for California's state and local employee pension systems is $846 billion, which is $530 billion more than the officially reported total," said co-author Edward Ring.

Even using the officially reported numbers for California's state and local governments' total unfunded pension liability, that, plus all other liabilities, totals $985 billion. Given the recent uncertainty in the stock market, and concerns about other investment assets such as bonds and real estate also being in bubble territory, that $985 billion is very likely a best-case amount.

As a matter of fact, using the methodology of the prestigious Stanford Institute for Economic Policy (which contends the "risk free" discount rate should be only 3.0 percent), we calculated the total unfunded pension liability at $1.26 trillion–$944 billion more than the officially reported total for pensions. That would put total state and local government liabilities in California at a whopping $1.9 trillion.

Read the full study in th Appendix titled: California's State and Local Liabilities Total $1.5 Trillion. The specific categories of debt tabulated in the study make clear that:

"California's state and local governments face serious financial challenges. Not only do they carry $1.5 trillion in debt and underfunded pensions. They also face billions in deferred costs to maintain and upgrade neglected public infrastructure," said co-author Marc Joffe. "And state revenues are dangerously dependent on income tax revenue from high income earners– revenue that will largely evaporate in the next economic downturn."

The Beholden State: How Public-Sector Unions Broke California

This section below is from the Spring 2010 *City Journal* article "The Beholden State: How public-sector unions broke California" by Steven Malanga:

The swelling government payroll made many California taxpayers uneasy, eventually encouraging the 1978 passage of Proposition 13, the famous initiative that capped property-tax hikes and sought to slow the growth of local governments, which feed on property taxes. Government workers rightly saw Prop. 13 as a threat. "We're not going to just lie back and take it," a California labor leader told the *Washington Post* after the vote, adding that Prop. 13 had made the union "more militant."

The next several years proved him right. In 1980 alone, unionized employees of California local governments went on strike 40 times, even though doing so was illegal. And once the

Supreme Court of California sanctioned state and local workers' right to strike in 1985—something that their counterparts in most other states still lack—the unions quickly mastered confrontational techniques like the "rolling strike," in which groups of workers walk off jobs at unannounced times, and the "blue flu," in which public-safety workers call in sick en masse.

But in post–Proposition 13 California, strikes were far from the unions' most fearsome weapons. Aware that Proposition 13 had shifted political action to the state capital, three major blocs—teachers' unions, public-safety unions, and the Service Employees International Union, which now represents 350,000 assorted government workers—began amassing colossal power in Sacramento.

Over the last 30 years, they have become elite political givers and the state's most powerful lobbying factions, replacing traditional interest groups, and changing the balance of power. Today, they vie for the title of mightiest political force in California.

The California Teachers Association (CTA)

Much of the CTA's clout derives from the fact that, like all government unions, it can help elect the very politicians who negotiate and approve its members' salaries and benefits.

Soon after Proposition 13 became law, the union launched a coordinated statewide effort to support friendly candidates in school-board races, in which turnout is frequently low and special interests can have a disproportionate influence. In often bitter campaigns, union-backed candidates began sweeping out independent board members. By 1987, even conservative-leaning Orange County saw 83 percent of board seats up for grabs going to union-backed candidates. The resulting change in school-board composition made the boards close allies of the CTA.

But with union dues somewhere north of $1,000 per member and 340,000 members, the CTA can afford to be a player not just in local elections but in Sacramento, too (and in Washington, for that matter, where it's the National Education Association's most powerful affiliate).

The CTA entered the big time in 1988, when it almost single-handedly led a statewide push to pass Proposition 98, an initiative—opposed by taxpayer groups and Governor George Deukmejian—that required 40 percent of the state's budget to fund local education. To drum up sympathy, the CTA ran controversial ads featuring students; in one, a first-grader stares somberly into the camera and says, "Pay attention—today's lesson is about the school funding initiative." Victory brought local schools some $450 million a year in new funding, much of it discretionary.

Unsurprisingly, the union-backed school boards often used the extra cash to fatten teachers' salaries—one reason that California's teachers are the country's highest-paid, even though the state's total spending per student is only slightly higher than the national average. "The problem is that there is no organized constituency for parents and students in California," says Lanny Ebenstein, a former member of the Santa Barbara Board of Education and an economics professor at the University of California at Santa Barbara. "No one says to a board of education, 'We want more of that money to go for classrooms, for equipment.' "

With its growing financial strength, the CTA gained the ability to shape public opinion. In 1996, for instance, the union—casting covetous eyes on surplus tax revenues from the state's economic boom—spent $1 million on an ad campaign advocating smaller classes. Californians began seeing the state's classrooms as overcrowded, according to polls. So Governor Pete Wilson earmarked some three-quarters of a billion dollars annually to cut class sizes in kindergarten through third grade.

The move produced no discernible improvements in student performance, but it did require a hiring spree that inflated CTA rolls and produced a teacher shortage. The union drew the line, however, when it faced the threat of increased accountability. Two years later, when Wilson offered funds to reduce class sizes even more but attached the money to new oversight mechanisms, the CTA spent $6 million to defeat the measure, living up to Wilson's assessment of it as a "relentless political machine."

During this contentious period, the CTA and its local affiliates learned to play hardball, frequently shutting down classes with strikes. The state estimated that in 1989 alone, these strikes cost California students collectively some 7.2 million classroom days. Los Angeles teachers provoked outrage that year by reportedly urging their students to support them by skipping school. After journalist Debra Saunders noted in *Los Angeles Daily News* that the striking teachers were already well paid, the union published her home phone number in its newsletter and urged members to call her.

Four years later, the CTA reached new heights of thuggishness after a business-backed group began a petition to place a school-choice initiative on the state ballot. In a union-backed effort, teachers shadowed signature gatherers in shopping malls and aggressively dissuaded people from signing up. The tactic led to more than 40 confrontations and protests of harassment by signature gatherers.

"They get in between the signer and the petition," the head of the initiative said. "They scream at people. They threaten people." CTA's top official later justified the bullying: some ideas "are so evil that they should never even be presented to the voters," he said.

Public-Safety Workers: Police, Sheriffs, Prison Guards & Highway-Patrol Officers

Public-safety workers—from police and sheriffs to prison guards and highway-patrol officers— are the second part of the public-union triumvirate ruling California.

In a state that has embraced some of the toughest criminal laws in the country, police, and prison guards' unions own a precious currency: their political endorsements, which are highly sought after by candidates wanting to look tough on crime. But the qualification that the unions usually seek in candidates isn't, in fact, toughness on crime; it's willingness to back better pay and benefits for public-safety workers.

The state's prison guards' union has exploited a similar message. Back in 1980, when the

California Correctional Peace Officers Association (CCPOA) won the right to represent prison guards in contract negotiations, it was a small fraternal organization of about 1,600 members. But as California's inmate population surged and the state went on a prison-building spree—constructing 22 new institutions over 25 years—union membership expanded to 17,000 in 1988, 25,000 by 1997, and 31,000 today. Union resources rose correspondingly, with a budget soaring to $25 million or so, supporting a staff 70 deep, including 20 lawyers.

Even more troubling are the activities of the California Organization of Police and Sheriffs (COPS), a lobbying and advocacy group that has raised tens of millions of dollars from controversial soliciting campaigns.

The results of union pressure are clear. In most states, police and other safety officers can typically retire at 50 with a pension of about half their final working salary; in California, they often receive 90 percent of their pay if they retire at the same age. The state's munificent disability system lets public-safety workers retire with rich pay for a range of ailments that have nothing to do with their jobs, costing taxpayers hundreds of millions of dollars.

California's prison guards are the nation's highest-paid, a big reason that spending on the state's prison system has blasted from less than 4.3 percent of the budget in 1986 to more than 11 percent today.

Third Big Public-Union Player is the Service Employees International Union (SEIU)

California's third big public-union player is the state wing of the SEIU, the nation's fastest-growing union, whose chief, Andy Stern, earned notoriety by visiting the White House 22 times during the first six months of the Obama administration.

Founded in 1921 as a janitors' union, the SEIU slowly transformed itself into a labor group representing government and health-care workers—especially health-care workers paid by government medical programs like Medicaid. In 1984, the California State Employees Association, which represented many state workers, decided to affiliate with the SEIU.

Today, the SEIU represents 700,000 California workers—more than a third of its nationwide membership. Of those, 350,000 are government employees: noninstructional workers in schools across the state; all non-public-safety workers in California's burgeoning prisons; 2,000 doctors, mostly residents and interns, at state-run hospitals; and many others at the local, county, and state levels.

The SEIU's rise in California illustrates again how modern labor's biggest victories take place in back rooms, not on picket lines. In the late 1980s, the SEIU began eyeing a big jackpot: tens of thousands of home health-care workers being paid by California's county-run Medicaid programs. The SEIU initiated a long legal effort to have those workers, who were independent contractors, declared government employees.

When the courts finally agreed, the union went about organizing them—an easy task because governments rarely contest organizing campaigns, not wanting to seem anti-worker. The

SEIU's biggest victory was winning representation for 74,000 home health-care workers in Los Angeles County, the largest single organizing drive since the United Auto Workers unionized General Motors in 1937.

Taxpayers paid a steep price: home health-care costs became the fastest-growing part of the Los Angeles County budget after the SEIU bargained for higher wages and benefits for these new recruits. The SEIU also organized home health-care workers in several other counties, reaching a whopping statewide total of 130,000 new members.

Armed with knowledge about California's three public-union heavyweights, one can start to understand how the state found itself in its nightmarish fiscal situation. The beginning of the end was the 1998 gubernatorial election, in which the unions bet their future—and millions of dollars in members' dues—on Gray Davis. The candidate traveled to the SEIU's headquarters to remind it of his support during earlier battles against GOP governors ("Nobody in this race has done anywhere near as much as I have for SEIU"); the union responded by pumping $600,000 into his campaign.

Declaring himself the "education candidate" who would expand funding of public education, Davis received $1.2 million from the CTA. Added to this was Davis's success in winning away from Republicans key public-safety endorsements—and millions in contributions—from the likes of the CCPOA.

Davis's subsequent victory over Republican Dan Lungren afforded public-worker unions a unique opportunity to cash in the IOUs that they had accumulated, because Davis's Democratic Party also controlled the state legislature. What followed was a series of breathtaking deals that left California state and municipal governments careening from one budget crisis to another for the next decade.

Surging Pension Costs Push More California Cities Toward Bankruptcy

The following sections are per the June 2020 article "Commentary: Surging pension costs push more California cities toward bankruptcy" by CalMatters' Dan Walters:

From one end of California to the other, hundreds of cities are facing a tsunami of pension costs that officials say is forcing them to reduce vital services and could drive some—perhaps many—into functional insolvency or even bankruptcy.

The system that manages pension plans for the state government and thousands of local governments lost a staggering $100 billion or so in the Great Recession a decade ago and has not recovered. The California Public Employees' Retirement System (CalPERS) is rapidly increasing mandatory contributions into its pension trust fund to make up for those losses, cope with a host of rising expenses and, it would appear, stave off the prospect of its own insolvency.

City managers, facing annual increases in contributions of 15-plus percent, are feeling the squeeze, which a new Stanford University study finds is crowding out "resources needed for public assistance, welfare, recreation and libraries, health, public works, other social services, and in some cases, public safety."

Marina Gallegos, the human resources officer for Salinas, spoke for many city officials when she told CalPERS representatives who briefed her city council on the increases: "This growth is unsustainable."

Unsustainable Pension Obligations

"Unsustainable" is a word that pops up frequently in public statements and interviews with local leaders. "We don't know how we're going to operate," Oroville's finance director, Ruth Wright, told the CalPERS board last year as a delegation of city officials pleaded for relief. "We've been saying the bankruptcy word."

While all CalPERS client agencies, including school districts, counties, and the state itself, are being hit by its rising demands for money, the state's 482 cities are being clobbered the hardest. They devote the vast majority of their budgets to personnel costs, particularly for firefighters and police officers who have the most generous pension benefit—up to 90 percent of their highest earnings—and thus incur the highest pension costs.

It's common for California cities to pay 50 cents into the pension fund for every dollar in salary for their police officers, and only slightly less for firefighters. Studies indicate that costs of police pensions could increase by 50 percent within a few years and even double as CalPERS continues to deal with a large "unfunded liability"—essentially a debt—for pension promises.

Lodi's city manager, Steve Schwabauer, told CalPERS' trustees, "I have the unfortunate obligation to tell you that Lodi is on a slow, inexorable slide toward insolvency if you maintain your present course." He and other city officials pleaded for relief but so far have not received it.

Three California cities have declared bankruptcy in recent years, and fast-rising pension costs have been major factors in all. One was Vallejo, whose recently retired city manager, Daniel Keen, joined his colleagues in seeking relief, saying he expected pension costs for police to reach 98 percent of payroll in a decade and hinting that Vallejo could slip into insolvency again.

A new study for the League of California Cities, conducted by a consulting firm, Bartel Associates, projects that over the next seven years overall city pension costs, excluding health care, will nearly double, reaching an average of 15.8 percent of their general fund budgets by 2024-25. Costs for police and fire personnel will climb to well over 60 percent of payroll.

"The results of this study provide additional evidence that pension costs for cities are approaching unsustainable levels," Bartel's report warns. As those burdens outstrip revenue growth, it says, "many cities face difficult choices that will be compounded in the next recession."

But CalPERS' officials, trying to steady the fund's own precarious financial position, are openly worried that if they don't increase the bite on public employers or see investment earnings rebound sharply, they will drift to a still-undefined point of no return, unable to meet obligations under any circumstances.

CalPERS is also facing a wave of retirements from baby-boom-generation workers, the need to adjust for retirees' longer lifespans and a tab for benefits that were increased sharply in the late 1990s and early 2000s.

It's a Perfect Financial Storm!

In 1999, the Legislature and a newly inaugurated Democratic governor, Gray Davis, retroactively expanded benefits by roughly 50 percent for state employees. Most cities, counties, and other local governments, under pressure from their unions to match the state, quickly followed suit. They all relied on CalPERS' assurances that its trust fund could absorb the costs without additional contributions.

As a state Senate analysis of its pension bill, SB 400, summarized: CalPERS "believes they will be able to mitigate this cost increase through continued excess returns."

That assertion crumbled a few years later, when "excess earnings" became immense losses. CalPERS has just 68 percent of the money it projects it needs to cover pension promises to millions of current and future retirees—down from 101 percent a decade earlier. Also, the funding level assumes that investment earnings will hit 7.5 percent per year now and slide slowly to 7 percent.

Critics, such as those behind the Stanford study, say that assumption, called the "discount rate," is unrealistically high. CalPERS' own staff says it cannot count on more than 6.1 percent in the next decade, partly because CalPERS is shifting to a more conservative investment strategy.

Despite that seeming anomaly, CalPERS officials say the 7 percent assumption is likely to be reached in the decades-long time frame in which they operate, as modest earnings in the near future are offset by higher earnings later. Its board decided in December not to lower the rate further, which would have required even higher contributions from client agencies.

Larger cities that operate their own pension systems are not immune to the syndrome, since they have also experienced weak investment earnings.

Officials in Los Angeles have calculated that its pension costs have more than doubled, from $435 million a year in 2005-06 to $1.1 billion currently, and are expected to hit $1.3 billion by the end of the decade.

San Diego's annual pension costs have leaped from $191 million to $228 million in the last two years. City finance director Tracy McCraner says, "We've been told that could possibly rise to the tune of about $10 million" next year.

Cities Need CalPERS to be More Conservative Regarding Their Earnings Assumption

Cities want CalPERS to explore other responses to a more conservative earnings assumption, beyond merely increasing employer payments. They want CalPERS to rein in its costs, by such means as modifying or even suspending cost-of-living increases for current retirees with especially high pensions.

However, the board's response has been negative, reflecting its domination by public employee unions and union-allied politicians who stoutly resist any downward pressure on pension benefits.

If, as city officials fear, they get no relief from CalPERS or in the Capitol, and their pension costs continue to escalate to unsustainable levels, they have several options, some of which are already being pursued:

- Negotiate lower levels of benefits with unions for pre-reform employees, to supplement the lower levels for new workers—an option that the pending state Supreme Court case could make more viable;

- Negotiate contracts that shift a greater share of pension costs to employees, particularly in cities that have been picking up employee shares;

- Reduce future obligations by making lump-sum payments, emulating a $6 billion extra payment that Brown included in his 2017-18 budget toward future state liabilities. Brown is borrowing the money from a state fund that invests extra cash, and some cities have floated "pension obligation bonds" to do the same;

- Cut city services to fund special reserves for future pension cost increases;

- Raise taxes;

- Declare bankruptcy.

As they await the Supreme Court's ruling and weigh their options for dealing with ever-increasing demands from CalPERS, city officials find that each one comes with its own set of difficulties. One city manager confided, for instance, that when he proposed to leave some parks positions vacant and shift the salary savings into a pension reserve, he told his council that it also would mean reducing park services, such as restroom maintenance. Fearing backlash from constituents, the council ordered that the jobs be filled.

Federal Law Could Allow Bankrupt Cities to Reduce Benefits

When Stockton went through bankruptcy, the federal judge handling the case, Christopher Klein, issued a lengthy opinion that despite the "California rule," federal law could allow bankrupt cities to reduce benefits. "I've had more than 138,000 bankruptcy cases," Klein wrote. "I've been party to impairment of millions of contracts and it's all constitutional."

Stockton, Vallejo, and San Bernardino, under pressure from CalPERS and their unions, did not try to reduce benefits while in bankruptcy. But Klein's opinion sits in the background, waiting for some insolvent public agency to test its validity.

The option that many cities have already taken, and dozens of others are considering, is to raise local taxes, especially sales taxes—although only rarely do they tell voters that the new revenue is needed for pensions.

More generally, they portray the tax boosts as ways to improve police and fire services and keep specific promises to voters, such as adding police patrols or opening fire stations. They know that eventually, as pension costs rise, they will have to rescind those steps.

Privately, some city officials are encouraging their unions to put pension-related tax increases on the ballot via initiative, because a recent court decision indicates that an initiative tax would have a lower vote requirement than one proposed by a city council. Thus it would be easier to enact.

That said, tax increases alone cannot deal with pension costs that are rising so quickly. State-local sales tax rates are now at or above 10 percent in many communities, and taxable retail sales have flattened out as a percentage of personal income. A final note: All of this is occurring during a period of general economic prosperity.

Were recession to hit, local revenue, particularly from sales taxes, would be adversely affected. And as the last big recession demonstrated, CalPERS and other pension funds would likely take another big hit and that could be a recipe for municipal fiscal disaster on a broad scale.

Jamming Janus–The Public Union Empire Strikes Back

This December 2018 article "Jamming Janus–The Public Union Empire Strikes Back" comes from the California Policy Center's Edward Ring:

In June 2018 the U.S. Supreme Court ruled on the *Janus v. AFSCME* case. The result of the decision is that public employees not only have the right to refuse membership in a union, but also the right to refuse to pay so-called "agency fees" to the union.

Unions had been preparing for years for a ruling like this. The Janus case was the successor to a similar case, Friedrichs vs the CTA, which after taking years to work its way through lower courts, ended up deadlocked after the untimely death of Justice Scalia in early 2016.

To hear the reports over the years, and especially in late 2017 and the first half of 2018, Janus was going to be a catastrophe for public sector unions. On the website of a California AFSCME Council, a news article late last year was titled "Judging Janus: Will California's Unions Survive?" When the Janus decision was announced last June, *Time* magazine published an article entitled "The Supreme Court's Union Fees Decision Could Be a Huge Blow for Democrats.

Not so huge, actually. What actually is happening post-Janus, at least so far, might remind one of the Y2K virus. Much ado about nothing. The unions were ready.

How public sector unions prepared for Janus, especially in California, is testament to their incredible power.

In June 2018 the California Policy Center published a list of the laws pushed by public sector unions in the state legislature, all of which were designed to minimize the impact of Janus. Here is an updated list:

1. Requires public employers to conduct a public employee orientation for new employees within four months of hire, and provide a union representative with at least 30 minutes to make a presentation–AB 2935 (2016, passed).

2. "Would require government agencies to negotiate the details of when, where and how unions could have access to recruit new employees; and to provide job titles and contact information for all employees at least every 120 days (as reported by EdSource)–AB 119 (2017, passed).

3. Expands the pool of public employees eligible to join unions–AB 83 (passed), SB 201 (passed), and AB 3034 (vetoed).

4. Makes it difficult, if not impossible, for employers to discuss the pros and cons of unionization with employees–SB 285 (passed) and AB-2017 (pending).

5. Requires the time, date, and location of new public employee orientations to be held confidential–SB 866 (passed).

6. Precludes local governments from unilaterally honoring employee requests to stop paying union dues–AB 1937 (pending) and AB-2049 (pending).

7. Makes employers pay union legal fees if they lose in litigation but does not make unions pay employer costs if the unions lose–SB 550 (passed).

8. Moves the venue for dispute resolution from the courts to PERB (Public Employee Relations Board), which is stacked with pro-union board members–SB 285 (passed) and AB 2886 (vetoed).

California's Largest School Districts Are Underwater

This August 2021 article "California's largest school districts are underwater: Massive debt raises questions about new spending proposals" comes from the California Policy Center's Brandon Ristoff:

The California Policy Center decided to look at California's ten largest school districts to examine their fiscal health, considering their three most recent, comprehensive annual financial reports and their unrestricted net positions.

The unrestricted net position (UNP), explained by Truth in Accounting, is a "magic number" of sorts that shows whether a government agency–school districts in this case–has the assets needed to cover costs funded by future generations of taxpayers. Prudent school boards will have a positive number that functions as a proxy for their financial health.

As seen in the table below, not one of California's largest school districts has the assets needed to pay future bills when they come due.

School District	FY 2018	FY 2019	FY 2020	FY 2018 UNP	FY 2019 UNP	FY 2020 UNP
Los Angeles Unified	621,414	607,723	596,937	-$19,556,239,000	-$16,044,626,000	-$16,376,450,000
San Diego Unified	126,400	124,105	122,916	-$1,715,465,812	-$1,718,781,280	-$1,765,970,592
Fresno Unified	73,455	73,249	73,381	-$1,488,180,172	-$1,625,637,591	-$1,724,228,253
Long Beach Unified	74,681	73,221	72,002	-$563,658,519	-$814,339,303	-$908,137,654
Elk Grove Unified	63,297	63,917	64,480	-$434,646,826	-$485,407,770	-$530,061,342
San Francisco Unified	60,263	60,390	61,031	-$1,212,350,457	-$1,287,870,699	-$1,395,173,956
San Bernardino City Unified	53,027	52,773	53,037	-$485,628,377	-$525,417,285	-$613,707,430
Capistrano Unified	53,622	53,269	52,794	-$459,268,865	-$470,858,912	-$498,027,861
Corona-Norco Unified	53,294	53,002	52,557	-$449,292,740	-$480,399,929	-$506,716,257
San Juan Unified	50,044	50,509	50,820	-$549,147,468	-$648,012,399	-$610,801,643

Credit: California Policy Center.

Breaking the number down to a per-pupil level demonstrates the gravity of the problem.

School District	FY 2018	FY 2019	FY 2020
Los Angeles Unified	-$31,471	-$26,401	-$27,434
San Diego Unified	-$13,572	-$13,849	-$14,367
Fresno Unified	-$20,260	-$22,193	-$23,497
Long Beach Unified	-$7,548	-$11,122	-$12,613
Elk Grove Unified	-$6,867	-$7,594	-$8,221
San Francisco Unified	-$20,118	-$21,326	-$22,860
San Bernardino City Unified	-$9,158	-$9,956	-$11,571
Capistrano Unified	-$8,565	-$8,839	-$9,433
Corona-Norco Unified	-$8,430	-$9,064	-$9,641
San Juan Unified	-$10,973	-$12,830	-$12,019

Credit: California Policy Center.

A link to the California's Largest School Districts Are Underwater full spreadsheet with the sources can be found in the Appendix.

14 – The Cost of Big, Bad & Wasteful Government Via Public Employee Unions

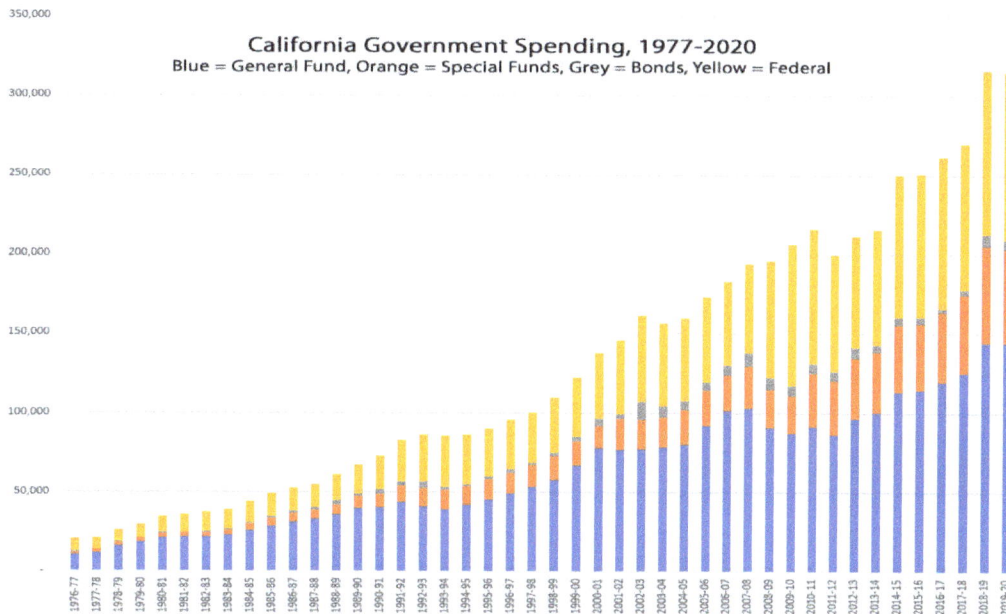

California Government Spending, 1977-2020
Blue = General Fund, Orange = Special Funds, Grey = Bonds, Yellow = Federal

Credit: *California Local Elected Officials (CLEO).*

Government unions have taken over California. Their agenda is inherently in conflict with the public interest, their rhetoric is compelling and formidable and utterly deceptive, their financial power is immense.

They are turning California into a feudal state, where the anointed and compliant corporations build monopolies, government workers lead privileged lives, the rich get richer, the middle class diminishes, and the poor become dependent on government. Nobody who is serious about reversing California's decline–or America's potential decline–can ignore the fundamental enabling role unionized government is playing in its demise.

California's unchecked progressive state-government rule—exemplified by an insatiable desire to raise taxes, a radical environmentalist agenda, and a predilection for social engineering and for micromanaging seemingly every aspect of people's lives—has raised the cost of living and diminished personal and economic freedoms so much that businesses, workers, and retirees have been fleeing the state for years.

Among the strongest special interests—and the chief beneficiaries of this state of affairs—are the state's labor unions, particularly its public-employee unions. From teachers to prison guards to police officers and firefighters to numerous other categories of state employees, unionized government workers exert a substantial influence on the Golden State's policies and finances, to the detriment of its other residents and taxpayers.

This union influence, combined with the monopolistic nature of government bureaucracies, has contributed to waste, fraud, abuse, and a lack of accountability, earning many state agencies and projects the dishonor of the California Golden Fleece Awards (conferred by the Independent Institute, where both authors of this article work) for such major issues as IT failures, housing, wildfires, and the state's ill-fated high-speed-rail project.

California Legislators Spend $200 Billion & Taxpayers Get Less And Less

This section is from the July 2020 report "California Legislators Spend $200 Billion And Taxpayers Get Less And Less" by the Hoover Institution's Lee Ohanian:

California's 2020–21 $202 billion state budget (prior to amendments) spends about three times as much per state resident, adjusted for inflation, compared to California's 1990–91 budget. And this is after $20 billion of COVID-19 related budget cuts. But as you look around the state, you will not see this much higher spending at work. You will instead observe public schools that are falling apart and potholes on major streets that are large enough and deep enough to take out your rear axle.

So why is the state government spending three times as much per Californian today and getting so little in return? One reason is that California taxpayers seem to be far too trusting that their politicians will represent their best interests. I suspect that very few taxpayers have any idea how much state lawmakers are spending, what they are spending it on, and whether the spending is cost-effective. If they did, they would be demanding accountability from the politicians who pass these budgets and who continue to spend more and more on budgets that deliver less and less.

Another reason is due to crony capitalism which is an economy in which businesses thrive not as a result of risk, but rather as a return on money amassed through a nexus between a business class and the political class. This is done using state power to crush genuine competition in handing out permits, government grants, special tax breaks, or other forms of state intervention.

Crony capitalism in its most obvious form is exemplified by massive public works projects of dubious value to society. California's grandiose and possibly doomed high speed rail project is the classic example. Even if the final project is restricted to the segment from Merced to Bakersfield, tens of billions will have been spent on a project that never passed any reasonably unbiased cost/benefit analysis, which is why it never attracted matching funds from the private sector.

There is an enormous disconnect between the value of state-provided goods and services taxpayers receive and how much is spent. By nearly every metric, Californians should be wondering where the money goes, because it is obvious that many priority public goods are not being supplied and this is imposing big costs on taxpayers, particularly on low-income households.

The state budget is increasingly being consumed by three broad categories: education, health and human services, and the state prison system. Those three now eat up more than 90 percent of the budget. And without reforms, these will just get even bigger, further crowding out other budget categories that are suffering woeful neglect.

Without Government Unions There Would Be No Gas Tax Increase

This section is from the November 2017 article "Without Government Unions, There Would be No Gas Tax Increase" comes from the California Policy Center's Edward Ring:

Nobody argues that California's roads need huge upgrades. But the solution didn't require the $0.12 per gallon tax hike that went into effect in November 2017. The root cause of these neglected roads–and the reason even more taxes will never be enough to fix them–is the power of public sector unions, whose agenda is consistently at odds with the public interest. Let us count the ways.

1 – CalTrans mismanagement:

CalTrans could have done a much better job of maintaining California's roads. One of the most diligent critics (and auditors) of CalTrans is state Senator John Moorlach (R, Costa Mesa), the only CPA in California's state legislature. Last year, Moorlach released a report on CalTrans which he summarized in "7-Step Fix for 'Mismanaged' Caltrans," an article on his official website. Just a few highlights include the following:

- In May 2014 the Legislative Analyst Office determined that CalTrans was overstaffed by 3,500 architects and engineers, costing over $500 million per year.

- While to an average state transportation agency outsources over 50% of its work, CalTrans outsources only 10% of its work. Arizona and Florida outsource more than 80%.

- 54% of CalTrans staff is at or near retirement age, so a hiring freeze would reduce staff merely through attrition, without requiring layoffs.

But Moorlach didn't make explicit the reason CalTrans is mismanaged. It's because the unions that run Sacramento don't want to outsource CalTrans work. The unions don't want to reduce CalTrans headcount, or hold CalTrans management accountable. Those actions might help Californians, but they would undermine union power.

2 – Bullet train boondoggle:

Money that could have been allocated to maintain and improve California's roads is being squandered on a train that will do nothing to ameliorate California's transportation challenges. A LOT of money. According to the American Road and Transportation Builders Association, California's freeways can be resurfaced and have a lane added in each direction at a cost of roughly $5.0 million per mile in rural areas, about twice that in urban areas.

Meanwhile, the latest estimate for California's "bullet train," is $98 billion (that's $245 million per mile), thanks to construction delays, and design challenges including nearly 50 miles of tunnels through seismically active mountains to the north and south. And hardly anyone is going to ride it. Ridership won't even pay operating costs. But Sacramento pushes ahead with this monstrous waste when that same money could (at the urban price of $10 million per mile) resurface and add a lane in each direction to 10,000 miles of California's freeways. Imagine smooth, unclogged roads. It's not impossible. It's just policy priorities.

But while bad roads destroy the chassis of millions of cars and trucks, and commuters endure stop-and-go traffic year after year, the California High Speed Rail Authority dutifully pushes on. Why?

Because that's what the government employee unions want. They don't want roads, with all the flexibility and autonomy that roads offer. They want to create a gigantic high-speed rail empire, with tens of thousands of new public employees to drive the trains, maintain the trains, maintain the tracks, and provide security, running up staggering annual deficits. But all of them will be members of public sector unions.

3 – All rapid transit boondoggles:

In a handful of very dense urban areas around the U.S., fast intercity trains make economic sense. But most light rail schemes, along with laughably absurd "streetcar" schemes that actually block urban lanes sorely needed by vehicles, do not achieve levels of ridership that even begin to justify their construction when the alternative is using that money for better, wider connector roads and freeways. The impact of ride sharing apps, the advent of non-polluting cars, and the option of using buses to accomplish mass transit goals all speak to the superior versatility of roads over rail for urban transportation.

So why do California's cities continue to poor billions into light rail and streetcars, when that money could be used to unclog the roads?

To reiterate: The public sector unions that run California want tens of thousands of new public employees to operate the trains and streetcars, maintain them, maintain the tracks, and provide security, running up staggering annual deficits. But doing this means that public sector union membership–hence public sector union power–will increase.

4 – CEQA reform so people can live closer to the jobs:

The median home value in the United States today is $202,700. The median home value in

California today is $509,600, 2.5 times as much! There is no shortage of land in California, and the alleged shortages of energy and water are self-inflicted as the result of policies enacted by California's state legislature. But instead of reforming California's Environmental Quality Act, SB 375, AB 32, and countless other laws that have made building homes in California nearly impossible, California's legislature is doubling down on more government solutions–primarily to subsidize either extremely high density housing, or subsidized housing for the economically disadvantaged, or both.

None of this is necessary. Outside of California's major urban centers, there is no reason homes cannot be profitably built and sold at a median price of $202,700, and there is no reason the people living in those homes cannot drive or ride share to work on fast, unclogged freeways.

But California's public sector unions want more regulations on home building, and they want more subsidized public housing. Because those solutions, even though inadequate and coercive, enable them to hire vast new bureaucracies to enforce the many regulations and administer the public assets. Unleashing the private sector to build affordable homes in a competitive market would rob these unions of their opportunity to acquire more power. It's that simple.

Insatiable Appetite For Pension Fund Contributions

According to a California Policy Center study, taking barely adequate annual employer pension contributions into account, the average unionized state/local government worker in California makes over $120,000 per year in pay and benefits. But to adequately fund their promised pension benefits, employers will need to pay at least another $20,000 per employee to the pension funds.

This funding gap, which equates to over $20 billion per year, is the additional amount that is required to cover the difference between how much California's public employee pension funds currently collect from taxpayers, and how much they need to collect to keep the promises that union controlled politicians have made to the government unions they "negotiate" with. That is a best-case scenario.

It could be much worse. A 2016 California Policy Center analysis estimated that under a worst-case scenario, the annual costs to fund California's public employee pension funds could cost taxpayers nearly $70 billion more per year than they are currently paying.

And by the way, California's pension funds are themselves almost entirely under the control of public sector unions–research the background of CalPERS and CalSTRS board directors to verify the degree of influence they have.

Absent significant reform, funding California's public employee pensions is going to continue to consume every dollar in new taxes for the next several decades. The cumulative financial impact of funding these pensions is easily triple that of the bullet train's $100 billion fiasco, probably much more.

Let's be perfectly clear. Government unions control California. They collect and spend over $1.0 billion every year, and spend most of that money on either explicit political campaigning and lobbying, or soft advocacy via expensive public relations campaigns and sponsored academic studies. Their presence is felt everywhere, from local transit districts to the governor's office. They make or break politicians at will, by outspending or outlasting their opponents. At best, California's most powerful corporate players do not cross these unions, often they collude with them.

California's public sector unions operate as senior partners in a coalition that includes left-wing oligarchs especially in the Silicon Valley, extreme environmentalists and their powerful trial lawyer cohorts, and the Latino Legislative Caucus–usurped by leftist radicals–and their many allies in the social justice/identity politics industry. The power of this government union led coalition is nearly absolute, and the consequences to California's private sector working class have been nothing short of devastating.

Government unions force California's agencies to over-hire, overpay, and mismanage, because that benefits their members even as it harms the public. These unions enforce absurd policy priorities that further harm the public in order to increase their power. They are the reason California has increased its gas tax.

The Cost of California's Public-Employee Unions

This April 2021 report below tiled "The Cost of California's Public-Employee Unions" comes from Independent Institute researchers Lawrence J. McQuillan and Adam B. Summers:

One of the most obvious ways that public-employee unions affect the political landscape in California is through their efforts to swell the size of government (and their own ranks) through tax increases. More money in state coffers means more money to public employees and larger numbers of dues-paying union members.

Union support has been important in a variety of major tax and fee increases, including Assembly Bill 32, the Global Warming Solutions Act of 2006. This measure established the state's cap-and-trade system, which forces energy and industrial companies to purchase emissions credits, with the revenues used to fund the high-speed-rail boondoggle and various environmental programs. Union backing was also instrumental in the imposition of online sales taxes in 2011 (AB 155 and AB 28X1); substantial personal-income-tax increases through.

Proposition 30, which added multiple higher-income tax brackets in 2012; and significant hikes to the state's gas taxes and vehicle fees via Senate Bill 1 in 2017. As a result, California has the highest gas tax in the nation (more than three times the national average), the highest state sales tax, and the three highest personal-income-tax brackets.

As detailed in the Independent Institute book *California Dreaming: Lessons on How to Resolve America's Public Pension Crisis*, generous pension benefits, overly optimistic assumptions about the returns on pension-fund investments, and politically motivated underfunding have led to the state's public-pension crisis, all facilitated by government-employee-union influence.

California's public-pension troubles began in earnest in 1999, when Senate Bill 400 raised government workers' pension benefits by as much as 50 percent. The new benefit formula allowed a California Highway Patrol officer, for example, to retire after 30 years, as young as age 50, with a pension equal to 90 percent of his final salary. To make matters worse, the benefit enhancements were made retroactive, meaning that workers who had made contributions for years based on a lower expected benefit suddenly received a windfall.

SB 400 was enthusiastically supported by a wide swath of public-employee unions and sponsored by the heavily union-influenced California Public Employees' Retirement System at the height of the dot-com boom. CalPERS argued that there would be little net cost to the state because of all the extra tax revenue it was raking in, as if the party was going to last forever.

The dot-com bubble inevitably burst, and stocks crashed the next year. But the damage had already been done, and taxpayers were now on the hook to make up pension-funding shortfalls for decades to come.

The Strongest Special interest in Sacramento is the Teachers' Unions

Perhaps the strongest special interest in Sacramento is the teachers' unions, including the California Teachers Association (CTA) and the California Federation of Teachers (CFT). Unfortunately for students, union rules and protections are not just expensive but have caused academic quality to deteriorate.

Things got so bad that a lawsuit was filed in 2014 on behalf of nine public-school students alleging that state laws granting teachers tenure after less than two years, establishing the "last in, first out" policy of laying off teachers based on seniority rather than effectiveness, and creating a lengthy, costly, and difficult process of getting rid of ineffective teachers so harmed students, particularly poor and minority children, that they violated the students' constitutional rights.

In *Vergara v. California*, Los Angeles County Superior Court judge Rolf Treu sided with the students, finding that "evidence has been elicited in this trial of the specific effect of grossly ineffective teachers on students. The evidence is compelling. Indeed, it shocks the conscience." The victory was short-lived, however, as the decision was overturned by the Court of Appeals two years later and the California supreme court refused to hear a further appeal.

The issue of unions' preventing public schools from getting rid of bad—and even abusive—teachers is not a new one. There have been many reports over the years of teachers' being paid to do nothing but sit in empty "rubber rooms" while their disciplinary procedures play out, or being given tens of thousands of dollars to go away or not to fight terminations, because it is cheaper than trying to fire them.

More recently, the teachers' unions have steadfastly refused to reopen schools that were closed because of the coronavirus outbreak, or have offered only limited and inadequate online instruction, even as teachers continue to collect full paychecks. Meanwhile, many private schools and other private businesses have managed to remain open and serve their students and customers.

Naturally, unions want to increase their ranks and influence, but sometimes they go about it in ways that use government coercion rather than simply offering workers an honest choice, and that harm both consumers and many of the workers on whose behalf they purport to act.

The SEIU-UHW West health-care workers' union has blatantly and repeatedly abused the state's ballot-initiative process in an attempt to pressure the dialysis industry into unionizing its workers. The union has done this by advancing measures (Proposition 8 in 2018, Proposition 23 in 2020) that would have punished dialysis centers with pointless regulations and added labor costs, threatening the health and the very lives of thousands of fragile dialysis patients across the state.

Fortunately, 2020 voters saw through both measures, which failed badly, by 20 and 27 points, respectively.

Banned Independent Contracting Work for Millions of Californians

Even more notorious is California's AB 5 legislation, ardently supported by the California Labor Federation and a host of other public and private-sector unions, which essentially banned independent contracting work for millions of Californians (though more than 100 politically connected professions were later exempted from the sweeping law).

While the stated purpose of the measure was to enhance worker protections, in reality it was a thinly veiled attempt to unionize hundreds of thousands of ride-share drivers. This nearly forced the shutdown of Uber and Lyft services statewide, but voters easily passed Proposition 22 to exempt ride-share and food-delivery drivers from the law.

Many other California entrepreneurs who prefer the flexibility of independent contract work but do not have the deep pockets or political connections to obtain exemptions have suffered substantial income losses from AB 5. It is clear that the unions do not care about these workers so long as they can add more union members—and their dues—to the rolls.

As the AB 5 example shows, California still has not learned the lesson that favoring narrow special interests while reducing employment opportunities, diminishing the quality of education, and continually increasing the cost of living is not a strategy for success. California illustrates the dangers of outsized public-employee-union influence and should serve as a warning to other states—and the federal government—that are following down the same path.

California's Public-Sector Unions Rake in $921 Million in Annual Revenue

This August 2020 article "California's Public-Sector Unions Rake in $921 Million in Annual Revenue" comes from the California Policy Center's Edward Ring:

There is no special interest in California that wields more influence over state and local politics than public sector unions. At every level of government, from the office of the governor to a school board managing a district with only a few hundred students, public sector unions are omnipresent. With rare exceptions, to defy their agenda is certain political suicide.

The reason for this power is money. Lots of money. Every two-year election cycle, not millions, but hundreds of millions of dollars are spent by California's public-sector unions to support or oppose candidates, campaign for ballot measures, lobby the legislature, and pay for public relations campaigns.

While wealthy individuals or powerful corporations may at times challenge these unions, their concerns are narrow in focus. Nothing matches the perennial torrent of public sector union money; the opposition may stir up a flash flood, but these unions are the Amazon.

Twice in the past five years the California Policy Center has attempted to estimate just how much money public sector unions collect and spend each year. In 2015, a rough top-down estimate that used US Census Bureau data on union membership and general assumptions on the average union dues payment came up with $1.0 billion per year. In 2018, exercising an abundance of caution, referring to the 990 forms that unions file with the IRS, as well as researching membership information that is often provided by the unions on their websites, the total public sector union spending estimate was $800 million per year.

This time, using the same methods as 2018, but going into somewhat more detail, the new estimate is $921 million. It should be noted that available information online is usually about 18-24 months behind. For example, our 2018 report referenced Form 990s that were filed for 2015. This 2020 report used Form 990 data for the year 2018, the most recent currently available.

The fact that data presented here represents 2018 numbers raises an important question: Has the Janus decision, which found that the application of public sector union fees to non-members is a violation of the First Amendment, had any effect on public-sector union revenue and membership? Because Janus took effect in mid-2018, the results shown here may only serve as a baseline. Form 990s for 2019 will not be available to the public for another year.

Moreover, unless the trends in total revenue estimates show truly dramatic changes, which is unlikely, there are too many variables at work to know what may be generating the variance.

If the numbers are up, would they have been up higher without the Janus decision? Will any downward results in 2019 merely be the impact of unions losing non-members who still had to pay agency fees, or would some of the downturn be the result of losing members? How will the bureaucratic obstacles put up by the unions delay individuals from exercising their new rights under Janus? And how would one account for new bargaining units, such as the 45,000 child care providers who in July 2020 voted to become new AFSCME members?

Much of this in-depth discussion will be covered in *Union Madness* and *Pension Madness* and falls outside the scope of this analysis.

Billions and Billions Spent of Political Donations

California's public-sector unions collect and spend well over $900 million per year, or $1.8 billion per two-year election cycle.

While only about one-third of this money is spent on explicitly political purposes such as campaign contributions and lobbying, this is still a staggering amount of money. What other special interest in California is willing and able to spend $600 million every two years on political advocacy, year after year, for decades on end?

And where the spending is not declared as political, it may still have a political impact. As the plaintiffs argued in the Janus case before the U.S. Supreme Court, and in the deadlocked *Friedrichs* case before that, all public sector union spending is inherently political. Public education campaigns, for example, are not considered "political," but unions rarely embark on these efforts, often at levels where they saturate California's expensive media markets, without at least an indirectly political motivation. And what about negotiations for compensation and work rules? Aren't these political decisions?

To get another glimpse of just how Sisyphean the task of identifying and tracking all of California's public-sector unions is, have a look at this website, put up by the Freedom Foundation. Scroll down this page and consider the following: Were all of these various Locals included in this analysis? Here's your answer: No. They weren't. There's simply too many of them. Some years ago, a professor at Pepperdine University who was considered an expert on public-sector unions in California was asked if there was an accurate compilation, anywhere, ever, showing how much, collectively, these unions rake in every year. His answer, emphatically to the negative, was too obscene to be repeated here.

California's public-sector unions are not only the most powerful political special interest in the state, but most of them are nakedly partisan.

To have all this power, and merely use it to push for more staff, more restrictive work rules (which equates to more staff), more pay, and more benefits, that would be bad enough. Not because workers shouldn't want to optimize their opportunities to work and live with security and dignity, but because public-sector unions simply do not have to deal with the natural checks on their demands that create more balance between management and private-sector unions.

But with only a few exceptions—primarily among the law enforcement unions—the websites of these public sector unions read like a pamphlet describing the agenda of the Democratic party. Is this appropriate? Does this represent the membership? And even if so, shouldn't public sector unions, with all the power they wield, be politically neutral?

A long-overdue reckoning with public sector unions faces California's electorate. It might start with the public schools, which labor under a public-sector union monopoly that has nearly destroyed accountability. The CTA, for example, has endorsed the absurd goal to "defund the police." Perhaps defunding the CTA itself might be a more appropriate way to rescue California's disadvantaged.

But between the political reality of public sector union power, and the necessary reforms that Californians desperately deserve, are nearly one billion dollars per year of cold hard cash.

Why Are Government Workers In California Paid Twice As Much As Private Sector Workers?

This section is from the April 2019 report "At $140,000 Per Year, Why Are Government Workers In California Paid Twice As Much As Private Sector Workers?" by the Hoover Institution's Lee Ohanian:

Nationwide, government-worker compensation has been growing more rapidly than private-sector compensation for several years, but this trend is on steroids in California, where some state and local government workers are now paid roughly twice as much as those in the private sector.

The California Policy Center recently examined public-sector compensation of full-time workers at two points in time: in 2012, when the California economy was still weakened from the recession, and in 2015. The study shows a high level of compensation for public-sector workers in 2012, and a subsequent high growth rate for compensation between 2012 and 2015.

The California Policy Center examined pay records for more than two million state and local government workers (not including those in K–12 or college education) and found that average total compensation in 2012 for a full-time employee was $124,058 in a California city, $102,312 for county workers, and $100,668 for state workers. By 2015, total compensation had increased to $137,392, $117,425, and $116,887, respective to these categories. Adjusting for inflation, these are increases of 7.3 percent, 11.2 percent, and 12.5 percent, respectively, over this three-year period, compared to roughly a 3 percent increase for the entire US economy over the same period. Full-time private-sector workers in California received average total compensation of $62,475 in 2015.

Both components of compensation, pay and benefits, are higher for government workers. Benefits contribute 40 percent to the overhead of a public-sector employee, which reflects significant public-sector pensions. However, this amount would be even higher if the pension contributions accurately accounted for the fact that pension funds are currently underfunded.

If the necessary increases in contributions to California's state and local pension funds were considered, then the average total compensation (pay and benefits) for a full-time city, county, or state worker in California during 2015 was $139,691, which is more than double private-sector compensation in that year.

So why are public-sector workers paid so much more? While there are important caveats in comparing compensation across workers of all types, differences in how competition guides public versus private-sector compensation practices are important in understanding this two-fold difference in compensation levels.

Private-sector employees must provide enough value to their organizations so that it covers their full cost of employment. Otherwise, the organization incurs a loss, and the employee loses their job. In the public sector, this relationship changes significantly.

One reason is that public-sector services are typically monopoly providers. They do not face any competition and thus do not confront the competitive pressure that private-sector organizations face. Of course, this competitive pressure in the private sector is what drives efficiency, innovation, and other business ideas that create new products, lower production costs, and offer higher value for consumers.

In the public sector, the lack of competition makes it is far easier to pass along higher costs, including employee costs. Not surprisingly, the unionization rate among public-sector workers in the state is about five times higher than in the private sector. The simple reason why unionization is so much more prevalent for government workers is that a typical union—one that raises its members' compensation above market rates—can only succeed if the organization faces little or no competition.

Government Unions and California Ballot Propositions

The sections below are from the December 2020 article "Government Unions and California Ballot Propositions" comes from the California Policy Center's Edward Ring:

Direct democracy, for better or for worse, has become California's most distinctive and emblematic political institution. Initiative, referendum, and recall elections were added to the state constitution in 1911 as part of Governor Hiram Johnson's "progressive" movement, which redeemed the state from control by "The Octopus", meaning the Southern Pacific Railroad monopoly that had a stranglehold on the state's economy and government. Progressive reformers expected that California voters would use direct democracy to tame the Octopus and to protect themselves against such wealthy special interests in the future. Over time, however, those same interests proved adept at using direct democracy to serve their own interests.

Californians voted on twelve state ballot propositions on November 3, 2020. On nine of these propositions, California's government and private sector unions spent significant amounts of money, over a million in five cases, and over ten million in two cases. But of these nine, the unions only got their way on one of them, Prop. 19, which changed some of the rules on how property taxes are applied. And Prop 19 was not a high priority for the unions, with barely over $100,000 in contributions, mostly from Firefighter unions. The big bucks in favor of Prop. 19, over $41 million, came from the real estate industry.

And if it weren't for Prop. 19, California's unions would have logged a perfect record on November 3, losing every battle. The real story on November 3 is that California's tech moguls, and big business, in that order, are willing and able to spend California's unions into the ground when they decide that's what is necessary to protect their interests. Before reflecting on the implications of that staggering fact, it's worth having a closer look at some of the battles.

Mostly Government Unions Spent $68 Million on 2020 Ballot Propositions

As reported by the California Secretary of State, unions, mostly government unions, spent $68 million on ballot propositions. That is based on information updated through October 17, 2020, and does not include in-kind contributions, so the actual spending was higher. The biggest fight, by far, was in support of Prop. 15, which would have required commercial properties to be reassessed at current market values for assessing property taxes.

It's no secret why passing Prop. 15 was a priority for government unions. Ever since the legendary Prop. 13 was passed back in 1978, it has been blamed for government budget deficits in California. Leaving aside the fact that administrative bloat, mismanaged overtime, and financially unsustainable pensions are the real reason for budget deficits, or the fact that inflation adjusted tax revenues in California have always kept pace with population growth despite the impact of Prop. 13, the relatively low property taxes that businesses pay in California is one of the last, if not the last, competitive advantage left for business in what is otherwise the most hostile business climate in America.

Protecting California's businesses, however, is not a priority these days for California's unions. The California Teachers Association, the California Federation of Teachers, and the Service Employees International Union (SEIU) joined with their local chapters and other unions to pony up nearly $38 million to push Prop. 15. And joining these union in a rare defeat was over $10 million in funding from the Chan Zuckerberg Initiative Advocacy PAC. Zuckerberg's PAC, along with other Zuckerberg controlled entities, drenched the political soil across America this election season, including $400 million to "get out the vote" in key swing states.

As the last few election cycles are making increasingly obvious, if you pair the deep pockets of government unions with the even deeper pockets of big tech, you're going to get whatever they want. But Prop. 15 was an existential threat that backed California's businesses, big and small, into a corner. Apparently not all of them are ready to flee to Texas, because led by the California Small Business Roundtable that kicked in $31.7 million, they came up with just over $60 million in opposition spending. Prop. 15 failed, only getting 48 percent of the vote. This time.

There Were Other Ballot Mega-Fights on November 3, 2020 Election

There were other mega-fights on November 3, 2020, most notable the limited war waged by big tech against AB 5, which took the form of Prop. 22. Limited war, because instead of repealing AB 5, a smashmouth union power play that turned most of California's over two million independent contractors into employees overnight, the big tech rideshare companies chose to only bail themselves out.

It wasn't as if these companies didn't have the wherewithal to come up with a more comprehensive reform. The war chest they amassed in support of Prop. 22 was almost ridiculous–almost, because nothing is ridiculous any more when it comes to the power of big tech–Uber kicked in $51 million, Door Dash threw down $51 million, Lyft added $47.5 million, Instacart was good for $31 million, and Postmates spent $11.5 million. All told, the rideshare industry raised $192.7 million to protect their interests.

Fighting against Prop. 22 were all the unions, with the biggest contributions coming from the SEIU and the International Brotherhood of Teamsters. Over $16 million of the $18.6 million spent against Prop. 22 came from unions, but it was a lopsided battle from the start. Prop. 22 passed easily, with 58.6 percent of the vote.

Another big spend by unions this election cycle was the SEIU's support for Prop. 23, which would have imposed new regulations on dialysis clinics and presumably opened the door to unionizing them. But where the SEIU spent almost $9 million, the renal care industry spent a whopping $104 million, with much of this money coming from out-of-state.

One of the most visible of the propositions on the November 3 ballot was Prop. 16, which would have brought back affirmative action. It's not clear why affirmative action is even required in California, since virtually every established institution in the state desperately adheres to proportional representation whenever possible. And while the unions came up with $1.7 million to support this bill, another $17.5 million came from private donors, including $5.5 million from M. Quinn Delaney–who along with her wealthy husband Wayne Jordan are among California's premier limousine liberals.

The defeat of Prop. 16 is perhaps one of the most encouraging signs in the 2020 election, because despite being outspent by more than ten-to-one, the opponents prevailed. Californians saw Prop. 16 for what it was, a transparently racist meal ticket for trial lawyers, "equity and inclusion" bureaucrats, and the victim industry, masquerading as anti-racism. With only 42 percent of Californians voting yes, it wasn't even close.

Another fight worth mentioning was the sad fate of Prop. 20. Losing badly with only 38.3 percent of the vote, it would have restored tougher penalties for drug and property crimes. Backed to the tune of $3.0 million by law enforcement unions, supporters for Prop. 20 were outspent overall, although not by much. Leading the charge against Prop. 20 was $2.3 million from Zuckerberg's PAC, and $2.0 million from Patty Quillin, whose husband Reed Hastings is the founder of Netflix. This power couple is better known for donating $2.2 million to the victorious campaign of district attorney George Gascon, who helped decriminalize San Francisco, and who is now going to reprise this role as district attorney to crime plagued Los Angeles.

Overall, Unions Did Not Do Well on Ballot Propositions in California Last Election Season

Overall, unions did not do well on ballot propositions in California this election season, despite maintaining their grip on nearly every other manifestation of political power in the state.

The real takeaway is the fact that big tech has consolidated its power and is firmly established as the new top dog in California politics. So far, the decisions they're making are not encouraging. They looked out for their own, in the case of Prop. 22, ostensibly to protect the rights of their drivers to remain independent contractors, while leaving all the rest still victims of AB 5.

Mark Zuckerberg, who has enough money to hire a private security force that could probably defeat the armies of small nations, saw fit to take down Prop. 20, apparently indifferent to the ongoing chaos on the streets of every major city in California.

To conclude with the obvious, how unions and tech billionaires decide they want to influence politics from now on is going to be decisive. But apart from the police unions peeling away from the pack to support Prop. 20, there is no sign that the coalition that already broke California–unions, government bureaucrats, extreme environmentalists, litigators, and liberal activists of every stripe–will be anything but more powerful with the arrival of politically active tech billionaires.

There are only two political forces that can match this sort of firepower. Other business interests, when confronting an existential threat, as shown by the massive opposition to Prop. 15 and Prop. 23, and populism, as shown by the landslide rejection of Prop. 16.

In most cases, if they chose to, these special interests could pursue an enlightened course of action. The law enforcement unions were right to back Prop. 20, and they should try again. While the tech billionaires haven't done much of anything right just yet, it would only take one of them to shake the system.

Maybe school vouchers will be the disruptive cause that attracts real money from Silicon Valley. And if the environmentalist leadership listened to their members, instead of just talking down to them and addling their minds, we would already be logging responsibly in California's forests to thin the tinder, instead of encouraging our feckless governor to cope with wildfires calling for more electric cars.

With only a few exceptions, on the dozen ballot initiatives they faced, California's voters made the right choices. This is an encouraging development. If only a few more special interests put common sense and the common welfare in front of their blinding ideologies and billion dollar enterprises, the political landscape in this state would swiftly realign.

However, California Union's Support of Governor Newsom's Anti-Recall Efforts Paid Dividends

Per an October 2021 post recall election report titled "An Indecent Proposal" from the California Policy Center you can never under-estimate union power:

It would be easy to look at Gavin Newsom's win as a rejection of the massive, grassroots movement that put him up for recall in the first place, or use it to dismiss citizen initiatives altogether. But, a closer look suggests Newsom's win may have less to do with his ideas and even the job he's done as governor, and more to do with money.

In his case, a lot more.

In total, Newsom and the various committees working to protect him from recall brought in just shy of $80 million. Together, Newsom's opponents raised just over $50 million, though the leading contender, Larry Elder, campaigned with around $20 million.

Over $11.5 million of Newsom's support came from government unions, and he received another $4.4 million from unions representing both public- and private-sector workers. Time and again, we saw government unions kick money collected through membership dues to Newsom during the recall cycle, and in exchange, receive nice payoffs.

With a contribution of over $1.8 million, the California Teachers Association was Newsom's top government union supporter, though gifts from other education unions brought the support from public school employees nearly $2.5 million. One could easily argue Newsom is repaying these donors in the best way he can: by supporting their vehement demands that all students be masked at school, and hinting he will mandate students be vaccinated against COVID-19.

The California Correctional Peace Officers Association's $1.75 million contribution is paying enviable dividends. Despite the Legislative Analyst's Office determining the raises lacked "clear justification," and a compensation study finding California guards receive 40% higher compensation than their counterparts in local government, Newsom signed off on $5,000 raises and 12 days' worth of wellness relief time for prison guards. Now, Newsom and his administration are actively fighting to exempt prison guards from his sweeping vaccine mandate for state workers.

The Service Employees International Union Local 1000—California's largest public-sector union—gave the governor $1 million to fight the recall attempt, and one can only assume it was a thank-you gift for the pay hikes the members received this summer. In addition to Newsom's administration restoring the 9.23% pay cuts the union members (like other government workers) took during the height of the COVID work stoppages, members will receive an additional 4.55% pay increase moving forward.

Public-sector unions elect politicians, who once in office, hold incredible power to return the favor. While many Americans are rightly concerned about preserving or restoring integrity to our election process, California government unions are buying politicians in broad daylight and stealing away one election after another.

15 – Stopping the State's Downward Spiral Into Progressivism Madness

Credit: WallpaperDog.

The start of this final chapter is from the Summer 2010 *City Journal* article "The Golden State's War on Itself" by Joel Kotkin:

Today's California represents most everything wrong with today's Progressivism movement, more often referred to as "Regressivism." In retrospect, California's progressive mistakes provide an incubator and testing ground to show America and prove the world, why it's not in the best interest of the overwhelming number of Californians and Americans.

In the 19th and 20th centuries, California was the destination for those seeking a better place to live. For most of its history, the state enacted sensible policies that created one of the wealthiest and most innovative economies in human history. California realized the American dream—but better—fostering a huge middle class that, for the most part, owned their homes, sent their kids to public schools, and found meaningful work connected to the state's amazingly diverse, innovative economy.

In the middle of the 20th century, the leadership of Governor Pat Brown and his practical Democrats made California, the Golden State, the envy of all others. These were the sapient leaders with old school Democrats values, ideas and policies that helped create the California dream.

However, since the dawn of the 21st century, the dream has been evaporating. Between 2003 and 2007, California state and local government spending grew 31 percent, even as the state's population grew just 5 percent. The overall tax burden as a percentage of state income, once middling among the states, has risen to the sixth-highest in the nation, says the Tax Foundation.

Since 1990, according to an analysis by California Lutheran University, the state's share of overall U.S. employment has dropped a remarkable 10 percent. When the state economy has done well, it has usually been the result of asset inflation—first during the dot-com bubble of the late 1990s, and then during the housing boom, which was responsible for nearly half of all jobs created earlier in this decade, and big tech most recently.

Guiding the agenda of California's Democrats are a ruling elite, small in number, but wielding incredible power. Among these elites are government union leaders, liberal billionaires from Hollywood to Silicon Valley, extreme environmentalists, and the social justice vanguard. The money and influence these elites bring to California politics cannot possibly be matched by the opposition. But all the money in the world cannot make up for the fact that their policies have made life miserable for millions of ordinary Californians.

We've heard all this before. Much of what Californians face are challenges confronting everyone in America. But California, the biggest state, and the bluest state, is a powerful trendsetter. California is broken, hijacked by opportunists wielding overwhelming financial and political power. How does this change?

Progressivism as the New Marxism

The ideological failure of California falls squarely on the shoulders of progressive politicians and activists, social justice reformers, civil rights workers, cultural appropriation enforcers, diversity, and inclusion warriors and the like who have spread into the media, government, college campuses, neighborhood organizations and workplaces.

In the twentieth century, Marxist revolutionaries sought to set things right by leading a revolution to overthrow the capitalist system and replace it with a just economic system. Progressives want to set things right through social change in order to create a just society. In a just society everyone is equal: men and women, immigrants and native-born, persons of various racial and ethnic groups, heterosexuals, and homosexuals, first and third world people, disabled and able-bodied. This will be a society free from the "isms" of sexism, nativism, racism, heterosexism, colonialism, and ableism.

To the progressive, the success of the newly liberated oppressed person must not be limited by the extent of his talent or effort. Success is merited by the very existence of his membership in an oppressed group. As in Marxist theory—"from each according to his ability, to each according to his needs"—even people of lesser abilities and efforts deserve equal outcomes. The progressive sees anything less than this as failure.

Undergirding all this is the assumption that a just society will be gained through the intervention of government. Only government can force the needed changes. This is achieved through a complex and extensive web of government mechanisms: civil rights laws; affirmative action programs; minimum wage laws; housing assistance; guaranteed income; income maintenance programs that seamlessly transfer wealth from haves to have nots; block grants to states; guaranteed health care for all; national disaster relief—and more.

In the progressive view there is little tolerance for government that cannot deliver equal outcomes for all. However, every human being is unique and not standardized widgets, so ultimately, government is incapable of creating a society of equals (which is impossible) and will fail.

Fixing California: The Themes That Make Anything Possible

This section is from the June 2021 article "Fixing California–Part One: The Themes That Make Anything Possible" comes from the California Policy Center's Edward Ring:

For conservatives across America, California has become the cautionary tale for the rest of the country. Anyone who actually lives in the Golden State, and enjoys the best weather and the most beautiful, diverse scenery on earth, knows there are two sides to the story of this captivating place. Nevertheless, the story keeps getting worse.

For every essential—homes, rent, tuition, gasoline, electricity, and water—Californians pay the among the highest prices in the continental United States. Californians endure the most hostile business climate in America, and pay the highest taxes. The public schools are failing, crime is soaring, electricity is unreliable, water is rationed, and the mismanaged forests are burning like hell. Yet all of this can be fixed.

The solutions aren't mysteries. Deregulate housing permits. End the disastrous "housing-first" policies and instead give the homeless safe housing in inexpensive barracks where sobriety is a condition of entry. Repeal Proposition 47, which downgraded property and drug crimes. Build reservoirs, desalination, and wastewater recycling plants. Build nuclear power plants and develop California's abundant natural gas reserves. Recognize that the common road is the future of transportation, not the past, and widen California's freeways and highways. Let the timber companies harvest more lumber in exchange for maintaining the fire roads and power line corridors. Implement school choice and make public schools compete with private schools on the basis of excellence. Done.

This isn't just about ideology. The politicians who governed California during what arguably were its greatest yesteryears were Democrats. Old-timers refer to them as the Pat Brown Democrats (not to be confused with his son Jerry Brown and his progressive Democrat constituents), leaders whose approach to politics was pragmatic and focused on serving the people.

During that heyday, homes were affordable, and freeways weren't crowded. Public schools were good, and the University of California campuses offered the best public higher education in the country. The California Water Project, taking barely more than a decade to construct, remains the most successful feat of interbasin water transfers in the world.

The Coalition That Will Realign California

This section is from the December 2020 article "Fixing California—Part One: The Themes That Make Anything Possible" comes from the California Policy Center's Edward Ring:

Across several areas of policy, the Democratic party, led by Gavin Newsom, has not merely alienated, but enraged millions of Californians.

The key to political realignment in California is not only to offer these groups a political agenda that incorporates solutions to all their grievances, but does so in a manner so coherent, so practical, and so promising, that a common solidarity is generated which transcends all the ways California's ruling class has thus far divided them

Hardcore populist support for Democrats in California comes primarily from millions of white liberals, living in inherited homes, who pay minimal property taxes and are hence immune from the consequences of an out-of-control public sector bureaucracy, along with the government employees that work in that bureaucracy.

The critical swing constituency, currently solidly in the Democratic camp, are black, Latino, and Asian voters—and the battle to turn back California's progressive downward spiral is in the hands of these critical groups.

The Battle for California is the Battle for America

These sections below are from the October 2020 article "The Battle for California is the Battle for America" comes from the California Policy Center's Edward Ring:

By now, this is a familiar story. California is a failed state. Thanks to years of progressive mismanagement and neglect, the cities are lawless, and the forests are burning. Residents pay the highest prices in America for unreliable electricity. Water is rationed. Homes are unaffordable. The public schools are a joke. Freeways are congested and crumbling. And if they're not still on lockdown or otherwise already destroyed by it, business owners contend with the most hostile regulatory climate in American history.

It is understandable that conservatives in the rest of the United States would be happy to write off California. But California is not writing off the rest of the United States, and therein lies grave danger to American prosperity and freedom.

What if California doesn't implode, a victim of its own political mismanagement? What if California instead completes its transformation into a successful plutocracy, run by a clique of multi-billionaires in a partnership of convenience with environmentalist extremists and backed by the power of a unionized state bureaucracy?

What if the people who would resist this tyranny leave, and the remaining population peacefully accepts universal basic income and subsidized housing? What if all it takes to be a feudal overlord in progressive California is to proffer to the proletarians a pittance of alms, while reliably spouting incessant, blistering social justice and climate change rhetoric?

Why won't that work? After all, it's worked so far. California has the most progressive electorate in America.

California is by Far the Wealthiest, Most Influential State in America

Not because of California's regulatory state, but in spite of it, California is by far the wealthiest, most influential state in America. With 40 million people, a diverse economy, and a gross domestic product of $3.2 trillion, California is almost a nation unto itself. And the progressive zealots who run California have been acting like an independent nation, with the avowed goal of transforming the entire United States to match its image.

What happens in California matters to the rest of the United States because California's internal market is huge, its political and financial influence is powerful, and it rallies political allies throughout the U.S. If what California does to transform its own culture and economy isn't stopped, the rest of the U.S. will fall into line. The result will be a comprehensive reinvention of society in all areas, political, economic, and cultural.

The difficult reality that conservative Americans must accept is that while California may be a failed state by the standards Middle America has come to take for granted, California may not fail by its own standards. The society California is building may prove viable, even if it is hideous to contemplate and morally wrong. It may prove viable even though the alternatives that it displaces offer more prosperity and freedom to more people. It amounts to an all-powerful tech plutocracy ruling over a micro-managed, dependent population, with rationing and redistribution in the name of social justice and saving the planet.

This model, which is a modern form of feudalism, may work not merely because it is politically and economically sustainable despite its many shortcomings, nor merely because it offers more power and profit to its handful of resident billionaires who already possess obscene levels of power and wealth. These reasons don't fully explain the popularity of progressive feudalism. There is one more piece in the puzzle.

The progressive model also becomes viable because of a moral narrative that is flawed but nonetheless compelling: We live in an inherently oppressive society, so we must reduce the privileged middle class in the interests of social justice. We live in an era of limited resources and a stressed planet, so we must reduce everyone's standard of living. Countering that narrative is the mission that must be sent into California. The misery that Californians have condemned themselves to live is not a moral choice. They are victims of a con job.

What follows are detailed examples of what's happening in California. These examples are selected based on the level of transformative impact they are having, as well as their potential to be rolled into the rest of the United States. But this compendium, while lengthy, only scratches the surface.

The Labor Movement is the Glue

At the forefront of California's populist progressive movement is organized labor. Assimilating the progressive battle cries on all the predictable topics—race, gender, climate change—California's labor movement wields both their billions in dues revenue and a perpetually mobilized field army that reaches into every locale and institution. And in a major escalation of a battle soon to rage across America, California's unions have taken on independent contractors.

Sailing through the state legislature and signed by Governor Gavin Newsom in September 2019, AB 5 outlawed most forms of individual independent contracting and threw most of the rest into legal ambiguity. While aimed at rideshare drivers on Uber and Lyft platforms, it affected all businesses that use independent contractors, from nail salons and graphic artists to thousands of badly needed nurses and other health care professionals.

The most powerful injured parties, led by Uber and Lyft, have funded a ballot initiative that will repeal AB 5 for their specific industries. But small businesses, including sole proprietors, are out of luck. The move to ban independent contractors has now gone national, with Biden and Harris endorsing the policy. The Biden campaign is even running ads against the Uber and Lyft-backed ballot proposition: "Now, gig economy giants are trying to gut the law and exempt their workers. It's unacceptable."

The consequences of outlawing most forms of independent contracting are obvious, and disgraceful. Within realistic constraints, people should be allowed to exchange services for money without having to become employees of a company. That such a basic expression of freedom should come under attack illustrates the gravity of the fight we're in. The motivation for this law is equally obvious and disgraceful; if people can be herded into companies as employees, then they can be organized and put under union representation.

It's worth reexamining exactly what unions in California represent, rather than leaving it at that. California's unions exist primarily in the public sector, where their "negotiations" are with politicians whose campaigns they've bankrolled, and their wage and benefit demands are paid for by taxes, not by businesses operating in a competitive environment.

Public Safety Employer-Employee Cooperation Act, HR 1154

California's state legislature doesn't have to do anything to unionize public employees including police and firefighters, that's already an established fact. But if Californian Democrats have anything to say about it, unionized public safety is coming to America. California's 45 Democrats in the U.S. Congress, by far the most numerous and influential coalition of Democrats from any state, have introduced federal legislation to that effect.

Legislation to unionize public safety, misleadingly dubbed the Public Safety Employer-Employee Cooperation Act, HR 1154, authored by Los Angeles-area Representative Karen Bass and co-sponsored by 201 other Democratic representatives (including all of California's Democratic House members), would impose exclusive California-style collective bargaining for police and emergency services to the roughly 20 states that don't already have it.

The consequences of unionized law enforcement and firefighting are many and dire. Every year these unions will collect hundreds of millions in dues, and they will use a significant percentage of that money on political spending to flip battleground states from purple to blue. This bill would also require union bargaining over police officers' wages, hours, and terms and conditions of employment, increasing costs to taxpayers.

These costs are not trivial. Police and firefighter pay, and benefits are breaking the budgets of cities and counties across California. The average sheriff in a California county in 2019 earned pay and benefits of $158,000. That's average, and that's on the low side compared to other categories of public safety. For example, on average, a police officer in a California city in 2019 earned pay and benefits of $176,000. And firefighters earned, on average, much more: In California's counties in 2019, $214,000; in California cities, also $214,000.

These averages, if anything, are understating the reality, insofar as they don't take into account the increased costs of prefunding their pension benefits if there isn't another bull market, nor do they take into account the full cost of prefunding their retirement health care. Most reasonable people agree that it is very important to support police and firefighters, and to pay them well. But these averages are so high they are often met with disbelief. They are unaffordable, compromising the ability to maintain adequate forces, and taking funding away from other vital public services. They are a direct result of unionization.

And if unionizing is not to save money, since clearly the opposite has happened, then what is the motivation? In contrast to Democrats' stated aims, unionizing police departments per this legislation would exacerbate systemic police violence, by protecting bad cops from accountability. So why support it? Because government unions want it. Passing the bill allows Democrats to expand the revenue of the unions that quietly fund their campaigns.

Environmentalist Extremism

In 2006, California passed AB 32, the "Global Warming Solutions Act." Signed by Republican Governor Arnold Schwarzenegger, AB 32 empowered the unelected bureaucrats on California's Air Resources Board (CARB) to regulate CO_2 emissions in California with the goal of reducing them to 1990 levels by 2020. Since the passage of AB 32 there has been an unceasing flow of follow-on legislation, executive orders, and CARB regulations. To name just a few:

In 2008 California's Public Utilities Commission released their "Long Term Energy Efficiency Strategic Plan," which, among other things, requires all new residential construction to be "zero net energy" (ZNE) staring in 2020, all new commercial construction to be ZNE by 2030, and 50 percent of all commercial buildings to be ZNE by 2030.

SB 350 in 2015 requires California to generate 50 percent of its electricity from "renewables" by 2050, with emissions-free nuclear power not eligible for inclusion.

More recently, Newsom has ordered CARB to implement the phaseout of new gas powered cars and light trucks by 2045, barely 14 years from now. He also called on the state legislature to ban fracking.

These recent executive orders from Newsom are motivated by the series of cataclysmic wildfires that have again claimed millions of acres of forest in California, wildfires that Newsom alleges were caused by climate change. But the biggest factor by far in causing these wildfires was forest mismanagement, thanks to environmentalist policies pioneered in California.

For decades, California's foresters and timber harvesters knew the forests were dangerously overgrown. Tree density had progressed in the vast Sierra Nevada from a historical and healthy norm of between 10-50 per acre to upwards of 300 per acre.

While natural fires were suppressed with increasing efficiency, for many years healthy forests were nonetheless maintained by logging and controlled burns. But between 1950 and 2020, California's timber industry's annual harvest declined from 6 billion board feet, which maintained an equilibrium between natural growth and annual removals, to less than 1.5 billion board feet.

California's powerful environmentalist nonprofits, such as the Sierra Club and the Center for Biological Diversity, used litigation and lobbying—not only within California, but in federal court and the U.S. Congress—to coerce sympathetic judges and legislators to nearly destroy California's timber industry, at the same time as CARB regulations and other onerous permitting obstacles prevented forest thinning or controlled burns.

When it comes to progressive ideology in general, and California's environmentalists in particular, irony abounds. Let this sink in: California's environmentalists destroyed California's forests. Any attempt to deflect this catastrophe onto climate change is sophistry. Densely packed, tinder dry forests will burn like hell, and that's exactly what happened. It doesn't matter one bit if summers are slightly drier and slightly hotter. They'll still burn.

Make Basic Necessities Unaffordable

The consequence of California's excessive, environmentalist-inspired policies is to make the state unaffordable. It comes from a fundamental worldview that California uses all of its cultural influence to reinforce in America and across the globe: Austerity is necessary to save the planet. This goes all the way back to Jerry Brown's "era of limits" philosophy which he promoted during his first terms as governor back in the 1970s.

The basic necessities of life—housing, transportation, energy, and water—cost more in California than anywhere else in America. This is because of artificially imposed scarcity, a choice that is entirely avoidable. Along with making it impossible to profitably build affordable market housing, California no longer makes significant public investments in energy, water, or transportation infrastructure—preferring instead to redirect available funds to public employee pay and benefits. They justify this by claiming they are protecting the environment, but the real winners are the special interests.

The fully co-opted, unionized public sector is a primary beneficiary of a hyper-regulated state where everything costs more than it should. Stratospheric home values translate directly into higher property tax receipts. Elevated utility and telecommunications prices to the consumer enable higher returns from the hidden taxes and fees embedded in the monthly billings. Public employee pension funds benefit when their real estate portfolios soar in value.

Also benefiting from artificial scarcity are landowners, established corporations, public utilities, and investment funds, all of which realize higher profits and returns when competitors are shut out and captive consumers bid up prices on limited supplies. Public utilities offer a particularly pernicious example of how artificial scarcity elevates profit.

The profits these regulated utilities can earn are limited to a percentage of their revenues. But when expensive renewable energy is delivered on this cost-plus basis to the consumer, they can sell the same or even fewer kilowatt-hours for far more revenue. Since they are allocated a fixed percentage of their revenue for profit, higher revenue always means higher profits.

This philosophy of limits and austerity, pioneered in California and pushed relentlessly into the culture, is as dangerous to the prospects of ordinary Americans in the rest of the country as the actual policies enacted by California's politicians.

The blessings of capitalism, where competitive development and innovation yield ongoing and broadly distributed prosperity, are assigned no credibility in California. They are discredited as harming the planet and inherently racist, in a stunning inversion of logic promulgated as much by high-tech billionaires as by the zealous millennials emerging from California's K-12 system of public school indoctrination. Which brings us to public education.

Destroy Public Education

There is one area where California's influence is felt every election cycle in the rest of the United States, and it comes courtesy of California's unionized public education system. California's public employee unions collect and spend over $900 million per year, mostly from member dues. More than half of that, nearly a half-billion per year, comes from public education unions, chief among them the California Teachers Association.

The leadership of these unions are willing to spend hundreds of millions every election cycle to support Democratic candidates and causes. Everywhere. With California's cities and counties and school boards almost universally dominated by California Teachers Association-approved Democrats, along with both houses of the state legislature and all higher state elected offices, the teachers' unions have money to burn in the rest of the United States. And that's exactly what they do, sending out millions to swing close elections to the U.S. Senate, House of Representatives, and state offices around the country.

Where there's money for politics, there's the political clout to completely dominate California's school system. Thanks to the influence of the teachers' union, state laws are slowly squeezing charter schools out of existence, with a rising assault on homeschoolers only deferred by the COVID-19 school shutdowns.

Thanks to the teachers' unions in California, the work rules that prevent teacher accountability and school accountability are already well-established law. Attempting to fire a teacher, or retain the best teachers in layoffs, or even to extend the period of time before a teacher gains tenure and has a job for life, are all rendered nearly impossible in California.

The ways teachers' unions have used their power to affect the curriculum of California's public schools are well documented. Most notably, the recent mandate to implement "gender studies" instruction across all age groups that borders on pornographic. Still pending, the mandate to require "ethnic studies" courses as a prerequisite for high-school graduation— something that would have already become law, except the various "stakeholders" haven't yet agreed on which victimized groups would occupy which positions on the victim hierarchy.

In general, California's teachers' unions have committed public schools to a pedagogy that indoctrinates students with their own political ideology. America is a flawed nation founded on racism. White men are oppressors. Capitalism is inherently exploitative. Socialism is the only path to social justice and environmental health.

The impact of the teachers' unions to reinforce and catalyze California's socialist vision for America and the world cannot be overstated. Year after year, their money pours over the Sierra Nevada to decisively influence countless political races in the rest of the nation. The national teachers' unions that lobby for similar curricula around America are dominated by the California leadership and California's dues revenue.

For over a generation, students thoroughly steeped in socialist ideology have graduated from California's K-12 schools. As graduates of this indoctrination, they have spread into every state, from the streets of Portland and Seattle to the precincts of Allegheny County. They staff HR departments and activist nonprofits. They are code warriors and social media influencers. The teachers' unions of California have done their job well. Their proteges are everywhere.

Foment Identity Group Tension

Fundamental to California's progressive culture is the deconstruction of meritocracy. It's all an illusion, of course. No start-up that aspires to be Google or Facebook's next unicorn acquisition expects to achieve such glory by hiring incompetent programmers. But the institutional drive towards erasing colorblind, genderblind criteria has progressed further in California than anywhere else in the United States. For any corporation still doing business in California, these policies have enterprise-wide impact.

In September 2020, for example, Newsom signed AB 979, which requires publicly traded corporations to "appoint directors from underrepresented communities to their boards." A close reading of this law reveals the brazen, punitive arrogance of California's Democrats, exemplified by the announced fine of $100,000 merely for "failure to timely file board member information with the Secretary of State."

A tactic of the Left, perfected in California, is to measure aggregate group achievement, by ethnicity or by gender, and then to ascribe all variation between groups either to racism or sexism. And to the argument that perhaps there are factors related to competence, qualifications, and merit, rather than racism or sexism alone explaining these disparities, the response has been to eliminate those factors as official evaluation criteria, or even as subjects we are allowed to discuss.

Why else is it that the regents of the University of California, yielding to pressure from the state legislature, have eliminated the use of the SAT and ACT tests as a method to evaluate college applicants? Why is it that California is lowering the score required to pass the bar exam and become a licensed attorney?

All of these steps and more are being pioneered in California. In November, California voters will even have the opportunity to bring back affirmative action, which would restore the explicitly racist (and sexist) requirement for public and private institutions to achieve proportional representation by race and gender in admissions, hiring, pay, and promotions. Where does this end?

It doesn't end there. Governor Newsom has just signed another bill, AB 3070, which will "establish a first-in-the-nation task force to study and make recommendations on reparations for slavery." Critics have suggested this is just Newsom's way to position himself to run for president in 2024 or 2028. Probably not now because of the recall because he's damaged goods. But meanwhile, given their record to-date, there is no evidence whatsoever that California's state legislature would not enact a reparations bill.

As part of their relentless, intrepid quest for social justice, California's woke Democrats are not just trailblazing quotas, affirmative action, and reparations and exporting them across the United States—another pioneering innovation is to declare racism to be a public health emergency. This notion gained national traction in the wake of the death of George Floyd in Minneapolis, but it was already being pushed by health providers in California.

Which brings us to California's excessive attention to public health, to the point of absurdity and beyond.

Health and Safety Mandates

The COVID-19 lockdowns may have grabbed the headlines, but California has been going off the deep end in pursuit of health and safety for decades. A good example is Proposition 65, the "Safe Drinking Water and Toxic Enforcement Act," sold to voters in 1986. This is the California law responsible for cancer-warning signs so ubiquitous that most Californians know it's better just to ignore them.

In bars and restaurants, on playground equipment, shoes, umbrellas, and golf club covers, even around Disneyland, consumers are warned that a product served on the premises—even the place itself—"is known to the state of California to cause cancer or reproductive harm."

While most Californians have gotten used to these warning labels, they are no laughing matter. They expose small businesses to ruinous lawsuits. Prop. 65 is often out of step with scientific consensus because it draws from a reference list of nearly 1,000 chemicals, chosen if, according to state regulators, they could cause "one excess case of cancer in 100,000 individuals exposed to the chemical over a 70-year lifetime." But with criteria like that, everything causes cancer.

Like so many regulations, the biggest victims of Prop. 65 are small businesses. Prop. 65 deputizes private trial lawyers to search for evidence of noncompliance. Small businesses, which generally don't have the resources to fight costly legal battles, are often compelled to settle. Because the penalties for "failure to warn" are so steep, businesses paid $35 million in Prop. 65 settlements in 2018, with more than three-quarters of this total going to attorney fees. Some lawyers who specialize in this area take home more than $1 million in fees per year.

The federal government is the only backstop against a law so broad that it applies to products produced anywhere in the world and that are sold in California. In August 2019, the U.S. Environmental Protection Agency took the unprecedented step of issuing guidance stating it won't approve of Prop. 65's "false labeling" on the weedkiller Roundup because the science doesn't support it. EPA didn't mince words: "It is irresponsible to require labels on products that are inaccurate when EPA knows the product does not pose a cancer risk," said EPA Administrator Andrew Wheeler. "We will not allow California's flawed program to dictate federal policy."

The California Battle for America is the Battle for the Future of the World

Most Californians have figured out that something is wrong, but they have been brainwashed into fearing the alternatives. They fear meritocracy. They fear capitalism. They fear racism. They fear climate change. They have slowly become accustomed to what is becoming tyranny, and they believe material poverty is necessary to save the planet and atone for racism. And in all these areas, the people who could offer common-sense solutions have been censored and disparaged.

But the progressive feudalists have one fatal weakness: They are wrong. The fundamental premises they use to justify their actions are flawed. Many maddingly—and a few idiotically.

Meritocracy is the only way a free people can create an efficient, prosperous, opportunity society. Without it, nobody has any incentive to innovate or work hard. The capable and hard-working become cynical and resentful, while the incompetent and the indolent know they don't have to step up, because they can live for free.

Capitalism is not dangerous, it is the engine of progress. It has been conflated with corporate monopolies and financial speculators. What a free nation does is use thoughtful regulations to amputate the gangrenous appendages of capitalist corruption, the predators, and the gamblers, leaving the pure and competitive heart of capitalist competition to thrive.

Finally, there is climate change, the trump card of the collectivists, played by progressive feudalists whenever they decide it's time to end the debate and get on with their agenda. But everything the environmental extremists have done in recent years has caused harm. Suburban expansion doesn't stop climate change, it just makes housing unaffordable. Forest "preservation" doesn't preserve forests, it turns them into tinderboxes that are periodically obliterated by fire. Natural gas is affordable and clean, and has already allowed Americans to lower their ratio of CO_2 emissions to energy consumption to the lowest of all industrialized nations. Are the Chinese and Indians going to lower their emissions? Because if they don't, so what if Americans do? And what about nuclear power? Why is the renewables lobby shutting down Diablo Canyon?

These are the messages that must be taken to California's voters, without apology or equivocation. Expand suburbs along the freeway corridors into the vast rangeland of California. Build new reservoirs and restore the aqueducts. Build desalination plants up and down the California coast and keep Diablo Canyon open. Thin the forests, restore the timber industry, and build biomass power plants to turn the trimmings into clean electricity.

Instead of squandering billions on the bullet train, widen the roads with smart lanes for high speed, high tech cars. Drill for natural gas in the Monterey Shale. Mine lithium in the Mojave Desert. Deregulate, so builders and business owners can spend their time, talents, and money on productive work instead of permits and fees. And launch a frontal assault on the teachers' union by enacting school choice with vouchers parents can redeem wherever they want.

This is a contract with California that would entice everyone. This is the enlightened, empowering capitalism that delivers the broad prosperity and freedom that progressive feudalism promises but cannot possibly deliver. This is the agenda that will enable voters in California to understand that competitive abundance is a morally preferable choice. California can be affordable again without compromising environmentalist values.

California can deliver opportunity to everyone again, no matter who they are or where they came from. Americans who want to prevent the Californication of America must step up, dollar for dollar, to counter the spending of California's public sector unions and resident billionaires.

California's seething population, searching for answers, must realize the premises used to justify their misery rely on convenient illusions, conjured by special interests for their own gain. But the battle must be fought. Somebody has to tell them.

What is at stake in California is not just California. It is the future of America. It is the future of the world.

Are You Part of the Solution? Or Part of the Problem?

I still believe the California Dream and so do millions of others and we need your help in making it golden again. Despite covering a lot of ground in this textbook of how California is transforming itself and the rest of the nation in the process, there are more examples of equal significance left unexamined or ones requiring greater detail that could make up a second volume of *California Madness*.

Nonetheless, I hope by now you get the straight-forward arguments and critical analyses presented and now recognize an idiocracy of epic proportions has put its own interests before the interests of its California residents. Sapient beings can fix this!

Idiocracy: Is democracy gone wrong through idiocy. It is the unfortunate situation where the vote of a person ignorant of even the most basic of facts surrounding an issue or candidate counts exactly as much as the vote of someone who is well-informed about the specific issue or candidate.

Sapience: Also known as wisdom, is the ability to think and act using knowledge, experience, understanding, common sense and insight. Sapience is associated with attributes such as intelligence, enlightenment, unbiased judgment, compassion, experiential self-knowledge, self-actualization, and virtues such as ethics and benevolence.

Being a sapient being is not about identity politics, it's about doing what is right and borrows many of the essential qualities of Centrism that supports strength, tradition, open mindedness, and policy based on evidence not ideology.

Sapient beings are independent minded thinkers that achieve common sense solutions that appropriately address America's and the world's most pressing issues. They gauge situations based on context and reason, consideration, and probability. They are open minded and exercise conviction and willing to fight for it on the intellectual battlefield. Sapient beings don't blindly and recklessly follow their feelings or emotions.

Their unifying ideology is based on the truth, reason, logic, scientific method, and pragmatism—and not necessarily defined by compromise, moderation, or any particular faith—but is considerate of them. The love of truth and the desire to attain it should motivate you to think for yourself. Open-mindedness, critical thinking, and debate are essential to discovering the truth.

Thinking for yourself means questioning dominant ideas even when others insist on their being treated as unquestionable. It means deciding what one believes not by conforming to fashionable opinions, but by taking the trouble to learn and honestly consider the strongest arguments to be advanced on both or all sides of questions—including arguments for positions that others revile and want to stigmatize and against positions others seek to immunize from critical scrutiny.

Are you a sapient being? For the sake of California—and America—I hope so!

Appendix

50 *MADNESS* Textbook Titles: https://www.fratirepublishing.com/madnessbooks
- *Fake News Madness*
- *Crime Rate Madness*
- *Voting Madness*
- *California Madness*

Ballotpedia: https://ballotpedia.org/Voter_identification_laws_by_state

California 2020 Propositions and Election Results: https://ballotpedia.org/California_2020_ballot_propositions

California Policy Center (CPC): https://californiapolicycenter.org/

California's Largest School Districts Are Underwater Full Spreadsheet With Sources: https://docs.google.com/spreadsheets/d/1kZWd9URNjQ1Uzzu8B7mqLeUPlucMy9sFvLrc5PWr8o0/edit#gid=2010638064

California's State and Local Liabilities Total $1.5 Trillion: https://californiapolicycenter.org/californias-state-and-local-liabilities-total-1-5-trillion-3/

CalMatters: https://calmatters.org/commentary/

Convention of States (COS): https://conventionofstates.com/take_action

Election Observer Training Program - Voter Integrity Project: https://voterintegrityproject.com/vip-launches-election-observer-training/

Hoover Institution: https://www.hoover.org/publications/californiaonyourmind

Independent Institute: https://www.independent.org/

Judicial Watch: https://www.judicialwatch.org/

Little Hoover Commission: https://lhc.ca.gov/about/history

Public Policy Institute of California (PPIC): https://www.ppic.org/

Redistricting - We Draw The Lines California; https://www.wedrawthelinesca.org/sign_up?recruiter_id=13418

San Francisco City and County, California Ballot Measures: https://ballotpedia.org/San_Francisco_City_and_County,_California_ballot_measures

Save Our States: https://saveourstates.com/

The Facts About Election Integrity and the Need for States to Fix Their Election Systems: https://www.heritage.org/election-integrity-facts

SAPIENT BEING PROGRAMS:
- **Make Free Speech Again On Campus (MFSAOC) Program:**

https://www.sapientbeing.org/programs
- **Sapient Conservative Textbooks (SCT) Program:** https://www.sapientbeing.org/programs
- **World Of Writing Warriors (WOWW) Program:** https://www.sapientbeing.org/programs
- **World Of Writing Warriors (WOWW) Journalism Code of Ethics, Practical Logic & Sapience Guidelines:** https://www.sapientbeing.org/resources

The S.A.P.I.E.N.T. Being: https://www.fratirepublishing.com/books

Voter's Defense Manual–2020 Edition: https://static.votesmart.org/static/pdf/2020_VSDM.pdf

Vote Harvesting - A Recipe for Intimidation, Coercion, and Election Fraud:
https://www.heritage.org/sites/default/files/2019-10/LM253_0.pdf

Glossary

Absentee Ballot Vote Fraud – A person attempts to fill out and turn in an absentee ballot containing false information. For example, this can occur when a person attempts to fill out and turn in an absentee ballot with the name of a false or non-existent voter. The term can extend to manipulation, deception, or intimidation of absentee voters.

American Dream -- Is a national ethos of the United States, the set of ideals in which freedom includes the opportunity for prosperity and success, as well as an upward social mobility for the family and children, achieved through hard work in a society with few barriers.

Ballot Harvesting – A Ballot collecting is the gathering and submitting of completed absentee or mail-in voter ballots by third-party individuals, volunteers, or workers, rather than submission by voters themselves directly to ballot collection sites.

Ballot Initiative – Is a means by which citizens may propose to create, amend, or repeal a state law or constitutional provision through collecting petition signatures from a certain minimum number of registered voters.

Californification – Is a word, an expression that refers to the influx of Californians into various western states in the U.S.

California Environmental Quality Act (CEQA) – Is a California statute passed in 1970 shortly after the United States federal government passed the National Environmental Policy Act, to institute a statewide policy of environmental protection.

Crony Capitalism – Is an economy in which businesses thrive not as a result of risk, but rather as a return on money amassed through a nexus between a business class and the political class. This is done using state power to crush genuine competition in handing out permits, government grants, special tax breaks, or other forms of state intervention.

Democracy – A government in which the supreme power is vested in the people and exercised by them directly or indirectly through a system of representation usually involving periodically held free elections; a political unit that has a democratic government.

Dystopia – An imagined state or society in which there is great suffering or injustice, typically one that is totalitarian or post-apocalyptic.

Global Warming Solutions Act – Or Assembly Bill 32, is a California State Law that fights global warming by establishing a comprehensive program to reduce greenhouse gas emissions from all sources throughout the state.

Hollywood Glitterati – Another name for Hollywood elites.

Homeless Industrial Complex – A situation where "non-profit" organizations utilize taxpayer dollars, ostensibly, to "fix" the homeless crisis.

Identitarian – A supporter or advocate of the political interests of a particular racial, ethnic, or national group, typically one composed of Europeans or white people.

Idiocracy – An idiocracy is a disparaging term for a society run by or made up of idiots (or people perceived as such). Idiocracy is also the title of 2006 satirical film that depicts a future in which humanity has become dumb.

Illiberalism – The 21st century term is used to describe an attitude that is close-minded, intolerant, and bigoted.

Intellectual Humility – A mindset that encompasses empathy, trust, and curiosity, viewpoint diversity gives rise to engaged and civil debate, constructive disagreement, and shared progress towards truth.

Intersectionality – A theoretical framework for understanding how aspects of one's social and political identities might combine to create unique modes of discrimination.

Judicial Fiat – Refers to an order or a decree especially an arbitrary one.

Libertarian – An advocate of the doctrine of free will; a person who upholds the principles of individual liberty especially of thought and action; a member of a political party advocating libertarian principles.

Little Hoover Commission – Formally known as the Milton Marks "Little Hoover" Commission on California State Government Organization and Economy, is an independent state oversight agency created in 1962.

Mainstream Media (MSM) – Traditional forms of mass media, as television, radio, magazines, and newspapers, as opposed to online means of mass communication.

Marxism – The political, economic, and social principles and policies advocated by Marx and a theory and practice of socialism including the labor theory of value, dialectical materialism, the class struggle, and dictatorship of the proletariat until the establishment of a classless society.

Meritocracy – Is the only way a free people can create an efficient, prosperous, opportunity society. Without it, nobody has any incentive to innovate or work hard. The capable and hard-working become cynical and resentful, while the incompetent and the indolent know they don't have to step up, because they can live for free.

Municipal Elections – Elections for sub-state municipalities, such as county government or city government. Mayors, councilmembers, city attorneys, school boards, and sheriffs are some of the people who may be elected by municipal elections.

New Suburbanism – Is an urban design movement which intends to improve on existing suburban or exurban designs.

New Urbanism – Is an urban design movement which promotes environmentally friendly habits by creating walkable neighborhoods containing a wide range of housing and job types.

NIMBY – Not in my backyard.

Occam's Razor – Is a principle of theory construction or evaluation according to which, other things equal, explanations that posit fewer entities, or fewer kinds of entities, are to be preferred to explanations that posit more.

Preen – Congratulate or pride oneself and (of a person) devote effort to making oneself look attractive and then admire one's appearance.

Progressivism – A political philosophy in support of social reform based on the idea of progress in which advancements in science, technology, economic development, and social organization are vital to improve the human condition.

Republic – A government having a chief of state who is not a monarch and who in modern times is usually a president; a political unit (as a nation) having such a form of government; a government in which supreme power resides in a body of citizens entitled to vote and is exercised by elected officers and representatives responsible to them and governing according to law.

Sage – Wise through reflection and experience. b archaic : grave, solemn. 2 : proceeding from or characterized by wisdom, prudence, and good judgment sage advice.

Sapience – Also known as wisdom, is the ability to think and act using knowledge, experience, understanding, common sense and insight. Sapience is associated with attributes such as intelligence, enlightenment, unbiased judgment, compassion, experiential self-knowledge, self-actualization, and virtues such as ethics and benevolence.

Section 8 Housing – The U.S. Department of Housing and Urban Development (HUD) operates a housing voucher program under Section VIII of Title 24 of the Code of Federal Regulations. This voucher program is commonly known as Section 8 assistance, and is designed to help low income, elderly, and disabled people afford decent, safe, and sanitary housing.

Smart Growth – Is an urban planning and transportation theory that concentrates growth in compact walkable urban centers to avoid sprawl.

Social Justice – A political and philosophical theory which asserts that there are dimensions to the concept of justice beyond those embodied in the principles of civil or criminal law, economic supply and demand, or traditional moral frameworks.

Socialism – Any various economic and political theories advocating collective or governmental ownership and administration of the means of production and distribution of goods. A system of society or group living in which there is no private property. A system or condition of society in which the means of production are owned and controlled by the state. A stage of society in Marxist theory transitional between capitalism and communism and distinguished by unequal distribution of goods and pay according to work done.

Soft Fascism – Is a process of anti-democratic governing that is not as overtly totalitarian or authoritarian as more historically memorable fascist states.

Supermajority – The current 2020 election condition in the California legislature where Democrats in both houses, Senate and Assembly, have a two-thirds voting threshold, which allows them to pass most legislation without Republican help.

Useful Idiot – Is attributed to Vladimir Lenin. It describes naïve people who can be manipulated to advance a political cause.

Viewpoint Diversity – Viewpoint diversity occurs when members of a group or community approach problems or questions from a range of perspectives.

Voter Registration Fraud – Filling out and submitting a voter registration card for a fictional person or filling out a voter registration card with the name of a real person but without that person's consent and forging his or her signature on the card.

Voter Suppression – An artificially created term that unfairly condemns any perfectly legal election reform with which liberal critics disagree. It is a linguistic trick designed to taint reasonable and commonsense safeguards that protect voters by lumping these policies together with illegal activities like poll taxes and literacy tests that did occur in the Democratic South prior to the Civil Rights Act of 1964 and Voting Rights Act of 1965.

Voting Rights Act of 1965 – The Voting Rights Act of 1965 expanded the 14th and 15th amendments by banning racial discrimination in voting practices. The act was a response to the barriers that prevented African Americans from voting for nearly a century.

YIMBY – Yes in my backyard.

References

An Indecent Proposal. California Policy Center. Oct. 1, 2021.
https://mailchi.mp/calpolicycenter/rkrqx2n9hd-375160?e=1f5da64d99.

Bernal, Rafael. "Yale, MIT Study: 22 million, Not 11 million, Undocumented Immigrants in US." *The Hill.*
09/21/18. https://thehill.com/latino/407848-yale-mit-study-22-million-not-11-million-undocumented-immigrants-in-us.

Beyer, Scott. "How San Francisco's Progressive Policies Are Hurting the Poor." Reason. 11.9.2014.
https://reason.com/2014/11/09/how-san-franciscos-progressive-policies/.

Billingsley, Lloyd. "California Imposes Diversity Dogma on Corporate Boards." Independent Institute.
October 12, 2020. October 10, 2020. https://www.independent.org/news/article.asp?id=13293.

Billingsley, Lloyd. "The Brown-Becerra Axis For Illegals." FrontPage Magazine. Dec. 6, 2016.
https://archives.frontpagemag.com/fpm/brown-becerra-axis-illegals-lloyd-billingsley/.

Buckley, Thomas. "What California Could Have Done With the $30 Billion Lost by the EDD All 40 million
Californians could dine at the French Laundry with Gavin Newsom." California Globe. July 19, 2021.
https://californiaglobe.com/section-2/what-california-could-have-done-with-the-30-billion-lost-by-the-edd/?fbclid=IwAR1wBO9r2ICVhSDCZaNWoRY-3D8GEKWJHdEmm_B4UfRSxtQ9O4WLNrRz6MU.

California Roars Back: Governor Newsom Signs $100 Billion California Comeback Plan to Accelerate
State's Recovery and Tackle Persistent Challenges. Office of Governor Gavin Newsom. July 12, 2021.
https://www.gov.ca.gov/2021/07/12/california-roars-back-governor-newsom-signs-100-billion-california-comeback-plan-to-accelerate-states-recovery-and-tackle-persistent-challenges/.

California's Ethnic Studies Mandate: A New Curriculum Rejects Merit and Sees Oppression Everywhere.
Editorial Board. *Wall Street Journal.* March 16, 2021. https://www.wsj.com/articles/californias-ethnic-studies-mandate-11615935133.

Del Beccaro, Tom. "Tom Del Beccaro: Newsom recall election—here's why California governor is in real
trouble." Fox News. Aug. 10, 2021. https://www.foxnews.com/opinion/newsom-recall-election-california-governor-tom-del-beccaro.

Elder, Larry. "California's Latino Education Crisis. Real Clear Politics. July 16, 2015.
https://www.realclearpolitics.com/articles/2015/07/16/californias_latino_education_crisis_127394.html.

Greenhut, Steven. "Reform California's Water Policies." *National Review.* April 1, 2021.
https://www.nationalreview.com/magazine/2021/04/19/reform-californias-water-policies/.

Grimes, Katy. "California Gov. Gavin Newsom Defeats Recall." California Globe. September 15, 2021.
https://californiaglobe.com/articles/california-gov-gavin-newsom-defeats-recall/.

Grimes, Katy. "New Lawsuit Alleges State of California Violated National Voter Registration Act:

California failing to verify citizenship before placing voters on the voter rolls." California Globe. October 1, 2019. https://californiaglobe.com/section-2/new-lawsuit-alleges-state-of-california-violated-national-voter-registration-act/.

Hanson, Victor Davis. *Mexifornia. Twenty Years Later.* Encounter Books: New York. 2021.

Herriges, Daniel. "The California High-Speed Train that Wasn't: The Opportunity Cost of Megaprojects." Strong Towns. February 13, 2019. https://www.strongtowns.org/journal/2019/2/13/what-is-the-problem-for-which-california-high-speed-rail-is-the-solution?gclid=Cj0KCQjwg7KJBhDyARIsAHrAXaFJEHCo5QOLC1zgQKuz2u_38wCIqn340FyMHxo1WKYnhtUu9tRgz68aAlCqEALw_wcB.

Immigrants in California. Public Policy Institute of California (PPIC). March 2021. https://www.ppic.org/publication/immigrants-in-california/.

Jaschik, Scott. "Why Did Prop 16 Fail?" Inside Higher Ed. November 9, 2020. https://www.insidehighered.com/admissions/article/2020/11/09/experts-discuss-failure-californias-proposition-16.

Joffe, Marc. "Analyzing the Cost and Performance of LAUSD Traditional High Schools and LAUSD Alliance Charter High Schools." California Policy Center. June 1, 2015. https://californiapolicycenter.org/analyzing-the-cost-and-performance-of-lausd-public-high-schools-and-la-alliance-charter-high-schools/.

Kotkin, Joel and Karla López del Río. "The Other California." *City Journal.* Winter 2021. https://www.city-journal.org/california-inland-empire.

Kotkin, Joel and Marshall Toplansky. *Beyond Feudalism: A Strategy to Restore California's Middle Class.* Chapman University Center for Demographics & Policy 2020 Research Brief. https://www.chapman.edu/communication/_files/beyond-feudalism-web-sm.pdf.

Kotkin, Joel and Marshall Toplansky. *California Feudalism: The Squeeze on the Middle Class.* Chapman University Press. 2018. https://www.chapman.edu/wilkinson/_files/Feudalism.pdf.

Kotkin, Joel and Wendell Cox. "California Squashes Its Young." *City Journal.* April 30, 2017. https://www.city-journal.org/html/california-squashes-its-young-15167.html.

Kotkin, Joel and Wendell Cox. "In Defense of Houses." *City Journal.* July 16, 2019. https://www.city-journal.org/single-family-housing-opposition.

Kotkin, Joel. "California and Its Contradictions Rumblings of realignment beneath a solid-blue surface." *City Journal.* November 6, 2020. https://www.city-journal.org/signs-of-weakness-in-californias-blue-alliance

Kotkin, Joel. "California's Woke Hypocrisy." *City Journal.* July 29, 2020. https://www.city-journal.org/california-woke-hypocrisy.

Kotkin, Joel. "Governor Preen." *City Journal.* November 20, 2020. https://www.city-journal.org/gavin-newsoms-woke-posturing-masks-dismal-california-economic-record.

Kotkin, Joel. "How Los Angeles Descended Into Neo-Feudalism—and How to Fix It." *Newsweek.* 5/16/21. https://www.newsweek.com/how-los-angeles-descended-neo-feudalism-how-fix-it-opinion-

1591004

Kotkin, Joel. "Left and Lefter in California." *City Journal.* March 7, 2018. https://www.city-journal.org/html/left-and-lefter-california-15755.html.

Kotkin, Joel. "Making America California." *City Journal.* January 25, 2021. https://www.city-journal.org/biden-touts-california-as-model-for-america.

Kotkin, Joel. "The Golden State's War on Itself." *City Journal.* Summer 2010. https://www.city-journal.org/html/golden-state%E2%80%99s-war-itself-13304.html

Lin, Judy and Adria Watson. "California migration: The story of 40 million." CalMatters. June 23, 2020. https://calmatters.org/explainers/california-population-migration-census-demographics-immigration/?gclid=Cj0KCQjwlMaGBhD3ARIsAPvWd6gw_b65_4wSzho6RWyFoHd6ui7_eO25GOEUbQt5pHjRWdA9EwE4LEIaAnrrEALw_wcB.

Mac Donald, Heather. California's Demographic Revolution: If the upward mobility of the impending Hispanic majority doesn't improve, the state's economic future is in peril." *City Journal.* Winter 2012. https://www.city-journal.org/html/california%E2%80%99s-demographic-revolution-13440.html.

Malanga, Steven. "Calculating the Californication: Will migrating Golden State residents bring left-wing politics to their new homes? Maybe not." *City Journal.* Winter 2020. https://www.city-journal.org/california-migration-politics.

Malanga, Steven. "Cali to Business: Get Out!: Firms Are Fleeing the State's Senseless Regulations and Confiscatory Taxes." *City Journal.* Autumn 2011. https://www.city-journal.org/html/cali-business-get-out-13419.html.

Malanga, Steven. "California's Split Personality: The Golden State's tech sector is booming, even as its industrial base flees." *City Journal.* Winter 2016. https://www.city-journal.org/html/california%E2%80%99s-split-personality-14169.html.

Malanga, Steven. "How Unskilled Immigrants Hurt Our Economy: A handful of industries get low-cost labor, and the taxpayers foot the bill." *City Journal.* Summer 2006. https://www.city-journal.org/html/how-unskilled-immigrants-hurt-our-economy-12946.html.

Malanga, Steven. "How Unskilled Immigrants Hurt Our Economy: A handful of industries get low-cost labor, and the taxpayers foot the bill." *City Journal.* Summer 2006. https://www.city-journal.org/html/how-unskilled-immigrants-hurt-our-economy-12946.html.

Malanga, Steven. "The Beholden State: How public-sector unions broke California." *City Journal.* Spring 2010. https://www.city-journal.org/html/beholden-state-13274.html.

McQuillan, Lawrence J. "How to Restore the California Dream: Removing Obstacles to Fast and Affordable Housing Development." Independent Institute. January 8, 2020. https://www.independent.org/publications/article.asp?id=13013.

McQuillan, Lawrence J. "New Study Concludes Prop 47 Caused California's 'Smash-and-Grab' Crime Wave." Independent Institute. June 28, 2018. https://www.independent.org/news/news_detail.asp?newsID=1247.

McQuillan, Lawrence J. and Adam B. Summers. "The Cost of California's Public-Employee Unions."

Independent Institute. April 2, 2021. https://www.independent.org/news/article.asp?id=13501.

McQuillan, Lawrence J. and Hayeon Carol Park. "California's High-Speed Rail Authority Wins Dishonor of the California Golden Fleece® Award. Independent Institute. April 13, 2016. https://www.independent.org/publications/article.asp?id=8995.

McQuillan, Lawrence J., Hayeon Carol Park, Adam B. Summers and Katherine Dwyer. "California Wildfires: Key Recommendations to Prevent Future Disasters." Independent Institute. June 25, 2019. https://www.independent.org/publications/article.asp?id=12834.

Miller, Andrew Mark. "40% of San Francisco residents plan to leave due to quality of life: Poll." *Washington Examiner*. July 1, 2021. https://www.washingtonexaminer.com/news/40-percent-san-francisco-residents-leave-quality-of-life.

Ohanian, Lee. "A Perverse Way To "Solve" California's Housing Crisis: People Are Leaving The Golden State." Hoover Institution. January 14, 2020. https://www.hoover.org/research/perverse-way-solve-californias-housing-crisis-people-are-leaving-golden-state.

Ohanian, Lee. "At $140,000 Per Year, Why Are Government Workers In California Paid Twice As Much As Private Sector Workers?" Hoover Institution. April 30, 2019. https://www.hoover.org/research/140000-year-why-are-government-workers-california-paid-twice-much-private-sector-workers.

Ohanian, Lee. "California Legislators Spend $200 Billion And Taxpayers Get Less And Less." Hoover Institution. July 7, 2020. https://www.hoover.org/research/california-legislators-spend-200-billion-and-taxpayers-get-less-and-less.

Ohanian, Lee. "California's Recall Election Is On—And Not Because 1.7 Million Signatories Are Racists." Hoover Institution. June 29, 2021. https://www.hoover.org/research/californias-recall-election-and-not-because-17-million-signatories-are-racists.

Ohanian, Lee. "Facing Recall, California's Governor Blows Out The State Budget." Hoover Institution. May 20, 2021. https://www.hoover.org/research/facing-recall-californias-governor-blows-out-state-budget.

Ohanian, Lee. "Only In San Francisco: $61,000 Tents And $350,000 Public Toilets." Hoover Institution. March 9, 2021. https://www.hoover.org/research/only-san-francisco-61000-tents-and-350000-public-toilets.

Ohanian, Lee. "Why Drug Addicts Outnumber High School Students In San Francisco." Hoover Institution. October 1, 2019. https://www.hoover.org/research/why-drug-addicts-outnumber-high-school-students-san-francisco.

Paine, Linda. "Questions Surround Irregularities in California's 2020 Election." Integrity Project California (EIPCa). https://www.eip-ca.com/.

Poverty in California. Public Policy Institute of California (PPIC). 2021. https://www.ppic.org/publication/poverty-in-california/.

Ring, Edward. "A Green Conundrum for the Golden State." American Greatness. August 21, 2021. https://amgreatness.com/2021/08/21/a-green-conundrum-for-the-golden-state/.

Ring, Edward. "A Strategy to Transform California in One Election." California Policy Center. June 26, 2019. https://californiapolicycenter.org/a-strategy-to-transform-california-in-one-election/.

Ring, Edward. "California is Ready to Get Rid of Newsom." California Policy Center. May 11, 2020. https://californiapolicycenter.org/california-is-ready-to-get-rid-of-newsom/.

Ring, Edward. "California's Budget "Surplus" Ignores Crushing Debt Burden." California Policy Center. January 9, 2019. https://californiapolicycenter.org/californias-budget-surplus-ignores-crushing-debt-burden/.

Ring, Edward. "California's General Fund Relies on Bailouts and Billionaires." California Policy Center. January 13, 2021. https://californiapolicycenter.org/californias-general-fund-relies-on-bailouts-and-billionaires/.

Ring, Edward. "California's One-Party State, the Blue Wave Machine." California Policy Center. November 5, 2020. https://californiapolicycenter.org/californias-one-party-state-the-blue-wave-machine/.

Ring, Edward. "California's Public-Sector Unions Rake in $921 Million in Annual Revenue." California Policy Center. August 5, 2020. https://californiapolicycenter.org/californias-public-sector-unions-rake-in-921-billion-in-annual-revenue/.

Ring, Edward. "California's Socialist Oligarchy, Part One: Making the State Unaffordable." California Policy Center. October 8, 2018. https://californiapolicycenter.org/californias-socialist-oligarchy-part-one-making-the-state-unaffordable/.

Ring, Edward. "California's Socialist Oligarchy, Part Two: Who They Are and How to Defeat Them." October 9, 2018. https://californiapolicycenter.org/californias-socialist-oligarchy-part-two-who-they-are-and-how-to-defeat-them/.

Ring, Edward. "California's State and Local Liabilities Total $1.5 Trillion." California Policy Center. January 6, 2019. https://californiapolicycenter.org/californias-state-and-local-liabilities-total-1-5-trillion-3/.

Ring, Edward. "Californians exempt from the consequences of Liberalism." California Policy Center. December 2, 2019. https://californiapolicycenter.org/californians-exempt-from-the-consequences-of-liberalism/

Ring, Edward. "Deceptive and Misleading Claims—How Government Unions Fool the Public." California Policy Center. September 8, 2015. https://californiapolicycenter.org/deceptive-and-misleading-claims-how-government-unions-fool-the-public/.

Ring, Edward. "Electricity and Ideology—Competing Priorities in California." California Policy Center. October 22, 2019. https://californiapolicycenter.org/electricity-and-ideology-competing-priorities-in-california/.

Ring, Edward. "Environmentalists Destroyed California's Forests." California Policy Center. September 10, 2020. https://californiapolicycenter.org/environmentalists-destroyed-californias-forests/.

Ring, Edward. "Fighting the One-Party State at the Local Level in California." California Policy Center. February 12, 2020. https://californiapolicycenter.org/fighting-the-one-party-state-at-the-local-level-in-california/.

Ring, Edward. "Fixing California–Part One: The Themes That Make Anything Possible." California Policy Center. June 30, 2021. https://californiapolicycenter.org/fixing-california-part-one-the-themes-that-make-anything-possible/.

Ring, Edward. "Government Unions and California Ballot Propositions." California Policy Center. December 17, 2020. https://californiapolicycenter.org/government-unions-and-california-ballot-propositions/.

Ring, Edward. "How Does a California Family Survive?" California Policy Center. July 1, 2019. https://californiapolicycenter.org/how-does-a-california-family-survive/.

Ring, Edward. "How Public Sector Unions Exploit Identity Politics." California Policy Center. November 7, 2017. https://californiapolicycenter.org/public-sector-unions-exploit-politics-race/.

Ring, Edward. "Investing in Infrastructure to Lower the Cost of Living." California Policy Center. March 14, 2016. https://californiapolicycenter.org/investing-infrastructure-lower-cost-living/.

Ring, Edward. "Jamming Janus–The Public Union Empire Strikes Back." California Policy Center. December 12, 2018. https://californiapolicycenter.org/jamming-janus-the-public-union-empire-strikes-back/.

Ring, Edward. "New Suburbanism–A Smart Alternative to 'Smart Growth.'" California Policy Center. June 6, 2019. https://californiapolicycenter.org/new-suburbanism-a-smart-alternative-to-smart-growth/.

Ring, Edward. "Pension reform waits for California Supreme Court." California Policy Center. December 2, 2019. https://californiapolicycenter.org/pension-reform-waits-for-california-supreme-court/.

Ring, Edward. "Public Education is Changing Forever." California Policy Center. May 20, 2020. https://californiapolicycenter.org/public-education-is-changing-forever/.

Ring, Edward. "Rhetoric to Challenge California's Statist Elites." California Policy Center. November 22, 2017. https://californiapolicycenter.org/rhetoric-challenge-californias-statist-elites/.

Ring, Edward. "The Battle for California is the Battle for America." California Policy Center. October 19, 2020. https://californiapolicycenter.org/the-battle-for-california-is-the-battle-for-america/

Ring, Edward. "The Coalition That Will Realign California." California Policy Center. December 31, 2020. https://californiapolicycenter.org/the-coalition-that-will-realign-california/.

Ring, Edward. "The CTA Empire Strikes Back." California Policy Center. July 28, 2015. https://californiapolicycenter.org/the-cta-empire-strikes-back/.

Ring, Edward. "The Manger vs The Monster–Housing California's Homeless." California Policy Center. December 18, 2019. https://californiapolicycenter.org/the-manger-vs-the-monster-housing-californias-homeless/.

Ring, Edward. "The Premises of California's Dysfunction." California Policy Center. March 3, 2020. https://californiapolicycenter.org/the-premises-of-californias-dysfunction/.

Ring, Edward. "The Seven Deadly Sins of California's Political Establishment." California Policy Center.

November 18, 2019. https://californiapolicycenter.org/the-seven-deadly-sins-of-californias-political-establishment/.

Ring, Edward. "Why Teachers Unions are the Worst of the Worst." California Policy Center. August 1, 2018. https://californiapolicycenter.org/why-teachers-unions-are-the-worst-of-the-worst/

Ring, Edward. "Why We Fight Government Unions." California Policy Center. November 24, 2020. https://californiapolicycenter.org/why-we-fight-government-unions/.

Ring, Edward. "Without Government Unions, There Would be No Gas Tax Increase." California Policy Center. November 1, 2017. https://californiapolicycenter.org/without-government-unions-no-gas-tax-increase/.

Ristoff, Brandon. "California's largest school districts are underwater: Massive debt raises questions about new spending proposals." California Policy Center. August 9, 2021. https://californiapolicycenter.org/californias-largest-school-districts-are-underwater/.

Singman, Brooke. "Republicans demand probe into Padilla's $35M grant to Biden-linked firm, claim 'misuse' of taxpayer funds." Fox News. December, 2020. https://www.foxnews.com/politics/republicans-demand-probe-into-padillas-35m-grant-to-biden-linked-firm-claim-misuse-of-taxpayer-funds.

Steinmetz, Katy. "California Just Became a 'Sanctuary State.' Here's What That Means." *Time*. October 5, 2017. https://time.com/4960233/california-sanctuary-state-donald-trump/.

Theroux, David J. "California Ranks Second Worst in U.S. on Economic Freedom Index: High Taxes, Overregulation Causing Exodus of Workers and Employers to Other States." Independent Institute. December 14, 2017. https://www.independent.org/news/news_detail.asp?newsID=1242.

Thornton, Bruce. "HOW ASSIMILATION WORKS: And how multiculturalism Has Wrecked It In California." *City Journal*. May 18, 2011. https://archives.frontpagemag.com/fpm/how-assimilation-works-bruce-thornton/.

Ulrich, Amanda. "Census 2020: California population grows 6%, becomes more diverse." *Desert Sun*. Aug. 12, 2021. https://www.desertsun.com/story/news/2021/08/12/census-2020-california-population-grows-diversity/8112412002/.

Walters, Dan. "'Roaring Back' Is Just a Campaign Slogan, Not Reality." CalMatters. July 18, 2021. https://calmatters.org/commentary/2021/07/roaring-back-newsom-recall-campaign-slogan-budget-surplus/.

Walters, Dan. "California's immense pension dilemma." CalMatters. August 10, 2020. https://calmatters.org/commentary/dan-walters/2020/08/california-court-pension-debt-unfunded/.

Walters, Dan. "Commentary: Surging pension costs push more California cities toward bankruptcy." California Policy Center. June 23, 2020. https://calmatters.org/economy/2018/02/commentary-surging-pension-costs-push-california-cities-toward-bankruptcy/.

Walters, Dan. "Identity Politics vs. Melting Pot Vision." CalMatters. November 25, 2020. https://calmatters.org/commentary/2020/11/california-senate-appointment-newsom-kamala/.

Walters, Dan. "Newsom Paints Rosy, But Flawed, Economic Picture." CalMatters. May 25, 2021.

https://calmatters.org/commentary/2021/05/newsom-economy-unemployment-rate-recall-california/

Walters, Dan. "Proposition 16: A New Fight Over Affirmative Action." CalMatters. October 4, 2020. https://calmatters.org/commentary/2020/10/california-proposition-16-affirmative-action/.

Walters, Dan. "We Have a Power Supply Problem." CalMatters. August 30, 2020. https://calmatters.org/commentary/dan-walters/2020/08/california-blackout-electrical-power-shortage-renewables/.

White, Jeremy B. "Newsom counting on labor union army to tank the California recall." Politico California. 06/03/2021. https://www.politico.com/states/california/story/2021/06/03/newsom-counting-on-labor-union-army-to-tank-the-california-recall-1384936.

Wilson, Corey Lee. "Electricity Prices in California Rose 5x More Than Rest of the USA." LinkedIn. 7-1-20. https://www.linkedin.com/pulse/electricity-prices-california-rose-5x-more-than-rest-usa-wilson.

Winkler, Matthew A. "California Defies Doom With No. 1 U.S. Economy." Bloomberg News. June 14, 2021. https://www.bloomberg.com/opinion/articles/2021-06-14/california-defies-doom-with-no-1-u-s-economy.

Zinshteyn Mikhail. "California State University now requires ethnic studies." CalMatters. August 18, 2020. https://calmatters.org/education/2020/08/csu-ethnic-studies-ab-1460/.

Index

F

G

M

N

Author Bio

Author: Corey Lee Wilson.

Corey Lee Wilson was raised an atheist by his liberal *Playboy* Bunny mother, has three Anglo-Latino siblings, a bi-racial daughter, a brother who died of AIDS, baptized a Protestant by his conservative grandparents, attended temple with his Jewish foster parents, baptized again as a Catholic for his first Filipina wife, attends Buddhist ceremonies with his second Thai wife, became an agnostic on his own free will for most of his life, and is a lifetime independent voter.

Corey felt the sting of intellectual humility by repeating the 4th grade and attended eighteen different schools before putting himself through college at Mt. San Antonio College and Cal Poly Pomona University (while on triple secrete probation). Named Who's Who of American College Students in 1984, he received a BS in Economics and won his fraternity's most prestigious undergraduate honor, the Phi Kappa Tau Fraternity's Shideler Award, both in 1985. In 2020, he became a member of the Heterodox Academy and in 2021 a member of the National Association of Scholars and 1776 Unites.

As a satirist and fraternity man, Corey started Fratire Publishing in 2012 and transformed the fiction "fratire" genre to a respectable and viewpoint diverse non-fiction genre promoting practical knowledge and wisdom to help everyday people navigate safely through the many hazards of life. In 2018, he founded the SAPIENT Being to help promote freedom of speech, viewpoint diversity, intellectual humility and most importantly advance sapience in America's students and campuses.

The SAPIENT Being has three programs: Make Free Speech Again On Campus (MFSAOC), World of Writing Warriors (WOWW) and the Sapient Conservative Textbooks (SCT) all working together to promote its mission and vision of sapience. The WOWW program plans to self-publish 50 *MADNESS* non-fiction textbooks in partnership with Fratire Publishing over the span of the 2020 decade in alliance with the MFSAOC program to start 50 chapters on America's high school and college campuses by 2030.

If you're interested in the MFSAOC Program and starting a S.A.P.I.E.N.T. Being club, chapter, or alliance please go to https://www.SapientBeing.org/start-a-chapter, e-mail SapientBeing@att.net, or call (951) 638-5562 for more information.

If you're interested as an author or journalist in the WOWW Program and their 50 MADNESS series of textbooks from the S.A.P.I.E.N.T. Being, please check them out at https://www.FratirePublishing.com/madnessbooks, e-mail SapientBeing@att.net, or call (951) 638-5562 for more information.

If you're interested as an educator or marketer in the SCT Program and their 50 MADNESS series of textbooks from the S.A.P.I.E.N.T. Being, please check them out at https://www.FratirePublishing.com/madnessbooks, e-mail SapientBeing@att.net, or call (951) 638-5562 for more information.

Hopefully, this book was enlightening and your journey through it—along with mine—made you aware of the issues and challenges ahead of us. If it has, your quest and mine towards becoming a sapient being has begun. If it hasn't, there's no better time to start than now. Come join us in creating a society advancing personal intelligence and enlightenment now together (S.A.P.I.E.N.T.) and become a sapient being.